Thackeray and Slavery

Thackeray
and Slavery

DEBORAH A. THOMAS

Ohio
University
Press
Athens

© Copyright 1993 by Deborah A. Thomas
Printed in the United States of America

Ohio University Press books are printed on acid-free paper ∞

97 96 95 94   5 4 3 2

Library of Congress Cataloging-in-Publication Data

Thomas, Deborah A.
    Thackeray and slavery / Deborah A. Thomas.
        p.   cm.
    Includes bibliographical references and index.
    ISBN 0-8214-1038-5
    1. Thackeray, William Makepeace, 1811-1863—Political and social
views.   2. Slavery and slaves in literature.   I. Title.   II. Title:
Thackeray and slavery.
PR5642.S56T48   1993
823'.8—dc20   92-43257
                                                       CIP

For G.A.T. and A.M.T.

Ordinary home questions . . . are as dull as lectures or sermons—
slavery has the excitement of a tragedy.

—*THE SPECTATOR, 31 MARCH 1838*

Contents

xi *Illustrations*

xiii *Acknowledgements*

xv *Introduction*

1   CHAPTER ONE: The Ties That Bind

17   CHAPTER TWO: *Barry Lyndon* and the Dynamics of
     Enslavement

40   CHAPTER THREE: "Oriental" Slavery in *Vanity Fair*

76   CHAPTER FOUR: Bondage and Freedom in *Pendennis*

96   CHAPTER FIVE: Henry Esmond as Slave and Master

114 CHAPTER SIX: "Selling of Virgins" in *The Newcomes*

140 CHAPTER SEVEN: Slavery as Touchstone in *The Virginians*

157 CHAPTER EIGHT: Seeming, Being, and Racism in *Philip*

188 CHAPTER NINE: Slavery as Creative Image

198 *Notes*

232 *Selected Bibliography*

240 *Index*

Illustrations

20 Depiction of an African ("Timbuctoo")

26 Auguste-Francois Biard, *The Slave Trade (Scene on the Coast of Africa)*

45 Slave for sale in Constantinople (*Notes of a Journey from Cornhill to Grand Cairo*)

47 The Fat Contributor in a Turkish harem ("An Eastern Adventure of the Fat Contributor"

48 John Frederick Lewis, *The Reception*

50 "The Lion of the Street" (*Our Street*)

53 "Mr. Jos's Hookahbadar" (*Vanity Fair*)

61 Becky fascinating Sir Pitt Crawley (*Vanity Fair*)

64 Becky on her knees to Sir Pitt Crawley (*Vanity Fair*)

65 Lord Steyne as "Oriental" potentate (*Vanity Fair*)

67 "The Triumph of Clytemnestra" (*Vanity Fair*)

77 Wedgwood medallion, "Am I Not a Man and a Brother?"

82 "Mr. Morgan at his ease" (*Pendennis*)

132 "Oriental" slavery and the "selling of virgins" (*The Newcomes*)

133 Lady Kew as auctioneer and Ethel as "Lot 1" (*The Newcomes*)

138 Eyre Crowe, "In the Richmond Slave Market"

145 Gumbo asleep on young George's bed (*The Virginians*)

155 "Sir George, my Lady, and their Master" (*The Virginians*)

162 "A Mississippi Bubble" (*Roundabout Papers*)

186 Othello wooing Desdemona (*Philip*)

191 Writing as slavery (*Philip*)

192 "On a Joke I Once Heard from the Late Thomas Hood" (*Roundabout Papers*)

Acknowledgements

NUMEROUS INSTITUTIONS have assisted in this examination of Thackeray and slavery, and they all deserve my thanks. A version of chapter 4 appeared in *Studies in the Novel* 17 (Summer 1985), as "Bondage and Freedom in Thackeray's *Pendennis* (copyright 1985 by North Texas State University; reprinted by permission of the publisher). The illustrations from Thackeray's works are reproduced, by permission of Oxford University Press, from *The Oxford Thackeray* edition of Thackeray's works, ed. George Saintsbury ([1908]). John Frederick Lewis's *The Reception* is reproduced by permission of the Yale Center for British Art, and the Wedgwood medallion is reproduced by permission of the Smithsonian Institution. Auguste-François Biard's *The Slave Trade (Scene on the Coast of Africa)* is reproduced by permission of the Wilberforce House, Hull City Museums, England. Quotations from Thackeray's *Letters and Private Papers* are reprinted by permission of the publisher from *The Letters and Private Papers of William Makepeace Thackeray*, Volumes I-IV, edited by Gordon N. Ray, Cambridge, Mass.: Harvard University Press, Copyright © 1945, 1946 by Hester Thackeray Ritchie Fuller and the President and Fellows of Harvard College, © renewed 1973, 1974 by Belinda Norman-Butler and Gordon N. Ray.

I am also grateful to the National Endowment for the Humanities for the 1985–86 fellowship that allowed me to do much of the research and part of the writing for this study. I am indebted to Harvard University for a 1985–86 appointment as a visiting scholar, permitting me to use that university's library facilities. In addition, I am grateful to Villanova University for summer research grants in 1984 and 1987 as well as a sabbatical leave in 1988–89 that helped me complete a preliminary draft of this book.

Along the way, many people have aided in this project, and it is a pleasure to acknowledge their help. In particular, thanks are due to the staffs of the libraries at Harvard, Princeton, and Villanova Universities, as well as the British Library and the Wilberforce House. I am indebted for helpful discussions to the other people involved in the special session on "Race, Gender, and Society in Thackeray" at the 1988 Modern Language Association convention—especially the other panelists, Carol Hanbery MacKay and Edgar F. Harden, and the moderator, Ina Ferris. For assistance and counsel of various kinds, I am indebted to Richard J. Dunn, George H. Ford, John R. Reed, and Mark Spilka. George H. Ford, in particular, deserves my gratitude for generously reading an early draft of this book. Finally, I would like to thank Gordon A. Thomas and Allen M. Thomas, to whom the book is dedicated, for their good humor and their patience.

Introduction

" A ND WHO CAN SAY: I have been always free," cries Empedocles in Arnold's *Empedocles on Etna*. By the end of his life, Thackeray too saw the human condition as one of bondage, as he explained at the conclusion of the Roundabout paper "On a Joke I Once Heard from the Late Thomas Hood." However, while Empedocles's response was suicide, Thackeray's reaction was resignation. In the same Roundabout paper, after comparing all human beings to galley slaves in the sense that we all have some work to do, Thackeray finishes with the wish, "So with stout hearts may we ply the oar, messmates all, till the voyage is over, and the Harbour of Rest is found" (17:472).

The image of slavery invoked in this Roundabout essay is recurrent in Thackeray's fiction, for reasons and with results that this study will explore. In the culture in which Thackery lived, slavery was a major social and political issue. Like the topic of nuclear power, following news of a near meltdown, in America today, the subject of slavery impinged on the consciousness of nearly everyone in Great Britain in Thackeray's lifetime. In recent years, slavery has aroused considerable interest among historians. Hitherto, however, the implications of this subject in terms of Victorian literature have, at best, received only passing attention. This book is the first to focus on the relevance of slavery to Victorian literature in general and to the work of Thackeray in particular. The subject of slavery is especially pertinent to Thackeray, who seems to have been fascinated with it. Throughout his career, he regularly alluded to literal or figurative slavery in his work. He was also eager to see slavery with his own eyes. In 1844, he witnessed slaves for sale in Constantinople and Cairo. On his lecture tours of the United States in 1852–53 and 1855–56, he observed slavery in the antebellum American South and described his observations in numerous personal letters. My purpose here is to analyze Thackeray's seven principal full-length novels—from *Barry Lyndon* to *The Adventures of Philip*—in terms of the idea of slavery (or in the case of *Philip*, the related topic of racism). My context for this analysis consists of Thackeray's own remarks about and reactions to slavery (demonstrated in his letters and some of his other writings outside these seven novels) as well as the changing Victorian climate of opinion regarding slavery. I have drawn on historical and sociological treatments of slavery, as well as biographical information about Thackeray, out of a belief that literary texts and the contexts in which they are produced are inevitably related. My aim has been to open a window on an important aspect of Victorian culture and show how light from that window enhances our understanding of Thackeray's work.

For Thackeray, as for most of his nineteenth-century British contemporaries, the major form of slavery was that to be found in the New World, although ideas about galley (penal) slavery as well as Western concepts of "Oriental" slavery also contributed to the image of bondage in Thackeray's mind. This book argues that—for both cultural and personal reasons—prior to his visits to the United States in 1852–53 and 1855–56, the idea of slavery had a powerful creative effect on Thackeray's novels but that after his contact with bondage in real life in the American South, the image of slavery waned in creative power in his fiction. The evidence of his novels suggests that what Thackeray imagined about slavery was artistically more fruitful than what he came to know. What Thackeray knew—or thought he knew—about actual slavery was conditioned by his time and place, although he believed throughout his life that the institution of slavery was flawed from the start. What he imagined about slavery he used with great skill in his fiction to explore the powers that compel and the chains that hold.

After an examination in chapter 1 of the social and biographical background of Thackeray's interest in slavery, the next six chapters will trace the image of slavery in his principal novels, beginning with *Barry Lyndon*—a work with which, as Dodds observes, Thackeray "leaves his apprenticeship behind."[1] Although Thackeray briefly mentions slavery in his only novel prior to *Lyndon*—the awkwardly written *Catherine,* which he later labeled "a mistake all through"[2]—the idea of slavery does not enter significantly into *Catherine* or lie behind it in some way, a fact that sets this early work apart from Thackeray's later novels. Perhaps, to view this apprentice novel in Foucault's terms, Thackeray was so preoccupied with the murder and the spectacle of capital punishment with which the historical tale of *Catherine* was to end that, for the moment, his imagination could not dwell on any other kind of "power over the body."[3] In any case, as chapters 2 through 7 will discuss, the concept of slavery is an important motif in all of Thackeray's subsequent novels, from *Barry Lyndon* to *The Virginians.*

Even *The Adventures of Philip,* as chapter 8 will explain, reflects Thackeray's thinking about slavery, although in this work, the last novel that Thackeray completed, overt references to slavery itself are largely absent. With *Philip,* much of which was written while the Civil War was raging in America, Thackeray seems to have decided that the subject of slavery was currently too touchy to mention. Instead, in this book, Thackeray substituted a prominent mulatto character of West Indian origin in place of the usual motif of slavery evident in the six full-length novels, starting with *Lyndon,* that preceded *Philip.* Chapter 9 explores some of the reasons why the image of slavery had such an especially rich hold on Thackeray's thinking.

References to slavery appear in many of Thackeray's writings outside his major novels, and some of these references will be incorporated into the discussion. Nevertheless, for the sake of clarity—in order to focus as sharply as possible on an emerging pattern in Thackeray's major fiction—the book as a whole will concentrate primarily on Thackeray's seven full-length novels from *Barry Lyndon* to *Philip.* The pattern that emerges from this analysis suggests that, before his American travels, slavery was an increasingly potent figure of speech in Thackeray's fiction. However, after his exposure to actual American slavery, this figure of speech became increasingly difficult for him to use, although his fascination with slavery made him unable to ignore the topic, and he retained his interest in slavery to the end of his career. For Thackeray in this regard, what was unseen was artistically more stimulating than what was seen.

CHAPTER ONE

The Ties That Bind

I heard a humorous balladist not long since, a minstrel with wool on his head, and an Ultra-Ethiopian complexion, who performed a negro ballad that I confess moistened these spectacles in the most unexpected manner. They have gazed at dozens of tragedy-queens dying on the stage, and expiring in appropriate blank verse, and I never wanted to wipe them. They have looked up, with deep respect be it said, at many scores of clergymen in pulpits, and without being dimmed; and behold a vagabond with a corked face and a banjo sings a little song, strikes a wild note which sets the whole heart thrilling with happy pity.

—THACKERAY, "CHARITY AND HUMOUR"

I

THE IDEA OF SLAVERY haunted Thackeray's imagination. A most kind-hearted man, he was paradoxically intrigued by one of the most brutal of human institutions. As a young writer, on the trip described in *Notes of a Journey from Cornhill to Grand Cairo* (1846), he visited slave markets at Constantinople and Cairo. Later, he echoed a famous anti-slavery slogan at the end of *The History of Pendennis* (1848–50). As he explained in "Charity and Humour" (1853), even a blackface minstrel—a performer with an artificially blackened face—stirred him to emotion.[1] On his first visit to the United States, he wrote to his mother in 1853, from Washington, "I feel as if my travels had only just begun—There was scarce any sensation of novelty until now when the slaves come on to the scene; and straightway the country assumes the aspect of the queerest interest."[2] Throughout Thackeray's fiction, allusions to slavery—both literal and figurative—recur. With such allusions, he makes a powerful statement about the ties that constrain and constrict human beings.

To be sure, Thackeray was not the kind of writer to advocate a political or social thesis in his novels. His treatment of the idea of slavery is no exception to this approach. Early in his career, in an important series of reviews in the *Morning Chronicle,* Thackeray clearly stated his opposition, on artistic grounds, to the kind of fiction that attempts to twist its reader's arm.[3] Thackeray's dislike of literature that, in Keats's words, "has a palpable design upon us" was a matter not only of artistic theory but of temperament.[4] One of Thackeray's underlying character traits was a habit of trying to see a subject from more than a single side. Hence, despite the incisiveness with which he anatomized society, Thackeray refused to commit himself in his fiction to rigid positions regarding the issues of his day. As G. H. Lewes declared in 1848: "Thackeray is not a man to create partizans. He espouses no 'cause;' has no party." For Lewes, Thackeray's unwillingness to promote any particular social doctrine was to be applauded: "The artist, unfettered by political or social theories, is better enabled to represent human nature in its truth, and his works thus leave a more permanent and satisfactory impression."[5]

Understandably, some readers have viewed Thackeray's refusal to express dogmatic—and readily quotable—statements in his novels regarding contemporary issues as a drawback. Admitting that he had been able to make little use of Thackeray's novels as source books when writing about the Victorian period, the historian G. M. Young contended that on the "Railway" that he envisioned as "the great Victorian symbol" he saw Thackeray as a rider oblivious to the vistas before him and simply worrying "if his ticket entitles him to travel first class."[6] While Young's image is amusing and his insight into Thackeray's social uneasiness may be accurate, the implication that this uneasiness blinded Thackeray to the larger issues of contemporary life is incorrect. Thackeray read widely. He travelled extensively. He was on friendly terms with many of the important social, political, and intellectual figures of his day including Carlyle, Browning, Tennyson, Macaulay, Palmerston, Gladstone, Milnes, and Delane (editor of the London *Times*). More charitably than Young, John W. Dodds has commented:

> To say . . . that Thackeray was not interested in the political currents of his time is to do an injustice to his active and inquiring mind. It would be foolhardy, however, to declare that his political opinions were always pertinent or ever really profound. In politics he was always more or less the big, beaming, enthusiastic outsider, with liberal instincts and a judgment guided by a warm and sympathetic heart rather than by a clear political head. The best that Thackeray had to say to his generation cut across political lines and went much deeper than party affiliations.[7]

Despite his keen interest in the subject of slavery, Thackeray deliberately tried to avoid polemics in his remarks about the topic. Consistently, in his handling of the idea of slavery in his fiction, he tried to take an imaginative rather than a political approach.

Nonetheless, Thackeray's imaginative grasp of the meaning of slavery was profound. As David Brion Davis has observed in his examination of *The Problem of Slavery in Western Culture,* slavery has "always been more than an economic institution; in Western culture it . . . [has] long represented the ultimate limit of dehumanization, of treating and regarding a man as a thing."[8] Repeatedly, Thackeray employs the image of slavery in his novels to suggest dehumanization carried to an extreme degree. In Orwell's twentieth-century satiric novel *1984,* a character observes, "Power is not a means; it is an end." Recurringly, in his fiction, Thackeray uses the idea of slavery to explore relationships in which people have been reduced to objects and power is indeed an end. These relationships include not only actual slaves and blacks but also servants and dependents of all races, upper-class women sold into marriage, and children struggling to escape parental domination.

Part of the problem in dealing with Thackeray's use of the image of slavery in his writing is the fact that he did not clearly distinguish between several different manifestations of enforced servitude. For Thackeray, as for many of his contemporaries, slavery included not only the New World—generally black—slavery evident during part of the nineteenth century in the West Indies and the Southern United States, but also an "Oriental" variety found in Islamic countries and, as Wylie Sypher has pointed out, present in "a literary tradition extending back to the Elizabethan drama."[9] For Victorians, "Oriental" slavery was mostly a vague literary motif (a reflection of the "constellation of ideas" Edward W. Said has called "Orientalism")[10] that provided an excuse for endless fantasies about harems and women being sold in slave markets. However, for the parents and grandparents of these Victorians, as well as people of earlier generations, North African and Near Eastern slavery was not simply a literary matter. Mediterranean travellers of both sexes for centuries had been in danger of being kidnapped and sold into slavery by Barbary pirates—a danger that had gradually lessened in the eighteenth and nineteenth centuries but was not finally ended until the conquest of Algiers by France in 1830. In addition, another type of involuntary servitude that went into Thackeray's thinking about slavery was the penal servitude traditionally known in France as galley slavery. In origin, this latter type of slavery was related to "Oriental" slavery, since one use of male slave labor in many Islamic countries bordering the Mediterranean had been to work the oars of the galley ships that plied its waters from classical times until the eighteenth century. Other Mediterranean countries possessed similar ships, which from the fifteenth into the eighteenth centuries were powered at first by prisoners of war and later by convicts. In France, even after man-powered vessels had become a matter of history, the term "galley slave" ("galérien") continued in common usage into the nineteenth century to describe a convict sentenced to forced labor. In summer 1836 (a time when Thackeray was living in Paris), the final chain gangs of such convicts travelled publicly across France— a spectacle so disorderly and disturbing that the government subsequently eliminated it by transporting convicts in closed carriages.[11] It is not known whether Thackeray witnessed any French chain gangs of contemporary galley slaves either in 1836 or on one of his earlier French sojourns. Nevertheless, the repeated references in his writing to the notion of a person doomed to labor at an oar suggest that the idea of galley (penal) slavery, along with "Oriental" (female) slavery and New World (black) slavery, was a significant ingredient in his thinking.[12]

The effect of Thackeray's lack of differentiation between different forms of slavery is both a limitation and a strength. Sometimes the blurring of distinction is evident in a single passage in his writing, as when Corporal Brock remarks in *Catherine,* while disparaging local wages in an attempt to recruit men from Warwickshire for the army: "and for this you toil like a galley slave, as I have seen them in Turkey and America,—aye, gentlemen, and in the country of Prester John!" (3:17). More commonly, Thackeray simply views one type of slavery as analogous to and implicitly no more serious than another. From a sociological or historical perspective, Thackeray's conception of slavery is obviously seriously flawed. From an artistic and literary point of view, however, the several types of slavery that fused together in Thackeray's mind enormously enriched the image of slavery in his novels. All three forms (New World slavery, "Oriental" slavery, and galley slavery) that went into his impression of the topic fundamentally involve treating persons like things. In any case, Thackeray's most significant depiction of slavery is not literal but figurative. By using slavery as a potent figure of speech in one book after another, he is able to make an enduring artistic statement about the nature of human bondage.

II

(a)

PART OF THE EXPLANATION for Thackeray's interest in slavery undoubtedly lies in the fact that New World slavery aroused a great deal of public attention during his lifetime. Four years before Thackeray's birth, Great Britain outlawed its involvement in the slave trade, but the effects of this involvement cast a shadow over much subsequent nineteenth-century social history. As William Law Mathieson observes, "Great Britain relinquished her slave trade in 1807 and for the next sixty years was largely occupied in the task of inducing other nations to make and to keep a similar renunciation."[13] Despite British repudiation of the African slave trade in 1807 in response to humanitarian pressure, slavery continued to be legal until the 1830s in the British West Indian colonies, where the often absentee plantation owners made huge profits cultivating crops (particularly sugar) with slave labor. When it became clear that simply abolishing the slave trade did not significantly improve the conditions endured by West Indian slaves, antislavery reformers in Great Britain launched a campaign to arouse British public opinion in favor of outright emancipation. According to James Walvin:

> The abolitionists had become hugely successful politically speaking by the mid-1820s. . . . Abolitionists' meetings and lectures proliferated; meetings through the country were crowded with people of all classes and both sexes. It became *de rigueur* for parliamentary candidates to denounce slavery as part of their electoral address. And the established abolitionist tactic of recruiting support via petitions continued to attract vast numbers of names.[14]

Throughout the late 1820s and early 1830s, the years of Thackeray's adolescence and young adulthood, pressure in Great Britain for the abolition of West Indian slavery continued to build.

By the start of the 1830s, the subject of West Indian slavery was evoking an extraordinary degree of British concern. Walvin remarks that "Between 1830 and 1832 the public flocked to the abolitionist cause as never before. Indeed the sole restraint on anti-slavery meetings in these years was the physical capacity of the meeting place."[15] Passage of the Reform Bill in 1832 greatly aided the antislavery cause since a number of the so-called "rotten boroughs" abolished by the bill had been represented in Parliament by West Indian magnates (just as near the beginning of *Vanity Fair* the Crawley family has sold one of the two seats associated with Queen's Crawley to Mr. Quadroon, an individual who the novel implies has no sympathy with the idea of slave emancipation—chaps. 7, 9).[16] In August 1833, with the planters' lobby weakened, the reformed Parliament passed a landmark bill abolishing slavery in the British West Indies effective 1 August 1834.

However, the emancipation that went into effect in August 1834 did not mean immediate freedom for the former slaves. Instead, all the ex-slaves aged six or older were declared to be "apprentices" who were required to work a legally mandated number of hours each week for their former owners for a period of six years in the case of field workers and four years in other cases. Parliament also granted a sum of £20,000 to be distributed among the plantation owners as compensation for the loss of their slaves. In practice, West Indian apprenticeship did not function very well. Many planters arranged the hours of labor so as to deny the apprentices the maximum amount of free time, and some planters refused to grant the apprentices privileges that had been customary during slavery. The most zealous British abolitionists—who favored immediate, total emancipation and opposed apprenticeship— publicized abuses and charged that large numbers of apprentices were being treated more brutally than during their days of slavery. Mathieson observes that the latter accusation probably had little basis in fact, along with the equally erroneous contention that the planters were working their apprentices to death in order to wring as much profit as possible out of them before their indenture period expired.[17] Nevertheless, such accusations aroused the British public. In Jamaica, the colony with the largest number of apprentices and the only colony where apprenticeship was investigated by a parliamentary committee, the planters were especially uncooperative, and numerous problems with the system were evident.[18] On 1 August 1838, in response to strong British pressure, the West Indian legislatures abandoned apprenticeship in its entirety.[19]

For the most part, Thackeray seems not to have been significantly involved in the remarkable British antislavery activities of the 1820s and 1830s. Part of this lack of involvement is undoubtedly due to his characteristic lack of aptitude for political affairs. As his daughter, Anne Thackeray Ritchie, later remarked: "He was never a keen politician. Pictures and plays form a much larger share of his early interests than either politics or law cases."[20] In 1832, when he allowed himself to be talked into electioneering on behalf of Charles Buller, who was running for a seat in the reformed Parliament, Thackeray made what Walvin describes as the obligatory antislavery declaration of this period on his friend's behalf. However, the tone with which Thackeray described his campaign activities in a letter to Edward FitzGerald suggests that Thackeray viewed his activity on this occasion, in the company of Charles's brother Arthur, as little more than a youthful lark:

> We canvassed for Charles very assiduously & successfully pledging him to reforms in politicks & religion of wh. we knew nothing ourselves. but nevertheless the farmers were highly impressed with our sagacity & eloquence. Then we published addresses in

the name of Charles Buller promising to lessen taxes & provide
for the agricultural and commercial interests, & deprecating that
infamous traffic, wh. at present legalizes the misery of the West
Indian slave.[21]

As throughout most of his later career (including his own unsuccessful
parliamentary campaign in 1857), Thackeray seems to have been temperamentally unable to embroil himself in partisan politics to any profound extent.

Yet another reason for Thackeray's lack of emotional engagement in
the antislavery events that were impinging on the political landscape
of his young manhood, especially the historically unprecedented events
of 1833 and 1838, may be the fact that he had other, more immediate
matters on his mind. In 1833, soon after the slaves won their modified
freedom, Thackeray lost his fortune. Within a few months after the
passage of the abolition bill, most of the considerable amount of money
left to Thackeray as an inheritance from his father was swept away in
an East Indian banking collapse. For the next fifteen years, until *Vanity
Fair* (1847–48) finally brought him fame and economic security, Thackeray's life was one of professional struggle, financial worry, and domestic ups and downs that periodically descended into tragedy. While
West Indian apprenticeship was being debated in England, Thackeray
was living for the most part in Paris, trying to establish a career for
himself—first (unsuccessfully) as an artist and then as a writer—falling
in love, marrying becoming a father, and engaging in a financially disastrous newspaper venture with his stepfather. In early 1838, Thackeray returned to London with his wife and daughter, and his problems
multiplied. His second daughter was born in July 1838 only to die in
March of the following year. In May 1840, a third daughter arrived,
and less than four months later his wife showed unmistakable evidence
of insanity when she attempted to drown herself on a family trip to Ireland. For several subsequent years, Thackeray sought desperately for a
cure for his wife's affliction, caring for her at home, trying remedies
with her, and sending her to the most enlightened institutions that he
could find for treatment until it finally became apparent that no cure
was possible.[22] In light of Thackeray's personal and professional preoc-
cupations for more than a decade after 1833, the fact that he does not
seem to have been significantly stirred by what happened in the West
Indies between 1833 and 1838 is understandable.

Nonetheless, while Thackeray may not have paid close attention to
the politics of emancipation in the 1830s, he could not have escaped the
fact that in Great Britain, during this period, the subject of slavery was
in the air. Indeed, two anonymous reviews published during August

1833 in the *National Standard*—the literary and artistic magazine Thackeray purchased in May 1833, prior to his loss of wealth, and edited until February 1834—indirectly reflect his awareness of the emancipation bill which became law at the end of August 1833 and his characteristic refusal to espouse either side in what had been a major parliamentary debate.[23] Although the *National Standard* generally avoided political topics, the four issues for 3, 16, 24, and 31 August hint at the contemporary excitement concerning abolition by presenting a review—consisting mainly of lengthy extracts—of *Domestic Manners and Social Condition of the White, Coloured, and Negro Population of the West Indies* by a Mrs. Carmichael (who describes herself as "Five Years a Resident in St. Vincent and Trinidad"). Mrs. Carmichael's view is definitely pro-planter. On 3 August, the reviewer remarks about her book, "The state of the slave is depicted somewhat *couleur de rose.*"[24] While the 3 August portion of the review focuses on the planters, the 16 and 24 August installments concentrate on the slaves and feature long excerpts from the book to support Mrs. Carmichael's view that the treatment of the slaves by their West Indian masters was generally humane.[25] However, to offset Mrs. Carmichael's rosy picture of the slavery issue, the 16 August issue of the *National Standard* also includes an installment from another review—again composed mainly of extracts—of *Men and Manners in America,* "By the Author of 'Cyril Thornton' " (Thomas Hamilton). This second review features an extract containing a highly critical, clearly antislavery description of a slave auction in New Orleans.[26] Lest any reader might have missed the balancing act that the *National Standard* was attempting to perform, the reviewer of Mrs. Carmichael's book observed on 24 August, "Our very copious extracts will have enabled the reader to see that there are two sides to the West India Question."[27] The authorship of these two reviews is unknown. According to Ray, "Though Thackeray boasted of 'the assistance of a host of literary talent,' he and his subeditor James Hume seem to have been responsible for most of the paper's contents, particularly in its later months."[28] In any case, whether Thackeray himself wrote one or both of these reviews, he presumably made the editorial decision to juxtapose their pictures of slavery in the 16 August issue. Furthermore, the opinion of the reviewer of Mrs. Carmichael's book reflects Thackeray's familiar tendency to try to look at any complex subject from more than a single side. Even at the outset of his career—at a time when passions regarding "the West India Question" were running high—he evidently viewed slavery as this kind of multifaceted subject.

Moreover, even if Thackeray had little direct involvement in the activity concerning slavery that caught up many of his contemporaries until the end of apprenticeship in 1838, he had an indirect connection with the important developments in the West Indies during this period through the family of his stepfather, Major Henry Carmichael-Smyth. Shortly before the passage of the abolition bill, Major Carmichael-Smyth's older brother—Sir James Carmichael-Smyth—became governor of British Guiana (located on the coast of South America but commonly perceived at this time as part of the British West Indies). From June 1833 until his untimely death from fever in March 1838, Sir James Carmichael-Smyth served as governer of this colony, supervising the transition from slavery to apprenticeship and administering the latter system so equitably and humanely that even visiting abolitionists could not find serious fault with apprenticeship in Guiana.[29] Thackeray would undoubtedly have been aware of Sir James's position during the latter's years in Guiana. Occasional positive references to Sir James Carmichael-Smyth occur in 1836 and 1837 in the *Constitutional,* the short-lived radical newspaper of which Major Carmichael-Smyth was a principal financial backer and Thackeray the Paris correspondent as well as eventually managing director.[30] Furthermore, the picture of apprenticeship presented by the *Constitutional* was that the system was working successfully—a point of view espoused by Sir James Carmichael-Smyth, in contradiction to the more negative opinion held by much of the British public at this point.[31] Clearly, although Thackeray was not immediately involved in the major antislavery events of the 1830s, these events were visible on the edge of his horizon. As chapters 6 through 8 will discuss, he was also acutely sensitive in the latter part of his career to the growing American controversy over slavery, a controversy that was still unsettled in the midst of civil war at the time of his death in 1863.

(b)

A SECOND FACTOR behind Thackeray's interest in the topic of slavery throughout his life was undoubtedly his East Indian background. The slavery that had been sanctioned for centuries by Hindu and Islamic tradition in what had become British India was not officially abolished until 1843, although at the time of the agitation concerning West Indian emancipation a decade earlier, much of the British public mistakenly believed that slavery did not exist on the opposite side of the globe in India itself.[32] Thackeray was born in Calcutta in 1811 as the son of a prosperous East India Company employee, and the actual status (slave or free) of the native servants who cared for young Thackeray in India is unknown. Since, in keeping with contemporary custom for Anglo-Indian children, the boy was sent to England at an early age, the question of whether any of these servants were literal slaves would probably have had little relevance for him at the time. What he would have been aware of, as a young child, was simply the experience of being waited on by another race. Consciously or unconsciously, this experience was surely etched into his memory by his traumatic departure at the age of five for England, leaving behind not only his familiar Indian home but also his widowed mother.[33]

Eventually, three and one-half years later, his remarried mother and stepfather joined young William Thackeray in England, but even after this reunion Thackeray's youthful life of English schools and adult life of personal and professional struggle was never so free from care as in his early Indian years. In India, not only was Thackeray enveloped in the attention his mother lavished on her only child, but he was also protectively surrounded by a large household of servants. As Gordon N. Ray has pointed out, the opulent Indian residence of William's father, Richmond Thackeray—prior to his marriage—was probably staffed by forty to sixty servants since "caste restrictions narrowly limited the functions that the individual Hindu was allowed to perform."[34] During his short-lived Indian childhood, William Thackeray himself, according to Ray, "possessed the retinue of a little prince."[35] A description appended by his great-aunt Anne Becher to Thackeray's first letter to his mother after his arrival in England evokes the world of the boy's Indian infancy and early childhood in which dark-skinned native servants played an integral part: "William drew me your house in Calcutta not omitting his monkey looking out of the window & Black Betty at the top drying her Towells."[36] Even on the long voyage from India to England, he was accompanied by an Indian manservant who took him to gaze at Napoleon when the ship stopped en route at St. Helena, as Thackeray later recounted in *The Four Georges:* "My black servant took me a long walk over rocks and hills until we reached a garden, where we saw a man walking. 'That is he,' said the black man: 'that is Bonaparte! He eats three sheep every day, and all the little children he can lay hands on!' " (13:753). As chapters 3 and 6 will discuss, Thackeray's fascination with the slavery that he later saw in the Near East and his emotional attachment to the slave culture that he eventually encountered in the antebellum American South surely stem, at least in part, from a yearning for the lost world of his Indian childhood.

While Thackeray may not have fully recognized the extent to which he was haunted by subliminal memories of Indian servants, there was one skeleton in his family's Indian closet of which he certainly was aware—his illegitimate half sister. In accordance with early nineteenth-century custom for unmarried British men in India, as Ray has pointed out, Thackeray's father kept a native—possibly Eurasian—mistress. The result of this union was a daughter, Sarah, born in 1804, six years before Richmond Thackeray married the woman who became William Thackeray's mother. To his credit, Richmond Thackery not only acknowledged his illegitimate daughter but also provided an annuity of £100 per year for her in his will, dated six months before his death in 1815. In 1820, in India, Sarah married another illegitimate Eurasian, James Blechynden. In 1841 she died; since her financially struggling half brother was the residuary legatee of annuities under his father's will, her death unexpectedly helped to free William Thackeray from immediate economic worry in the agonizing year after discovering his wife's insanity.[37] References to Mrs. Blechynden in some of Thackeray's early letters reveal sporadic feelings of guilt regarding this generally neglected Indian relative. In 1832, in a fit of repentance during his period of youthful extravagance prior to his loss of wealth, Thackeray wrote to his mother regarding a plan of self-economy that he thought might allow him to send £60 a year to his less fortunate sister.[38] In 1841, after learning of his sister's death, Thackeray wrote in his diary, "It is the sorest point I have on my conscience never to have taken notice of her."[39] However, in 1848, when Sarah Blechynden's "black" daughter—Thackeray's niece—visited Thackeray in London, he was only too glad to get rid of her.[40] Tangible evidence of the type of extramarital, interracial liaison taken for granted in early nineteenth-century India was clearly out of place in the home of a paterfamilias and prominent author in Victorian England.

The implications of the interracial element in Thackeray's Indian background are worth pondering. Phillips George Davies has argued that the repeated allusions to miscegenation in Thackeray's work—from the comical Indian amours of Goliah Gahagan in *The Tremendous Adventures of Major Gahagan* (1838–39) to the unpleasant treatment of Woolcomb in *The Adventures of Philip* (1861–62)—reflect Thackeray's uneasiness regarding the place of Sarah Blechynden in his own personal history.[41] This biographical reading of the impact of an often overlooked aspect of what Ray has elsewhere called Thackeray's "buried life" on his fiction seems well grounded.[42] Thackeray's efforts to submerge the guilty feelings that he felt regarding Sarah Blechynden may indeed partly explain the recurrence of racially mixed characters and unions in his writings, as well as the racist tone that often marks his attempts to depict such individuals and relationships. The fact that, according to Ray, Thackeray's own maternal grandmother may have "had some Asiatic blood" would only have compounded Thackeray's uneasiness on the subject of interracial unions.[43] As Patrick Brantlinger has recently emphasized, Thackeray was guilty of racism in his outlook on the world.[44] However, as chapter 8 here will discuss, what Hannah Arendt has called "race-thinking" was an accepted part of the Victorian culture in which Thackeray lived.[45] Not only did the circle of returned Anglo-Indians in which he grew up retain its condescending view even of prosperous Indian natives like Rummun Loll in *The Newcomes,* but as chapter 8 will explain, Victorian racism became increasingly pronounced as the century advanced.

An example of this shift in Thackeray's racial outlook can be seen in the contrast between his relatively tolerant treatment of the result of miscegenation in "Cox's Diary" (1840) and his far more hostile treatment of the same subject more than twenty years later in *The Adventures of Philip.* "Cox's Diary" is a short story in twelve episodes corresponding to the months of the year, written for Cruikshank's *Comic Almanac.* The story traces the barber Cox's own telling of his rise and fall. Originally entitled "Barber Cox and the Cutting of his Comb," "Cox's Diary" begins with the announcement in the first episode that Cox's wife has just inherited a fortune from her uncle Tuggeridge, who amassed great wealth in India, retired to England, and apparently died without a will. In the absence of a will, the uncle's illegitimate Eurasian son cannot inherit his father's property. Much of the humor of the story derives from the ludicrous efforts of the Cox family—propelled by Mrs. Cox—to live in accordance with the higher social sphere to which their new affluence has brought them. As a reader might predict in a comic tale of this type, eventually a will is found, leaving everything to the illegitimate son and crashing the Coxes back to their humble social level. This reversal of fortune lands Cox himself in debtors' prison. However, an unpredictable and remarkable feature of the story is the fact that it ends with an extraordinary act of generosity by the much maligned, illegitimate but rightful heir. Forgiving both the groundless lawsuit waged against him by the Coxes and the racial epithets heaped upon him by Mrs. Cox (who calls him such names as "a base-born blackamoor" [3:266]), the lawful heir John Tuggeridge pays Cox's debt for the unsuccessful lawsuit and rescues Cox from prison. John Tuggeridge also gives Cox £500 to set up in business again as a barber and provides a position for the latter's son. The good-natured tone with which the charitable and forgiving Tuggeridge is depicted at the end of this story contrasts strikingly with the consistently negative depiction of the mulatto Woolcomb in 1861–62 in *Philip.* The racial overtones of *Philip* and their relationship to the unfortunate intensification of racism that characterized British thinking in the 1850s and 1860s are examined in detail in chapter 8. Like Thackeray's interest in slavery, with which it is linked, the racism increasingly evident in Thackeray's writing in the latter part of his career stems partly from his Indian background and partly from the nineteenth-century British environment in which he lived.

(c)

IN ADDITION to the widespread early nineteenth-century concern with slavery and his own Anglo-Indian upbringing, a third ingredient in Thackeray's lifelong fascination with the subject of slavery was probably his mother's evangelicalism. In the British fight against slavery, religion was a major force. As David Brion Davis explains, "From the 1770s onward, devout Quakers were always the backbone of active antislavery organization and communication; from Sharp and Wilberforce to Buxton and Joseph Sturge, religion was the central concern of all the British abolitionist leaders; the grass-roots support, especially after 1823, came overwhelmingly from Baptist, Methodist, and Presbyterian Dissenters."[46] Most of these Protestant Dissenters, as well as individuals like Sharp and Wilberforce within the Church of England, were profoundly affected by the variety of faith known as "evangelical"—a term commonly used in a nineteenth-century context, as both a noun and an adjective, in two overlapping senses. In a general sense, the word "evangelical" refers to a powerful religious movement, originating in the eighteenth century, that stressed spiritual awakening and personal conversion. In a more limited sense, the term describes one part of the Church of England (the section sometimes labeled "Low Church") which was strongly influenced by this general movement. Early nineteenth-century evangelicals, both within the Anglican church and without, typically emphasized strict moral rectitude and Bible reading and disapproved of such conduct as gambling and breaking the Sabbath. They also became active in a number of humanitarian causes, the most notable of which was the antislavery movement. According to Roger Anstey, "In the very warp and woof of evangelical faith, slavery, of all social evils, stood particularly condemned."[47] Evidence indicates that the evangelical influence on Thackeray's childhood was strong.

Soon after her return to England from India in 1820, Mrs. Carmichael-Smyth became an enthusiastic adherent of the evangelical wing of the Church of England who banned card playing in her household and mandated church attendance.[48] Her view of the Bible was fundamentalist. As Thackeray later described her, she was "a dear old Gospel mother who is a good Christian, and who has always chapter and verse to prove everything."[49] In 1852, with her granddaughters in her care for an extended period of time while their father was absent in order to make his first lecture tour of America, Mrs. Carmichael-Smyth seized what must have seemed to her a splendid opportunity to try to indoctrinate the girls in her own strenuous brand of religious faith. Thackeray's response when he learned of his mother's effort provides an illuminating glimpse of the religious atmosphere in which he himself grew up. In reply to a letter from his older daughter, evidently imploring his advice, Thackeray wrote: "I should read all the books that Granny wishes, if I were you: and you must come to your own deductions about them as every honest man and woman must and does. When I was of your age I was accustomed to hear and read a great deal of the Evangelical (so called) doctrine and got an extreme distaste for that sort of composition—for Newton, for Scott, for the preachers I heard & the prayer-meetings I attended."[50] Of the two evangelical divines cited by Thackeray, Thomas Scott (1747–1821) was a well-known contemporary Biblical commentator, while John Newton (1725–1807) is today sometimes remembered as simply a good friend of the poet William Cowper and author of the hymn "Amazing Grace." However, Newton was also a former seaman and captain who had engaged in the African slave trade for almost a decade before leaving this occupation and ultimately becoming a clergyman. Newton eventually condemned his former involvement with the slave trade and became a close ally of William Wilberforce, who led the successful struggle in Parliament against this traffic in human beings. In 1788, Newton published his *Thoughts upon the African Slave Trade,* describing his firsthand knowledge of the horrors of such commerce. It seems likely that Thackeray's youthful exposure to the ideas of Newton would have included Newton's repudiation of the slave trade. As a well-brought-up child in an evangelical household, Thackeray would have been taught not only to attend church faithfully, read his Bible literally, and examine his conscience regularly, but also to believe that slavery was a thing to loathe.

In later life, Thackeray's reaction to his mother's evangelicalism was undoubtedly an element in his complex view of slavery. Biographers beginning with Trollope have pointed out that, despite his personal affection for his mother, Thackeray strongly disagreed in adulthood with her rigid approach to religious faith. As Trollope dryly commented, "Mrs. Carmichael Smyth was disposed to the somewhat austere observance of the evangelical section of the Church. Such, certainly, never became the case with her son."[51] While Thackeray seems to have held on to a few simple religious beliefs—in Greig's words, a rather vague "devotion to Jesus Christ and the doctrine of love"[52]—he emphatically objected to his mother's rigid insistence that all aspects of the Bible were literally true and that anyone who differed from her religious opinions was headed for destruction. When Mrs. Carmichael-Smyth insisted that he omit some negative remarks about the Old Testament he had intended to include in *Notes of a Journey from Cornhill to Grand Cairo*, Thackeray exploded in a letter to her, "What right have you to say that I am without God because I can't believe that God ordered Abraham to kill Isaac or that he ordered the bears to eat the little children who laughed at Elisha for being bald."[53] Near the end of the same tirade, he observed, "It seems to me hence almost blasphemous: that any blind prejudiced sinful mortal being should dare to be unhappy about the belief of another; should dare to say Lo I am right and my brothers must go to damnation."[54] Thackeray's eventual insistence, after witnessing the institution firsthand in America, that slavery per se was not so bad as it was often painted needs to be understood in the context of his long-standing rebellion against the evangelical doctrines inculcated in him during his youth. However, as Greig has noted, while Thackeray as an adult rejected his mother's rigidly doctrinaire approach to religion, he could never completely repudiate her values.[55] In a similar manner, while he tried to look at slavery as broadly as possible after encountering it in the Southern United States, he never abandoned the evangelical position that slavery was wrong.

The effect of these different influences leading Thackeray's attention to the topic of slavery was both powerful and contradictory. All of them, together, caused slavery to be a topic that exerted a powerful magnetism on Thackeray, yet this magnetic force had two north poles that worked against one another. As one pole, the prevailing early nineteenth-century antislavery climate of opinion reinforced the evangelical view of the wrongness of slavery which Thackeray absorbed from his mother. As another pole, his adult skepticism concerning his mother's religious views combined with a positive emotional feeling, derived from his Anglo-Indian childhood, regarding the presence of dark-skinned servants, and this combination made Thackeray far more tolerant of the institution of slavery than he might otherwise have been. His Anglo-Indian background also contributed to a degree of personal racism which the increasingly widespread racism in Great Britain during the last decade of his life only reinforced. The effect of these influences was to make slavery a potent metaphor for Thackeray when the topic was still largely a theoretical one for him, prior to his visits to the United States. In America, in the 1850s, his interest in the subject led him to pay particular attention to actual slavery (insofar as the lecture-tour framework of his visits permitted), and the result of his contradictory perspectives on slavery was a determination to present in his letters what he considered a fair-minded treatment of a subject that he found too fascinating to ignore. Such an approach was congruent with his characteristic habit of trying to see both sides of any complex issue. G. H. Lewes remarked about Thackeray in 1850 that one of his major traits was "a predominating tendency to *antithesis*. . . . the law of Thackeray's mind seems to be a conception of opposites, which makes him a perfect Janus Bifrons." In Lewes's words, Thackeray "shows a soul of goodness in things evil, as well as the spot of evil in things good."[56] Unfortunately, from a modern perspective, Thackeray's treatment of real-life slavery does not seem as fair-minded as he intended it to be. In general, what he has to say about slavery in a figurative sense in his fiction is of far greater significance than his racially tinged and uninsightful remarks about slavery in real life. Despite the contradictions in his outlook, Thackeray was convinced that slavery was a social evil that would eventually disappear as civilization advanced. Modern readers may dismiss his views about literal slavery as naive. What remains of lasting value, as the following chapters will discuss, is his use of the image of slavery as a vital part of much of his creative work.

CHAPTER TWO

Barry Lyndon and the Dynamics of Enslavement

Thus discipline produces subjected and practised bodies, 'docile' bodies.

—FOUCAULT, *DISCIPLINE AND PUNISH*

I

WHEN BARRY LYNDON YEARNS to be free from "slavery" in chapter 8 (161) of the novel that bears his name, the word that he chooses to describe his experience in the Prussian army of Frederick the Great would readily, for many Victorian readers, have evoked a compassionate response.[1] By 1844 when *The Luck of Barry Lyndon* was published, a great number of persons in England routinely accepted antislavery principles. As the historian C. Duncan Rice points out, "After West India emancipation, the British public soon reached the stage where it was no longer necessary to think out or justify an anti-slavery standpoint. . . . Anti-slavery views seldom had to be articulated, except when writing for American audiences, or to raise support for American abolitionists."[2] By the 1850s, according to Rice, this antislavery attitude had become a consensus. "For mid-Victorians," he writes "the anti-slavery position had become a reflexive part of their belief system."[3] As we shall see, Thackeray's thinking about slavery later in his career—especially in the 1850s—was not so reflexive or so simplistic as Rice's remarks suggest. Nonetheless, in 1843–44, at the time of writing *The Luck of Barry Lyndon*, Thackeray seems to have generally accepted the current antislavery position. Even before *Lyndon*, his youthful fascination with the motif of slavery is apparent in some of his short creative works, and several of his nonfictional remarks in the

17

early 1840s offer clear evidence of his contemporary antislavery views. In turn, this antislavery attitude, along with his imaginative awareness of the figurative dimensions of slavery and sophisticated handling of these dimensions, can be seen in *Barry Lyndon*.

II

THE IMPORTANCE, as well as the development, of slavery as an image in Thackeray's thinking is demonstrated by two very different works that span his early career: "Timbuctoo" (1829) and *Men's Wives* (1843). The first of these is a short poem that originally appeared in *The Snob*, an undergraduate magazine, while Thackeray was a student at Cambridge University. Written as a parody of a typical entry in a Cambridge poetry contest, the subject of which for 1829 was "Timbuctoo," the poem demonstrates not only Thackeray's youthful penchant for burlesque but also his youthful interest in slavery. As Hallman B. Bryant has argued, the topic for the contest was undoubtedly selected as a result of the furor generated by reports of the entry into the heretofore mysterious African city of Timbuctoo by the French explorer René Caillié. (The latter's account of his journey was published in 1829 and attacked by the British press.)[4] The contest itself was won by Tennyson, whose prize-winning entry reflects his lifelong concern with the role of imagination in a world of fact and reason.[5]

In contrast to Tennyson's serious composition, Thackeray's "Timbuctoo" is merely a clever *jeu d'esprit*. Thackeray's prefatory note, as well as the poem's date of publication (30 April 1829), indicates that the piece was not actually entered into the poetry competition, whose deadline for entries was 31 March 1829.[6] As Thackeray wrote "To the Editor of *The Snob*," with tongue in cheek, at the beginning of the poem:

> Though your name be 'Snob,' I trust you will not refuse this tiny 'Poem of a Gownsman,' which was unluckily not finished on the day appointed for delivery of the several copies of verses on Timbuctoo. I thought, Sir, it would be a pity that such a poem should be lost to the world; and conceiving *The Snob* to be the most widely circulated periodical in Europe, I have taken the liberty of submitting it for insertion or approbation. (*Works* 1:1)

Since Thackeray's burlesque was published well before 6 June 1829 when the winner of the competition was announced, it is also evident that what Thackeray is spoofing in this piece is not Tennyson's poem but the prize-poem genre in general. Ray points out that "Thackeray's heroic couplets neatly parody the fading eighteenth-century style of verse-writing which still prevailed among prize poets, just as his elaborate notes effectively burlesque the paraphernalia of erudition by which their effusions were often accompanied."[7] For example, although Tennyson's poem has only one brief footnote, Arthur Henry Hallam's poem for the same competition is accompanied by six notes, four of which are lengthy.[8] Nonetheless, just as Tennyson's poem foreshadows his enduring concern with the theme of imagination, so Thackeray's poem anticipates his enduring fascination with the motif of slavery.

Of the thirty-two lines and eleven paragraphs of footnotes in Thackeray's "Timbuctoo," a significant amount of material deals with the notion of slavery. The poem itself proceeds by logic of association. For the speaker, the thought in lines 1–4 of the fabled city of Timbuctoo simply suggests its African location:

> In Africa (a quarter of the world)
> Men's skins are black, their hair is crisp and curl'd;
> And somewhere there, unknown to public view,
> A mighty city lies, called Timbuctoo.

That thought then leads to a description of the black inhabitants of Timbuctoo, who are hunted by the lion, whom they hunt in turn. Next, in a meditation evocative of the medieval view of tragedy as a fall from high estate, the speaker contemplates how the happy denizens of Timbuctoo are sometimes kidnapped and sold into slavery:

> At home their lives in pleasure always flow,
> But many have a different lot to know!
> They're often caught, and sold as slaves, alas!
> Thus men from highest joy to sorrow pass.
> Yet though thy monarchs and thy nobles boil
> Rack and molasses in Jamaica's isle!
> Desolate Afric! thou art lovely yet!!
> One heart yet beats which ne'er shall thee forget.
>
> (15–22)

Then, after alluding to a broken romance between a West Indian slave and a sweetheart left behind in Africa (and punctuating with a hyperbolic series of five "oh nos" the speaker's claim that he will never forget this sweetheart), the poem turns to prophecy:

> The day shall come when Albion's self shall feel
> Stern Afric's wrath, and writhe 'neath Afric's steel.
> I see her tribes the hill of glory mount,
> And sell their sugars on their own account;
> While round her throne the prostrate nations come,
> Sue for her rice, and barter for her rum!
>
> (27–32)

Fig 1. Fanciful depiction of an African ("Timbuctoo").

Most of Thackeray's footnotes draw attention to the nature of this work as literary burlesque. Nevertheless, two of them deplore the existence of slavery, and the work itself concludes with a small drawing of a black man in what is apparently Thackeray's fanciful version of an African costume (fig. 1). How serious Thackeray is in the condemnation of slavery in the peroration that concludes his last footnote is open to question: "Yes—Africa! If he can awaken one particle of sympathy for thy sorrows, of love for thy land, of admiration for thy virtue, he shall sink into the grave with the proud consciousness that he has raised esteem, where before there was contempt, and has kindled the flame of hope, on the smouldering ashes of Despair!" (1:3).[9] The work as a whole seems to suggest sympathy on his part with the enslaved Africans, although Thackeray obviously is not viewing anything very earnestly in this youthful, designedly humorous composition. What is notable is the extent to which, in his first significant publication and on a topic that suggested far different ideas to both Tennyson and Hallam, Thackeray's mind is running on the idea of slavery.

In contrast, the series of four short stories Thackeray entitled *Men's Wives* shows a remarkable growth in his imaginative grasp of the implications of the image of slavery. All four of the stories originally published under this heading in *Fraser's Magazine* in 1843 touch on the territory where love between two persons becomes an obsession for one of them, leading to abnegation of selfhood by the obsessed person and exploitation by the other. The first and last of the stories explicitly invoke the metaphor of slavery to characterize this kind of relationship. The first and most pedestrian tale, "Mr. and Mrs. Frank Berry"

(March 1843), describes a schoolboy fighter who metamorphoses into a henpecked husband. Frank Berry himself refers to his marriage as happy. However, according to his old schoolmate—the narrator of the *Men's Wives* series, George Fitz-Boodle—who encounters Frank Berry in a married state in Paris and vainly attempts to liberate him from his subjugation to his wife Angelica, "In a word I found that Berry, like many simple fellows before him, had made choice of an imperious ill-humoured, and underbred female for a wife, and could see with half an eye that he was a great deal too much her slave" (4:334). The last and most sensational story, "The ——'s Wife" (November 1843), recounts how, long ago, another even less angelic Angelica is tricked into marrying an executioner by the brother of a young man whom she had spurned after encouraging the young man to spend all his money on her behalf. Again, the metaphor of slavery is used to describe the older brother's servitude—in this case, feigned—to a selfish and imperious woman: "Of all the devoted slaves Angelica had in her court, this unhappy man became the most subservient" (4:492). Moreover, the Angelica of "The ——'s Wife" herself thinks in terms of slavery to characterize her relationship with this apparently devoted wooer (who gradually becomes perceived as her eventual husband although he says he cannot marry her until his mother's death): "Meantime . . . I can dress Max [the older brother] to the *ménage* of matrimony; which meant, that she could make a very slave of him, as she did" (4:493). The tables are turned when Angelica herself is bullied by the man whom Max maneuvers her into marrying, but her marital relationship with this man is brief since she succumbs to madness as soon as she discovers her husband's occupation.

While the two middle works in the *Men's Wives* series do not explicitly use the image of slavery to describe the oppressive relationships they depict, the examination of marital domination and submission in these tales continues. The second and longest of these four stories, "The Ravenswing" (April–June, August, and September 1843), chronicles the marriage of a lowly but musically talented young woman to a despotic, worthless husband. To support herself and her child, after her husband is imprisoned for debt, she pursues a career as a singer under the name of "the Ravenswing." However, once her husband learns of her professional potential, he exploits her by making her musical supporters arrange his release from prison before he will permit her debut, receiving and spending her earnings, and taking a mistress. Only after her selfish husband's death, as explained in a postscript at the end of the story, does she finally achieve happiness in a new marriage with an early admirer and faithful friend who has supported her through her troubles.

In contrast, while "The Ravenswing" offers a conventional happy ending in its postscript as an antidote to the bleak picture presented by the story itself, the remaining tale in the collection concludes with no such ameliorating note. Of the four tales in the *Men's Wives* series, the most somber and powerful is "Dennis Haggarty's Wife" (October 1843). This story in the series relates how the honest and faithful Dennis Haggarty is tricked into marrying a dull, selfish, and demanding woman whom he mistakenly idolizes and to whom he once proposed, although unbeknownst to Haggarty, in the interim between his first and second proposals, she has had smallpox and become blind. Unlike the ludicrous Guppy a decade later in Dickens's *Bleak House,* Haggarty is far too decent to retreat from his offer when he learns of his would-be wife's disfigurement, even though Haggarty would have a better excuse than Guppy, since Esther in *Bleak House* has regained her eyesight and merely suffers from facial scarring. Rather, in Thackeray's story, Haggarty marries his beloved despite her altered appearance and loss of vision, settles all his money on her, and devotes his life to caring for her and their eventual children. According to the narrator, who visits Haggarty at what the latter eventually remembers as a high point of his married life, "He was so thoroughly beaten down and henpecked, that he, as it were, gloried in his servitude, and fancied that his wife's magnificence reflected credit on himself" (4:473). Haggarty's reward for this loyalty and devotion is to have his wife leave him, retaining his property and the children and telling him finally that her love for him was never genuine. Within the framework of the first and last tales in the *Men's Wives* series, which openly invoke the metaphor of slavery to suggest a perverse degree of submission in a love relationship, the idea of slavery also appears implicit in "The Ravenswing" and "Dennis Haggarty's Wife," whose mundane, naturalistic settings make this kind of obsessive self-abnegation seem much too ordinary for comfort.

Indeed, further evidence that Thackeray was consciously—if not entirely consistently—working with the image of slavery in this series is evident in "The Ravenswing," where Mrs. Walker (eventually known under the name in the story's title) is described as endlessly practicing her music while her husband neglects her. Reference to Mrs. Walker's interminable musical exercise in turn leads the narrator into a biting comment about the routine of the average Victorian young lady's life as she goes through a typical day of acquiring or demonstrating the conventional feminine accomplishments:

> What evidences of slavery, in a word, are there! It is the condition of the young lady's existence. She breakfasts at eight, she does

Mangnall's Questions with the governess till ten, she practises till one, she walks in the square with bars round her till two, then she practises again, then she sews or hems, or reads French, or Hume's *History,* then she comes down to play to papa, because he likes music whilst he is asleep after dinner, and then it is bedtime, and the morrow is another day with what are called the same 'duties' to be gone through. (4:390)

One sign of Thackeray's relative inexperience in this 1843 story is the fact that this digressive indictment of feminine "slavery" is somewhat misdirected in regard to the genuinely talented Mrs. Walker, who "in the snug little cage in the Edgware Road, sang and was not unhappy" (4:388). Nonetheless, Thackeray's picture of Mrs. Walker during her early married life as a bird in bondage contributes to the implication that she occupies a slavelike position in her relationship with her husband: "Morgiana . . . was one of those women who encourage despotism in husbands. What the husband says must be right, because he says it; what he orders must be obeyed tremblingly. Mrs. Walker gave up her entire reason to her lord. Why was it? Before marriage she had been an independent little person; she had far more brains than her Howard. I think it must have been his moustachios that frightened her and caused in her this humility" (4:388). Her slavish status is further suggested by her first name, Morgiana, after the clever slave girl in "Ali Baba and the Forty Thieves" (a part, in a musical adaptation of this familiar Eastern tale, that the mother of the Ravenswing formerly performed as a dancer "with unbounded applause both at the Surrey and the Wells" [4:342]). Yet, like her namesake, who destroys the robbers that try to kill her master, Morgiana Walker proves to be more resourceful than her servile condition might indicate. In "The Ravenswing," as well as in the *Men's Wives* collection as a whole, Thackeray's handling of the image of slavery is somewhat fuzzy, but he has definitely moved from the literal view of slavery jokingly present in "Timbuctoo" to a more sophisticated sense of the imaginative potential of slavery as a figure of speech. The next step in this imaginative development is his more elaborate use of the image of slavery to depict emotional and marital bondage in *The Luck of Barry Lyndon,* a novel begun in October 1843, while the *Men's Wives* series was in progress.

III

BEFORE FOCUSING on *Barry Lyndon,* however, it is helpful to look briefly at some of Thackeray's contemporary nonfictional remarks concerning slavery—remarks which provide a context for his figurative treatment of slavery in this novel. In the 1840s prior to *Lyndon,* what Thackeray had to say about slavery in his nonfictional writings was indirect. Throughout his career, as indicated in chapter 1, Thackeray rarely wrote specifically on political topics. He commented in 1844, in connection with his work for the *Morning Chronicle,* "I cant write the politics," a disability he lamented because "the literary part is badly paid."[10] As Gordon Ray has observed, on those sporadic occasions when Thackeray did attempt political articles for the *Morning Chronicle,* "they invariably missed fire."[11] Hence, for the *Morning Chronicle,* Thackeray generally confined himself to reviews of books and art and what he termed "occasional jeux d'esprit."[12] Thackeray's appreciation of history gradually deepened in the course of his periodical work in the 1840s, but he continued to find political writing uncongenial.[13] When he outlined his talents in 1845 to Thomas Longman, the *Edinburgh Review*'s proprietor, in the hope of obtaining a commission to write something for this prestigious journal, Thackeray simply excluded political subjects from his areas of expertise:

> I hardly know what subjects to point out as suited to my capacity—
> light matters connected with Art, humorous reviews, critiques of
> novels—French subjects, memoirs, poetry, history from Louis XV.
> downwards and of an earlier period—that of Froissart and Mon-
> strelet. German light literature and poetry—though of these I
> know but little beyond what I learned in a years residence in the
> Country fourteen years ago: finally subjects relating to society in
> general where a writer may be allowed to display the humourous
> *ego,* or a victim is to be gently immolated.[14]

In the context of this bias against political writing on Thackeray's part, combined with the widespread contemporary tendency of English readers to take antislavery principles for granted, it does not seem surprising that Thackeray did not address the topic of slavery directly in his journalism during this period. In passing, nonetheless, he made a number of revealing comments about the topic in connection with other subjects.

"A Pictorial Rhapsody," which Thackeray published in *Fraser's Magazine* in June 1840 and concluded in the following month, contains several pertinent remarks about slavery in a review of a Royal Academy exhibition (and some other exhibitions of pictures). One of the paintings at the Academy exhibit was J. M. W. Turner's *Slavers Throwing Overboard the Dead and Dying,* while another was Auguste-Francois Biard's *The Slave Trade (Scene on the Coast of Africa).* Both paintings dealt with what contemporary viewers would have considered current events. Turner's painting shows the cargo of a slave ship being jettisoned before an oncoming typhoon. As Rice points out, the picture may have been "a response to the atrocity stories based on the *Zong* case— . . . anachronisms—which were circulated in London before and during the World's Anti-Slavery Convention of 1840."[15] Biard's painting (fig. 2) depicts an African scene in which a group of slaves is being sold by a native king to a European dealer, presumably for transatlantic transport, an activity the British navy had been endeavoring to stop since 1807. Thackeray responds to these two pictures, as well as the others that he discusses in this article, as an art critic. However, what he says about these two particular paintings also reveals some of his assumptions about slavery.

Speaking through the persona of Michael Angelo Titmarsh, Thackeray demonstrates both his critical biases in judging art and his disapproval of the international slave trade, which British efforts had thus far failed to stop. As Helene E. Roberts has noted, Thackeray's Victorian commitment to realism as a major criterion of good art made it difficult for him to comprehend Turner's style of painting.[16] Like other art critics of the day, Thackeray also tended to judge a work of art in terms of its potential for arousing a sentimental response in the viewer.[17] Operating with these assumptions, Thackeray found Biard's picture more moving than Turner's although he recognized the power of the latter's work. In Thackeray's words about Turner's painting, "the slaver throwing its cargo overboard is the most tremendous piece of colour that ever was seen; it sets the corner of the room in which it hangs into a flame" (2:514). However, Thackeray also asks the question, "Is the picture sublime or ridiculous?" and answers, "Indeed I don't know which" (2:514). In contrast, Biard's painting requires no such hesitation. Thackeray observes after his remarks about Turner: "And here, as we are speaking of the slave-trade, let us say a word in welcome to a French artist, Monsieur Biard, and his admirable picture. Let the friends of the negro forthwith buy this canvas, and cause a plate to be taken from it. It is the best, most striking, most pathetic lecture against the trade that ever was delivered" (2:515). In Thackeray's assessment, Turner's "incendiary" (2:516) painting may lead a committed abolitionist like Thomas Fowell Buxton to "shudder" (2:514) or cause the statue of the emancipator William Wilberforce to "fly away in terror" (2:515). However, for Thackeray, Biard's painting elicits more critical enthusiasm, partly because its "lecture against the trade" is in a style that can arouse a sense of pathos in a general audience.

Thackeray continues his comments with a detailed description of Biard's picture. The intensity of Thackeray's response to this painting is worth quoting at length:

Fig. 2. Auguste-François Biard, The Slave Trade (Scene on the Coast of Africa). [COURTESY WILBERFORCE HOUSE, HULL CITY MUSEUMS, ENGLAND.]

The scene is laid upon the African coast. King Tom or King Boy has come with troops of slaves down the Quorra, and sits in the midst of his chiefs and mistresses (one a fair creature, not much darker than a copper tea-kettle), bargaining with a French dealer. What a horrible callous brutality there is in the scoundrel's face, as he lolls over his greasy ledger, and makes his calculations. A number of his crew are about him; their boats close at hand, in which they are stowing their cargo. See the poor wretches, men and women, collared together, drooping down. There is one poor thing, just parted from her child. On the ground in front lies a stalwart negro; one connoisseur is handling his chest, to try his wind; another has opened his mouth, and examines teeth, to know his age and soundness. Yonder is a poor woman kneeling before one of the Frenchmen. Her shoulder is fizzing under the hot iron with which he brands her; she is looking up, shuddering and wild, yet quite mild and patient; it breaks your heart to look at her. (2:515)

While Thackeray's parenthetical remark about the African slave-seller's "fair" mistress—"not much darker than a copper tea-kettle"—reveals a mild form of racism, the thrust of this passage is clear. Thackeray is in full sympathy with the "poor wretches" who are being sold.

As Roberts has pointed out, Thackeray had a preference for works of art that clearly displayed emotion on human faces.[18] Thackeray writes in "A Pictorial Rhapsody: Concluded" (*Fraser's Magazine,* July 1840), "the most sublime, beautiful, fearful sight in all nature is, surely, the face of a man; wonderful in all its expressions of grief or joy, daring or endurance, thought, hope, love, or pain" (2:522). Not surprisingly, then, Thackeray was strongly moved by the facial expression of the woman being branded in Biard's painting: "I never saw anything so exquisitely pathetic as that face. God bless you, Monsieur Biard, for painting it! It stirs the heart more than a hundred thousand tracts, reports, or sermons: it must convert every man who has seen it" (2:515). Thackeray's response to this woman's face demonstrates not only his high opinion of the painting of which it forms a part but also his unmistakable disapproval of the slave trade.

Furthermore, Thackeray's enthusiastic suggestion that the British government purchase this painting shows his support of West Indian emancipation, a costly arrangement for Britain in which the planters had been compensated for the loss of their slaves with twenty million pounds. In Thackeray's words, "You British Government, who have given twenty millions towards the good end of freeing this hapless people, give yet a couple of thousand more to the French painter, and don't let his work go out of the country, now that it is here" (2:515). Thackeray then makes the somewhat facetious Titmarshian suggestion that the picture be purchased by Thomas Babington Macaulay, "who has a family interest in the matter, and does not know how to spend all the money he brought home from India" (2:515). The "family interest" to which Thackeray is alluding is the fact that T. B. Macaulay's father, Zachary Macaulay, was a noted abolitionist and the first governor of Sierra Leone (an African colony established by British abolitionists for freed slaves). Although Thackeray eventually became a good friend of the younger Macaulay, they did not meet until 1849.[19] Thus, in these remarks in 1840, Thackeray is appealing to Thomas Babington Macaulay simply on the basis of the latter's public image—"from Titmarsh in his critical *cathedra* to your father's eminent son" (2:516). Nonetheless, this allusion to Zachary Macaulay, like the earlier reference to the statue of Wilberforce, reveals Thackeray's awareness of at least some of the leading abolitionists of the previous generation. Similarly, his remark about the money spent by the British government on the cause of emancipation demonstrates that Thackeray viewed the recent "freeing [of] this hapless people" in the British West Indies as a "good end."

In addition, one of Thackeray's letters shows his indirect association with a major British antislavery activity of the early 1840s—the disastrously unsuccessful Niger Expedition of 1841–42, an undertaking promoted by Buxton and supported by the British government. The purpose of the expedition was to undercut the lucrative slave trade which had been ravaging a section of West Africa. The expedition intended to achieve this purpose by establishing other kinds of commerce and extending western civilization to this region. According to the visionary scheme of the operation, "Commerce and Christianity would provide a dual antidote to slave-trading and barbarism."[20]

Unfortunately, although the expedition was elaborately equipped, it proved a failure. The model farm that the group established on bank of the Niger in 1841 was in a condition that warranted abandonment when a small part of the original expedition struggled back to inspect it in 1842. The native chiefs with whom antislave-trading treaties had been made in 1841 were found in 1842 to be again involved in the business of selling their fellow Africans.[21] Moreover, as William Law Mathieson points out, "Of the 145 whites who had taken part in the expedition, 43 died of fever, in addition to 6 other deaths, and only 9 retained their health."[22]

Among the dead was Commander Bird Allen, who had been in charge of the *Soudan,* one of three ships that had taken part in the expedition. Bird Allen was the brother of the Reverend John Allen, Thackeray's good friend, and the fiancé of Andalusia FitzGerald, the sister of Edward FitzGerald, another of Thackeray's close friends. Thackeray wrote to FitzGerald in 1842 after learning of Bird Allen's fate, "I began a letter some time back that was lugubrious too, for I was very much shocked with reading in an old Galignani the result of that fatal Niger Expedition, and thought of that kind gentle sister of your's suffering & being unhappy."[23] Unlike Dickens, who publicly denounced the Niger Expedition (*The Examiner,* 19 August 1848) as an early example of what he later characterized in *Bleak House* as "Telescopic Philanthropy," Thackeray refrained from criticizing the undertaking. His silence on this score is perhaps due to his awareness of the idealism that had motivated Bird Allen and that other members of the Allen family shared.[24] Nonetheless, his brief remark to FitzGerald makes clear that Thackeray thought more about the unfortunate Niger Expedition than he allowed himself to say and that he felt a secondhand but still emotionally moving connection with its fate.

Other remarks commonly attributed to Thackeray, which appeared near this time, support slave emancipation even more emphatically than his observations in "A Pictorial Rhapsody." A strong antislavery stand is evident in a review essay entitled "French Romancers on England," published in the *Foreign Quarterly Review* in October 1843 and probably written by Thackeray.[25] This essay severely criticizes *Le Bananier,* a proslavery novel by Frédéric Soulié. The review explains near the beginning, "The tale has been manufactured, we take it, not merely for a literary, but also for a political purpose. There is a colonial-slavery party in France; and the book before us is written to show the beauties of slavery in the French colonies, and the infernal intrigues of the English there and in the Spanish islands, in order to ovethrow the present excellent state of things" (5:482–83). The terms "beauties" and "excellent" are ironic as the even greater irony of the following sentences makes clear: "To paint negro slavery as a happy condition of being; to invent fictions for the purpose of inculcating hatred and ill will; are noble tasks for the man of genius. We heartily compliment Monsieur Soulié upon his appearance as a writer of political fictions" (5:483). Although there is no external evidence for assigning this essay to Thackeray, the attitude toward slavery in it is consistent with his 1840 remarks about Biard's picture. In addition, the essay's strong disapproval of what it perceives as the political purpose of Soulié's novel is consistent with Thackeray's well-known dislike of political fiction.[26] Thus it seems safe to follow the lead of those scholars who attribute the review to Thackeray on stylistic grounds. The piece provides another example of Thackeray's unhesitating antislavery assumptions in the early 1840s.

The essay's denunciation of Soulié's proslavery attitude is explicit. Since this piece may not be widely known, its condemnation of *Le Bananier*'s position regarding slavery warrants extensive quotation. The essay declares about Soulié's novel:

> If the romancer's epilogues have any moral to them, as no doubt they are intended to have, we should argue from his story, not only that slavery is not an evil, but actually a blessing and a laudable institution. We will not say that this is the opinion in France, but we will say that in that sentimental and civilized country the slave-question has been always treated with the most marked indifference, the slave sufferings have been heard with scepticism. Is it that the French are not far enough advanced and educated to the feelings of freedom yet, to see the shame and the crime of slavery? or, rather, that they are inspired by such an insane jealousy of this country, as to hate every measure in which it takes the lead? When the younger Dupin said in the Chamber that the abolition of slavery by England was 'an immense mystification,' and spoke what was not unacceptable to the public, too—he satirized his own country far more severely than the country he wished to abuse. . . . A people living by the side of ours, who can take no count of the spirit of Christian feeling in England, of the manly love of liberty, which is part of our private and public morals, shows itself to be very ignorant and very mean, too, and as poorly endowed with the spirit of Christianity as with that of freedom. There was not a meeting-house in England where sober, quiet, and humble folk congregated, but the shame and crime of slavery was soberly felt and passionately denounced. It was not only the statesmen and the powerful that Wilberforce and Clarkson won over; but the women and children took a part, and a very great and noble one, too, in the abolition of that odious crime from our legislation. (5:489)

In this attack on Soulié's book, the review makes its own antislavery position clear.

If the diatribe quoted above is indeed by Thackeray (whose antislavery comments three years earlier in "A Pictorial Rhapsody" are much less strident), it corroborates Rice's contention that one of the few situations in which Englishmen in the 1840s tended to give explicit expression to their antislavery principles was when addressing potentially proslavery foreigners.[27] The essay continues about the subject of British West Indian emancipation:

> It was the noblest and greatest movement that ever a people made—the purest, and the least selfish: and if we speak about it here, and upon such an occasion as this trumpery novel gives us, it

is because this periodical, from its character, is likely to fall into some French and many foreign hands; and because, such is the persevering rage of falsehood with which this calumny is still advocated by a major part of the French press, that an English writer, however humble, should never allow the lie to pass without marking his castigation of it, and without exposing it wherever he meets it. (5:489–90)

The review seems determined to spell out its disagreement with Soulié's proslavery position.

Ultimately, the review objects to Soulié's book on the grounds of both its proslavery content and its perversion of what a novel ought to be. The content is objectionable. As the reviewer declares near the end of the essay, "This novel is an argument for the slave-trade, proved by pure lying. Its proofs are lies, and its conclusion is a lie" (5:501–2). In the reviewer's eyes, Soulié's transposition of political "doctines" (5:490) into the realm of fiction is also to be deplored. The essay further emphasizes in its final remarks:

A romancer is not called upon to be very careful in his logic, it is true; fiction is his calling; but surely not fictions of this nature. Let this sort of argumentation be left to the writers of the leading articles; it has an ill look in the *feuilleton,* which ought to be neutral ground, and where peaceable readers are in the habit of taking refuge from national quarrels and abuse; from the envy, hatred, and uncharitableness that inflame the patriots of the *Premier Paris.* All the villains whom the romancer is called upon to slay are those whom he has created first, and over whom he may exercise the utmost severities of his imagination. Let the count go mad, or the heroine swallow poison, or Don Alphonso run his rival through the body, or the French ship or army at the end of the tale blow up the English and obtain its victory; these harmless cruelties and ultimate triumphs are the undoubted property of the novelist, and we receive them as perfectly fair warfare. But let him not deal in specific calumnies, and inculcate, by means of lies, hatred of actual breathing flesh and blood. This task should be left to what are called *hommes graves* in France, the sages of the war newspapers. (5:502)

The antislavery stand of the reviewer is as clear in this essay as is his concern with the nature of fiction, and the reviewer is probably Thackeray. The attitude toward slavery in the essay as a whole is similar to that enunciated in Thackeray's June 1840 remarks about Biard's painting. The preoccupation with what a novel ought to be is similarly indicated by some of Thackeray's 1845 *Morning Chronicle* essays as well as his 1847 series of parodies called *Punch's Prize Novelists.*[28] Here in October 1843 (the month in which he began writing his first major novel, *Barry Lyndon*), Thackeray is evidently revealing not only some of his present thinking about the "calling" of the "romancer" but also his endorsement of the contemporary British antislavery position.

IV

IN VIEW OF THACKERAY'S CONSCIOUSNESS of West Indian emancipation, as well as his familiarity with Britain's continuing work against the slave trade and his sympathy with the antislavery position, his use of the metaphor of slavery in *The Luck of Barry Lyndon* does not seem accidental. He first began thinking about this novel—set in the eighteenth century—in 1841 but did not actually start writing it until 1843. It was serialized in 1844 in *Fraser's Magazine* (from January to December, with the exception of October). As readers have often noted, *Barry Lyndon* is a masterpiece of irony, in which Thackeray is indicting not just Barry himself but the false gentlemanly system of conduct by which Redmond Barry (later called Barry Lyndon) operates.[29] Like D. H. Lawrence in "The Rocking-Horse Winner," Thackeray is also often seen in this book to be exploring the meaning of the term "luck" and showing that luck—in the sense of material prosperity—is not synonymous with happiness.[30] What readers have not commonly recognized, however, is the role that the idea of slavery plays in *Barry Lyndon*.

The most explicit part of the book in which the concept of slavery appears is the section describing Barry's service in the Prussian army of Frederick II, commonly known as Frederick the Great. Barry repeatedly refers to his involuntary servitude in Frederick's army as "slavery," as in the passage mentioned at the outset of this chapter. The young man's motives for desiring freedom are not noble: "I sighed to be out of slavery. I knew I was born to make a figure in the world" (161–62). These motives simply reveal the self-aggrandizing nature of his character. However, before Barry is free to fulfill his desires, Thackeray emphatically stresses the slavish quality of Prussian military life that Barry has experienced.

Although Barry serves in the English army before he unwillingly enters the Prussian one and finds the English service so distasteful that he deserts, he reserves the metaphor of slavery for what he encounters in the Prussian army. Moreover, this metaphor is not confined to his experiences alone. As Barry describes it, slavery is a pervasive condition of Prussian private soldiers, a condition that contradicts the positive public image of Frederick II. Barry declares at the end of chapter 5, "While . . . we are at the present moment admiring the 'Great

Frederick,' as we call him, and his philosophy, and his liberality, and his military genius, I, who have served him, and been, as it were, behind the scenes of which that great spectacle is composed, can only look at it with horror. What a number of items of human crime, misery, slavery, to form that sum-total of glory!" (121).

Thackeray's emphasis in this novel on Prussian military recruitment as enslavement is striking. When describing his naive journey toward Dusseldorf with the Prussian recruiter Galgenstein (of whose identity he is then ignorant), Barry remarks, "The prince in whose dominions we were was known to be the most ruthless seller of men in Germany" (130). As Barry continues his description—reminiscent of Thackeray's comment about the "troops of slaves" depicted in Biard's painting— "even the children of twelve years old were driven off to the war, and I saw herds of these wretches marching forwards, attended by a few troopers, now under the guidance of a red-coated Hanoverian sergeant, now with a Prussian sub-officer accompanying them, with some of whom my companion exchanged signs of recognition" (130). Galgenstein's comment on this scene is, "These recruiters whom you see market in human flesh" (130). When explaining how he finally recognizes that he too has been trapped and that his companion is none other than one of these recruiters, Barry says bitterly: "The great and illustrious Frederick had scores of these white slavedealers all around the frontiers of his kingdom, debauching troops or kidnapping peasants, and hesitating at no crime to supply those brilliant regiments of his with food for powder" (135). Barry is by no means an innocent young man at this point in the novel. However, he still holds the reader's sympathy to some extent as an individual who has been unwittingly enslaved.

Furthermore, Barry and his fellow recruits are treated like slaves not only in the way they are entrapped into the Prussian army but also in the way they are disciplined once they become part of that service. The strict discipline of Frederick II's army was well known.[31] Nonetheless, Thackeray's stress on the abusive aspect of Prussian service seems remarkable. Barry observes that by the end of the Seven Years' War, "the Prussian army, so renowned for its disciplined valour, was officered and under-officered by native Prussians, it is true, but was composed for the most part of men hired or stolen, like myself, from almost every nation in Europe" (153). In the case of his own entry into Prussian military life, after Barry and the other injured recruits have been discharged from the hospital where their wounds are treated, they are sent "to the town prison of Fulda, where we were kept like slaves and criminals" (147). Loss of physical freedom is not their most serious problem. Speaking in general, Barry explains: "The punishment was incessant. Every officer had the liberty to inflict it, and in peace it was more cruel than in war" (153). The purpose of this constant punishment is to bend the minds of the soldiers as well as their bodies into subordination to Prussian authority—to produce what Foucault describes as "political puppets, small-scale models of power."[32] In Barry's words:

> I have seen the bravest men of the army cry like children at a cut of the cane; I have seen a little ensign of fifteen call out a man of fifty from the ranks, a man who had been in a hundred battles, and he has stood presenting arms, and sobbing and howling like a baby while the young wretch lashed him over the arms and thighs with the stick. In a day of action this man would dare anything. A button might be awry *then* and nobody touched him; but when they had made the brute fight then they lashed him again into subordination. Almost all of us yielded to the spell—scarce one could break it. (154)

When he meets one of his fellow soldiers two decades later (a French officer who had been kidnapped into the Prussian army and "caned like a dog"), Barry recalls: "He turned quite pale and sick when I spoke to him of old days. 'For God's sake,' said he, 'don't talk of that time; I wake up from my sleep trembling and crying even now'" (154). Like slaves flogged into physical and mental submission, the Prussian privates are incessantly lashed.

In writing the self-justifying memoirs of which the novel is composed, Barry contends that he managed to escape most of the physical abuse inflicted on the other private soldiers. As he explains in the paragraph that follows the description of the flogging just quoted: "As for me, after a very brief time, in which it must be confessed I tasted, like my comrades, of the cane, and after I had found opportunities to shew myself to be a brave and dexterous soldier, I took the means I had adopted in the English army to prevent any further personal degradation. I wore a bullet round my neck, which I did not take the pains to conceal, and I gave out that it should be for the man or officer who caused me to be chastised. And there was something in my character which made my superiors believe me" (154). Nevertheless, though Barry egotistically insists that he was generally above the worst manifestations of Prussian discipline, his own words indicate that for a while, at least, he too "tasted . . . of the cane" and that he did not escape the cane until he reached the goal that this punishment was intended to achieve, showing himself as "a brave and dexterous [Prussian] soldier." In other words, while Barry claims that he experienced

little of the humiliating Prussian brutality, it is clear that he was suffi-
ciently affected by it to have reached "the condition of the proper
fighting beast" (155). In his relationship with Captain de Potzdorff,
the Prussian officer whom Barry serves as a spy in order to escape
from the oppressive routine of ordinary military life, Barry is ob-
sequiously servile to a degree that he later tries to disguise when
writing his memoirs. As one of Thackeray's footnotes in the first edition points out, "In the original MS. the words 'my master' have often
been written, but afterwards expunged, by Mr. Barry, and 'my captain' written in their stead" (160n). It is in this context of his enslavement and brutalization in the Prussian army, that Barry's treatment of
others after he finally leaves the Prussian service should be seen.

Although critics have sometimes called attention to the contrast between the likeable young rogue that Barry is at the beginning of the
novel and the wife-abusing villain that he becomes in the end, they
have generally overlooked the role that his Prussian military experiences play in the brutalization of his character.[33] However, these experiences are critical. In general, Thackeray conceived of characters as
unfolding, rather than changing. Nonetheless, just as in *The Newcomes*
(1853–55) circumstances eventually evoke a streak of vindictiveness in
Colonel Newcome latent in him from the beginning, so Barry's Prussian military experiences bring out "faults for which there had hitherto been no occasion" (*Newcomes,* in *Works* 14:836).[34] While another
man (like the French officer) might simply experience nightmares after
his liberation from Prussian service, Barry's Prussian enslavement com-
bines with his innate tendency toward self-aggrandizement to produce
a dire effect. After serving as a slave himself, Barry as a free man desires slaves of his own. In the duchy of W——— (called X——— in the
1856 edition), where Barry and his uncle live prosperously for a time as
gamblers, Barry is served by a black man named Zamor, "a tall negro
fellow habited like a Turk" (200). Although the text does not indicate
whether Zamor is an actual slave or simply a hired servant, the point
that Thackeray seems to be subtly making with this detail about the
man Barry calls "my black" (201) is that only two chapters after his
own escape from slavery in the Prussian army Barry has quickly
adopted the appearance of being served by a slave.

In other experiences at W———, Barry reveals a strong urge for
power and domination. When he manages to get the Chevalier de
Magny and the Princess Olivia into his power by obtaining damning
evidence of their liaison, he is not content with simply blackmailing
them into supporting his proposed marriage to the wealthy Countess
Ida, even though the marriage is his primary object. He enjoys bullying

these two high-born victims, and his admission of this fact links his treatment of Magny and the princess with the treatment that Barry had previously received in the Prussian army: "I had him under my thumb, and her highness too,—I, the poor private of Bülow's regiment" (204). Barry recounts with evident pleasure that the unfortunate princess "trembled before me as a child before his schoolmaster" (205). However, although the princess trembles in front of Barry, in public she proudly vents her hatred of him by outspoken rudeness, which Barry in turn punishes by his remarks to Magny. As Barry explains, "My revenge was, when the princess attacked me to say something bitter to *him*—to pass it on as boys do at school" (205). In general, what Barry seems to be doing in his relationship with Magny and Princess Olivia is passing on a form of the bullying that he experienced in the Prussian service. At this stage in the book he is no longer the ingenuous young man who wooed Nora Brady with such wild but natural passion in the opening chapters of the novel or even the shortsighted young British deserter who was duped by Galgenstein. Barry has become a bully with an impulse to victimize someone weaker than himself.

Given this bent in Barry's thinking, any marriage is bound to be a disaster. Although the Countess Ida escapes (through the events that cause Barry's and his uncle's expulsion from W_____), Lady Lyndon is not so lucky. Significantly, the courtship of Barry and Lady Lyndon evokes the language of slavery. When he forces this courtship upon her after her first husband's death, Barry declares, "Do not let your cruelty drive a desperate slave to fatal measures" (279). The irony in this statement is evident to the reader. Barry is hypocritically adopting the polite language of romance in order to press his suit but has no intention of ever becoming emotionally enslaved by Lady Lyndon. On the contrary, while wooing her, he secretly arranges to read her letters in order to "obtain a power over her by which I was not slow to profit" (283). In an ominous fantasy, Lady Lyndon's growing sense of Barry's power causes her to imagine herself as his slave. As she writes to one of her friends (in a letter that Barry reads), "Can this monster . . . indeed do as he boasts, and bend even Fate to his will?—can he make me marry him though I cordially detest him, and bring me a slave to his feet?" (284). In her subsequent marriage to Barry, this prenuptial enslavement fantasy comes horribly to life.

While the marriage between Barry and Lady Lyndon recounted in the last three chapters of the novel is not explicitly described as slavery, the imagery of slavery is clearly present. Where Lady Lyndon had earlier fantasized about herself as a "slave" at Barry's "feet," she is in reality forced by her husband to assume this position in order to remove his boots. Barry explains near the end of the novel: "I brought my high-born wife to kiss my hand, to pull off boots, to fetch and carry for me like a servant, and always to make it a holiday, too, when I was in good humour" (376). Barry himself makes the connection between the servile situation to which he reduces his wife and the bullying discipline that he encountered in his military experience:

> I had got my lady into such a terror about me, that when I smiled it was quite an era of happiness to her; and, if I beckoned to her, she would come fawning up to me like a dog. I recollect how, for the few days I was at school, the cowardly, mean-spirited fellows would laugh if ever our schoolmaster made a joke. It was the same in the regiment whenever the bully of a sergeant was disposed to be jocular—not a recruit but was on the broad grin. Well, a wise and determined husband will get his wife into this condition of discipline. (376)

Barry's self-justification to the contrary, only a foolish or a sadistic husband would attempt to treat his wife like a Prussian recruit.

An element of sadism does indeed seem to be present in Barry's treatment of Lady Lyndon, and as Juliet McMaster has pointed out, an element of masochism is present in Lady Lyndon's adoration of Barry despite her terror of him.[35] Just as the Prussian recruits were "lashed . . . into subordination," so Lady Lyndon suffers physically from her second husband's hands. Barry willingly admits this abuse, although he tries to discount it: "For the first three years I never struck my wife but when I was in liquor" (319). With his adolescent stepson Viscount Bullingdon—Lady Lyndon's child from her first marriage—Barry has no such reservations. Bullingdon is openly insubordinate and Barry flogs him repeatedly until an incident when "his behaviour to me was so outrageous (it was in the hunting-field and in a large public company), that I lost all patience, rode at the urchin straight, wrenched him out of his saddle with all my force, and, flinging him roughly to the ground, sprung down to it myself, and administered such a correction across the young caitiff's head and shoulders with my horsewhip as might have ended in his death, had I not been restrained in time" (343). After this beating Bullingdon runs away, and Barry finds that he has acquired a public reputation for domestic violence. In his unsuccessful campaign to retain his seat in Parliament, Barry complains, "I was held up as the Irish Bluebeard, and libels of me were printed, and gross caricatures drawn representing me flogging Lady Lyndon, whipping Lord Bullingdon, turning him out of doors in a storm, and I know not what" (349). When, at Barry's insistence, Lady Lyndon goes into town to campaign for him, "the brutal mob had the insolence to ask her why she dared to go back, and how she liked horsewhip for supper" (349). As Zacharay Macaulay wrote to Buxton prior to West Indian emancipation, the whip is "the grand badge of slavery."[36] In the eyes of those who observe her situation, Lady Lyndon's relationship with Barry at this point is that of a slave. Like a slave's, her freedom is restricted by Barry. She is held, in her own words, as a "captive" (368) until—with the help of her relatives and motivated at the critical moment by Barry's description of her as an "old fool" (380)—she manages to escape.

IV

THE IMAGE OF SLAVERY traced in this analysis is by no means the only motif in *The Luck of Barry Lyndon,* but it is one that warrants careful thought. Prompted by the antislavery climate of the early 1840s, Thackeray seems to be exploring the dynamics of slavery as reflected in a temporarily enslaved young man and his subsequent relationships with others. What Thackeray is suggesting is that slavery can have a psychologically damaging effect. After being treated as a brute, one may be led to brutalize others. Thackeray's exploration of the dark side of power relationships in this novel, as well as the book's suggestions of sadism and masochism, may explain why he once remarked to his daughter, "You needn't read 'Barry Lyndon,' you won't like it."[37]

However, whether one likes this book or not, one cannot fail to recognize, in Anne Thackeray Ritchie's words, "its consummate power and mastery."[38] Trollope declared, "In imagination, language, construction, and general literary capacity, Thackeray never did anything more remarkable than *Barry Lyndon.*"[39] Not only is the book artistically powerful, but it is also intimately concerned with the psychology of power, manifested in Barry's experience through the metaphor of slavery. From August to November 1844, while he was still composing *Barry Lyndon,* Thackeray was making the Mediterranean tour described in *Notes of a Journey from Cornhill to Grand Cairo,* during which he witnessed both Islamic slavery and the autocratic rule of Arab potentates. Undoubtedly, his Eastern journey enhanced his thinking about bondage and freedom in the September, November, and December installments of the novel—i.e., the last three chapters, depicting Barry's tyrannical treatment of his wife. This tyrannical behavior was also evident in the source from which Thackeray originally took his idea of the book—a description of the Countess of Strathmore's unfortunate marriage in 1777 to Andrew Robinson Stoney (who, like Barry, adopted his spouse's family name after their nuptials).[40] In the end, the most memorable aspect of the novel remains the aspect that Thackeray derived from this source, Barry's power over his wealthy wife and his abuse of this power, although the story of Bowes (as contained in the primary written account by Jesse Foot) did not attempt to explain why this man became the bully that he was.[41]

With Thackeray's treatment, the pattern of slavery that emerges in *The Luck of Barry Lyndon* provides at least a partial explanation for Barry's eventual behavior toward his wife. Barry's own figurative enslavement in the Prussian army in the middle of the novel is presented as an antecedent to Lady Lyndon's figurative enslavement at Barry's hands in the latter part of the book. In each case, the reader's sympathy is with the slave—with Barry as an unwilling Prussian recruit (insofar as his ethical shortcomings do not alienate the reader) and with Lady Lyndon as a victim (insofar as her follies do not weaken the reader's compassion). In both cases, Thackeray is artistically employing the antislavery values that he and many of his readers shared in 1844. The metaphor of slavery that Thackeray uses in this early novel is not so well worked out as in some of his later novels, such as *Pendennis*. However, even intermittently, it is an important motif in *The Luck of Barry Lyndon*. At the end of the book, the epilogue points out that Barry has unsuccessfully attempted to blackmail Lord George Poynings by threatening to publish his earlier correspondence with Lady Lyndon and thus prevent his marriage with a "Miss Driver, a great heiress, of strict principles and immense property in slaves in the West Indies" (384). Lord George is a former suitor and kinsman of Lady Lyndon. He helps her escape from Barry near the end of the book and, until the epilogue, has appeared to represent as good a person as can be found in the grimy world of this novel. What Thackeray seems to be indicating by this small but significant detail is that even Lord George is not completely admirable. By his eventual marriage to the West Indian heiress, he is at least tainted by the same kind of enslaving mentality that has brutalized Barry. Against this background of Lord George's enrichment from Miss Driver's "immense property in slaves," Barry's urge to enslave others—stemming from his own enslavement—can be seen as ultimately inseparable from the flaws of the larger society in which he lives.

CHAPTER THREE

"Oriental" Slavery in Vanity Fair

The Pacha woo'd as if he deem'd the slave
Must seem delighted with the heart he gave;
—BYRON, *THE CORSAIR*

I

THE WORLD OF *VANITY FAIR* is a world of predators. While human rapaciousness is vividly evident in *The Luck of Barry Lyndon* as Barry's adventures demonstrate, in Thackeray's next novel—*Vanity Fair*—human greed is depicted on a far greater social scale. According to Thackeray's own description of this work, subtitled "A Novel without a Hero," the story portrays "a set of people living without God in the world."[1] There are exceptions to the selfishness and self-seeking that otherwise pervade *Vanity Fair*. Nonetheless, in this work—serialized from January 1847 to July 1848 and "brilliantly illuminated with the Author's own candles" (iv)—Thackeray provides a searing indictment of the human urge to help oneself at one's neighbor's expense.[2] Recent critics have called attention to the paramount role of aggression in the book, and some have mentioned the suggestions of slavery in certain episodes or relationships.[3] However, the concept of slavery in this novel as a whole has not been systematically examined. Such examination reveals an ironic pattern of contrasts as slavery relates to the three major characters, Amelia, Becky, and Dobbin. The pattern seems rooted in Thackeray's interest in "Oriental" ways as well as his particular fascination with "Oriental" slavery. This set of contrasts also reveals Thackeray's awareness of the connection between slaves and things and reflects his underlying concern with power relationships in *Vanity Fair.*

II

DESPITE ITS POTENTIAL vagueness and imperialist connotations, the term "Oriental" seems appropriate to describe the type of slavery Thackeray envisioned in the Islamic Near East, for the word "Oriental" was one that Thackeray himself, like many of his contemporaries as well as writers of other generations, freely used. Wylie Sypher has observed that the motif of " 'oriental' slavery" was common in Restoration and eighteenth-century drama and that it can be found as early as Elizabethan drama on the English stage.[4] However, as Edward W. Said has argued, Orientalism itself is a Western construct, posited on an antithesis between familiar Western culture and an Eastern culture that to Western observers seems both fundamentally different and inferior. As Said explains, "The Orient is not only adjacent to Europe; it is . . . one of its deepest and most recurring images of the Other. In addition, the Orient has helped to define Europe (or the West) as its contrasting image, idea, personality, experience."[5] Thackeray's view of the culture that he called "Oriental" is based on this kind of ethnocentric dichotomy between European ways and other ways prevailing in India and more importantly in the Islamic Near East, the area Said designates along with India as "the Orient" in the eyes of early nineteenth-century British observers.[6] For Thackeray, with his Anglo-Indian background, "the Orient" certainly encompassed India, as can be seen with Jos Sedley in *Vanity Fair.* However, perhaps because Thackeray left India as a child and visited Constantinople and Cairo as a man, the most powerful "Oriental" images in his fiction are Near Eastern (or as he sometimes called them, "Turkish").[7] While the male and female slave labor sanctioned by Islamic tradition could fulfil a variety of functions in the Near East, one of the most sensational manifestations of slavery from the nineteenth-century British point of view was the presence of female slaves in the harems that were also part of traditional Islamic culture. As Said has pointed out, among the many Western stereotypes regarding the Orient, the "association between the Orient and sex" is "remarkably persistent."[8] When Thackeray travelled to the Near East in 1844, his impressions of the area were filtered through such Western stereotypes. In particular, he seems to have made the common Occidental error of assuming that all of the inhabitants of "Oriental" harems were slaves, either literally or metaphorically. (In this assumption, Englishmen like Thackeray failed to realize that, as Lady Mary Wortley Montagu remarked in 1717, many Turkish women possessed freedoms that Englishwomen lacked.)[9] As Thackeray conceived it, "Oriental" slavery carried connotations of Ottoman harems and pashas and basically consisted of abject, total submission of a woman to a man. This notion of "Oriental" slavery forms an important substratum in *Vanity Fair*, a novel Thackeray began serializing approximately two years after his return from his Eastern Journey.

III

FROM THE TURKISH BATH George Osborne takes at "the Hummums" on the morning of his marriage (187; ch. 22) to Dobbin's and Amelia's vacation at Pumpernickel, where the statue of a former ruler with "his foot on the neck of a prostrate Turk" decorates the town bridge (569; ch. 63), *Vanity Fair* contains a series of "Oriental" motifs. One purpose of some of these references is to give an aura of historical authenticity to the fictive landscape. The Turks were indeed forced to abandon their seige of Vienna in 1683 in the military action commemorated by the Pumpernickelean statue. The Hummums (Turkish baths) indeed existed in Covent Garden in the early nineteenth century when the action of the novel takes place. On the level of setting, such references also remind the reader of the early nineteenth-century interest in Eastern ways, an interest likewise shown by the popularity of Byron's so-called Oriental Tales. What we might today call this Near-Eastern or Middle-Eastern vogue continued into the 1830s and 1840s. (The vogue can also be traced through *The Rubáiyát of Omar Khayyám,* translated by Thackeray's friend Edward FitzGerald in 1859, into the aesthetic movement of the 1890s.) By the late 1840s, books of Eastern travels were commonplace. As Thackeray's persona, M. A. Titmarsh, observes in the Christmas Book *Our Street* (1848):

> What people can find in Clarence Bulbul, who has lately taken upon himself the rank and dignity of Lion of Our Street, I have always been at a loss to conjecture.
>
> 'He has written an Eastern book of considerable merit,' Miss Clapperclaw says; but hang it, has not everybody written an Eastern book? I should like to meet anybody in society now who has not been up to the second cataract. An Eastern book, forsooth! My Lord Castleroyal has done one—an honest one; my Lord Youngent another—an amusing one; my Lord Woolsey another—a pious one; there is the *The Cutlet and the Cabob*—a sentimental one; *Timbuctoothen*—a humorous one, all ludicrously overrated, in

my opinion, not including my own little book, of which a copy or
two is still to be had, by the way. (10:122)

Among the books Thackeray undoubtedly had in mind here are recently published ones by two of his friends—*The Crescent and the Cross*
by Eliot Warburton and *Eōthen* by A. W. Kinglake. However, the
work that most vividly reveals Thackeray's interest in the Eastern
world, as well as his complex attitude toward "Oriental" material, is
his "own little book," produced while he was evolving the novel that
became *Vanity Fair*.[10]

Published in January 1846, *Notes of a Journey from Cornhill to Grand
Cairo*—Thackeray's "Eastern book"—describes the Mediterranean trip
that he took on short notice in 1844. When an acquaintance who was
about to embark on a journey to the East invited Thackeray (at a farewell dinner) to join the travelling party, and the steamship company
being used for the tour offered him free passage, Thackeray rose to the
occasion and went, despite the fact that he was in the midst of writing
Barry Lyndon and had only two days to prepare for the voyage.[11] Em-
barking on 22 August from Southampton, Thackeray visited Lisbon,
Cadiz, Gibralter, Malta, Athens, Smyrna (now Izmir, in Turkey),
Constantinople (now Istanbul, also in Turkey), Beirut, Jaffa, (now part
of a municipality with Tel Aviv), Jerusalem, Bethlehem, Alexandria,
and Cairo, as well as a few other places along the way. He returned via
Malta, spending seventeen days in quarantine, and then went to Naples, before ending his tour in Rome on 26 November. The mere fact
that Thackeray undertook this ambitious itinerary so eagerly reflects
his interest in the East, to which he had tried to arrange a visit as early
as 1835.[12]

Thackeray's response was generally positive to the non-Western
culture he encountered in his 1844 journey. Despite seasickness, insect
bites, and other unpleasant consequences of travel, once out of Europe
he enjoyed the exotic sights and sounds that he experienced. In *Cornhill
to Grand Cairo,* he presents his "First Glimpses of the East" at Smyrna
with enthusiasm:

> Some of us were querulous up to that time, and doubted of the
> wisdom of making the voyage. Lisbon, we owned, was a failure;
> Athens a dead failure; Malta very well, but not worth the trouble
> and sea-sickness; in fact, Baden-Baden or Devonshire would be a
> better move than this; when Smyrna came, and rebuked all muti-
> nous cockneys into silence. Some men may read this who are in
> want of a sensation. If they love the odd and picturesque, if they
> loved the *Arabian Nights* in their youth, let them book themselves
> on board one of the Peninsular and Oriental vessels, and try one

dip into Constantinople or Smyrna. Walk into the Bazaar, and the East is unveiled to you. (9:131)

As Thackeray's rhapsodic reaction suggests, recollections of his boyhood reading of the *Arabian Nights* affected his response. As Lionel Stevenson has pointed out, however, Thackeray's enthusiastic impressions were probably also colored by dimly recalled memories of his early childhood in India, "the only period of his life when he had been completely happy, before his banishment into self-reliance."[13] For Thackeray, with his painter's eye, the ordinary street life of Smyrna was full of interest:

> I wonder that no painter has given us familiar views of the East: not processions, grand sultans, or magnificent landscapes; but faithful transcripts of everyday Oriental life, such as each street will supply to him. The camels afford endless motives, couched in the market-places, lying by thousands in the camel square, snorting and bubbling after their manner, the sun blazing down on their backs, their slaves and keepers lying behind them in the shade: and the caravan bridge, above all, would afford a painter subjects for a dozen of pictures. (9:135)

Here and elsewhere in this travel book, Thackeray describes slaves as an integral part of the Eastern scene.

Later in his journey, Thackeray toured slave markets at Constantinople and Cairo. Although he remarked about "the horrible market at Constantinople" (9:244), neither his travel book nor his private letters and diary otherwise register any kind of strong disapproval of what he saw on these occasions. Nonetheless, the fact that he witnessed human beings literally owned by others and openly displayed for sale (fig. 3) undoubtedly contributed to his overall impression that the Islamic Near East was a land of autocratic power. To some extent, this impression of power was a preconception. As Barry observes about Lord Tiptoff in the September 1844 installment of *The Luck of Barry Lyndon*, perhaps finished by Thackeray in the frantic days before he left on the Eastern tour, "Old Tiptoff . . . issued his mandates as securely as if he had been the Grand Turk, and the Tippletonians no better than so many slaves of his will" (320).[14] However, what Thackeray observed on his journey only confirmed his preconception. For example, in Constantinople, in a royal mausoleum, he saw "the tombs of Mahmoud's grandsons, nephews of the present Light of the Universe" (9:150). These two children were strangled in their infancy in one case by order of their grandfather, the late sultan, and in the other case by command of their uncle, the present sultan. Their mother, the current sultan's sister, died of a broken heart. In connection with this incident,

Fig. 3. Slave for sale in Constantinople (Notes of a Journey from Cornhill to Grand Cairo).

Thackeray remarked about the present sultan, "After the murder of that little child, it seems to me one can never look with anything but horror upon the butcherly Herod who ordered it" (9:150). Thackeray hastened to add that the people of Constantinople as a whole appeared very fond of children, but the incident showed the way in which the "Orient" (9:151) sanctioned what to nineteenth-century British sensibilities could only appear a horrifying abuse of power.

As the vignette about the heartbroken mother of the murdered children demonstrates, women and children seemed to Western observers like Thackeray to be especially vulnerable under autocratic "Oriental" rule. Also in Constantinople, Thackeray toured the sections of the seraglio open to public view and recalled rumors about the way in which the sultan occasionally murdered "some luckless beauty" (9:149) by having her dropped in a sack through a trap door into the Bosphorus. Thackeray's imagination was undoubtedly stimulated by the secrecy and eroticism associated with the proximity of harems and the sight of veiled women in the streets. A squib called "An Eastern Adventure of the Fat Contributor" (published in *Punch's Pocket Book,* 1847) allowed him to indulge in a fantasy about some of these secret and erotic suggestions in a comic vein that would have been out of place in the *Cornhill to Grand Cairo* book. In this short piece about the Fat Contributor (Thackeray's facetious persona for some of his *Punch* writings, including ones related to his Eastern tour), Thackeray describes how the Contributor surreptitiously enters a Turkish harem, or rather what he *thinks* is a Turkish harem (fig. 4). He is in the process, or so he believes, of proposing elopement to the daughter of Soliman Effendi when the latter enters, apparently kills the girl and starts to arrange the demise of the Contributor by inviting him to enter a suitably large sack in preparation for being thrown into the Nile. Fortunately, the affair proves to be a hoax, perpetrated by the Fat Contributor's friends. Although this "Eastern adventure" is set in Cairo, the language, customs, and setting of the scene are described as "Turkish" (*Works* 8:79–82). For Thackeray and his Victorian readers, "Oriental" ("Turkish") society epitomized an extreme of patriarchal subordination of women.

Furthermore, while Thackeray may have allowed himself to be temporarily titillated by the outward signs of "Oriental" customs regarding women, he apparently found what he considered the reality of sexual slavishness behind these outward signs appalling, just as in the end he found the East an interesting place to visit but not a place to stay. At Malta, on his way home from his tour, he met an Egyptian young gentleman who, in Thackeray's words, "gave a detail of the practices of private life which was anything but edifying" (9:234). The specific practice "of private life" that Thackeray cites in *Cornhill to Grand Cairo* seems to be that of amusing one's husband by telling jokes involving sexual *double entendres*. Nevertheless, the vehemence with which Thackeray denounces this behavior makes one wonder if the young Egyptian might have also mentioned other sex-related acts. As Thackeray recounts and editorializes on this conversation in *Cornhill to Grand Cairo,* the young gentleman explained: "The great aim of woman . . . in the much-maligned Orient, is to administer to the brutality of her lord; her merit is in knowing how to vary the beast's pleasures" (9:234–35). Thackeray's assessment of this conversation is that "the life of the East is a life of brutes. The much-maligned Orient, I am confident, has not been maligned near enough; for the good reason that none of us can tell the amount of horrible sensuality practised there" (9:235). In another situation, in Cairo, Thackeray enjoyed his dinner with the painter John Frederick Lewis ("our old friend J——, who has established himself here in the most complete Oriental fashion" [9:245]) in the magnificent home depicted in the latter's *Reception* (fig. 5). However, Thackeray indirectly criticized his friend for allowing himself to

Fig. 4. The Fat Contributor in a Turkish harem ("An Eastern Adventure of the Fat Contributor").

be "detained . . . from his natural pleasures and occupations in London" and implied that Lewis had come to resemble one of Tennyson's drugged escapists in "The Lotus-Eaters": "Here he lives like a languid lotus-eater—a dreamy, hazy, lazy, tobaccofied life" (9:249). In view of Thackeray's emphatic repudiation of the Eastern "practices of private

*Fig. 5. John Frederick Lewis, The Reception. [*Courtesy Yale Center for British Art, Paul Mellon Collection.*]*

life" and implicit disapproval of Lewis's rejection of his Western past, it is not surprising that on those occasions in Thackeray's fiction when he depicts European men and women enacting "Oriental" roles (such as in *Our Street* when Clarence Bulbul sits cross-legged on a sofa at an evening party, rests his feet on a young woman's dress, and tells her she "would fetch twenty thousand piastres in the market at Constantinople" [10:125; fig. 6]) an element of irony is likely to be involved.

IV

IN THE OVERALL SATIRE of *Vanity Fair,* references to all types of slavery are generally ironic. For example, in a passing allusion to New World slavery in chapter 9 of the novel, the conspicuously religious Mr. Pitt Crawley is described as a man who, prior to the time at which the action of the book begins in 1813, "took a strong part in the negro emancipation question" (75) and who is also a friend and admirer of William Wilberforce. Like his disreputable father, however, Mr. Crawley is quite willing to sell one of the two Parliament seats supplied by their rotten borough of Queen's Crawley to Mr. Quadroon, "with carte-blanche on the Slave Question" (75). During this period, many West Indian planters resided in England while reaping the benefit of their plantations in places like Jamaica, Barbados, or St. Kitts.[15] Some of these planters became members of Parliament, and Mr. Quadroon is apparently one of this group. Presumably, as a member of the planter class, Mr. Quadroon would not favor either the abolition of the British slave trade in 1807 or the emancipation of slaves in the British West Indies in 1833 (effective 1834)—antislavery actions that Wilberforce supported but the West Indian lobby opposed and Parliament hotly debated before the final bills were passed. This ironic juxtaposition of details about Mr. Crawley and Mr. Quadroon suggests the hypocrisy of Mr. Crawley's idealistic pretensions. In another small, ironic example, Lady Emily (the evangelical author of *The Washerwoman of Finchley Common*) is presented as "A mature spinster . . . [with] but faint ideas of marriage, her love for the blacks occupied almost all her feelings" (293; ch. 33).[16] A composite precursor of Mrs. Pardiggle and Mrs. Jellyby in Dickens's *Bleak House* (1852–53), Lady Emily seems, in her passion for helping the far-off blacks, to have become oblivious to the kinds of ordinary domestic feeling exemplified by her sister Lady Jane. However, the most significant ironic allusions to slavery in *Vanity Fair* involve the "Oriental" type. Most of these allusions cluster around three principal characters, although it is the corpulent Jos Sedley who strikes the "Oriental" keynote near the book's beginning.

Fig. 6. "The Lion of the Street" (Our Street). The figure in the background wearing glasses may be a representation of M. A. Titmarsh, Thackeray's persona in Our Street.

(a)

NEAR THE START of the novel, Jos Sedley, the fat "Collector of Boggley wollah" on leave from his employment in the East India Company, evokes a comic aura of Eastern associations. When dining alone, as he normally does since he knows virtually no one except his family in London and is too thin-skinned to bear his father's jokes, he eats in solitary splendor "at the fashionable taverns (for the Oriental Club was not as yet invented" [18; ch. 3]). When dining with his family, as he does in chapter 3, he gobbles curry that his mother has prepared especially for him. However, the most striking "Oriental" imagery connected with Jos at the beginning of *Vanity Fair* occurs not in his presence but in his absence. Even before he actually appears in the novel, the "big beau" (17; ch. 3) stimulates an Eastern fantasy in the mind of Becky Sharp. Upon hearing that Amelia's visiting brother from India is affluent and unmarried, Becky promptly constructs a farfetched "Oriental" vision:

> She had a vivid imagination, she had besides, read the "Arabian Nights" and "Guthrie's Geography," and it is a fact that while she was dressing for dinner and after she had asked Amelia whether her brother was very rich, she had built for herself a most magnificent castle in the air of which she was mistress, with a husband somewhere in the back-ground (she had not seen him as yet, and his figure would not therefore be very distinct). She had arrayed herself in an infinity of shawls, turbans, and diamond-necklaces, and had mounted upon an elephant to the sound of the March in Bluebeard, in order to pay a visit of ceremony to the Grand Mogul. (18; ch. 3)

Becky's fantasy is comically unrealistic woven from her reading and recollection of a contemporary opera, but it is worth noting that her "castle in the air" features herself in a position of power, "mounted upon an elephant . . . in order to pay a visit of ceremony to the Grand Mogul." After meeting Jos and suffering with curry-cum-chile at dinner, Becky's joke again calls upon the world of the *Arabian Nights' Entertainments* and again suggests a female position of power: "I ought to have remembered the pepper which the Princess of Persia puts in the cream-tarts in the Arabian Nights" (20; ch. 3).

   In contrast, Jos's line of thought after Becky leaves the table obliquely hints at the "sensuality" and subjection of women that Thackeray saw as intrinsic to "Oriental" life, as evidenced by his remarks about his conversation with the young Egyptian in *Notes of a Journey from Cornhill to Grand Cairo*. Although Jos "thought a great deal about" Becky and is tempted to follow the sound of her singing to the drawing-room where she has retired with Amelia and Mrs. Sedley, instead he decides to "go and see the *Forty Thieves* . . . and Miss DeCamp's dance" (21; ch. 3). In other words, while Jos at this point is too shy to reveal his attraction to Becky, he finds vent for his suppressed feelings by indulging in the erotic pleasure of watching a woman dance before him. As John Carey has observed, Thackeray was aware of the erotic element involved when women dance on the stage in front of men. In Carey's words, Thackeray sensed that "the ballet gave Western man a chance of feeling like the masterful voluptuaries of the orient, with girls exhibiting themselves at his command."[17] By watching "Miss DeCamp's dance," Jos is enjoying this kind of "Oriental" fantasy. Moreover, the "Oriental" components of the fantasy are heightened by the fact that, like the mother of the Ravenswing in Thackeray's story, Miss DeCamp is dancing the role of Morgiana, the slave girl in "Ali Baba and the Forty Thieves," a tale traditionally considered part of the *Arabian Nights*.[18] The servile role of women in Jos's fantasy is thus clear, as is the incompatibility of this fantasy with Becky's earlier one.

On his second return from India, the comical "Oriental" aura associated with Jos is even more pronounced. Having amassed "a considerable sum of money" in the East India service (517; ch. 57), he is free to return to England with nothing to do but indulge his tastes in food and splendid clothing. Just as he adopts the persona of Waterloo Sedley in India, so on his progress from Southampton, where the ship arrives, to London he adopts the pose of a returning colonial potentate: "At length, he drove leisurely to London on the third day, and in the new waistcoat. The native, with chattering teeth, shuddering in a shawl on the box by the side of the new European servant, Jos puffing his pipe at intervals within, and looking so majestic, that little boys cried Hooray, and many people thought he must be a Governor-General" (533; ch. 59). The "native, with chattering teeth" is a valet whom Jos has brought from India, and the "pipe" is a hookah or water pipe (both comically depicted in the illustration "Mr. Jos's Hookahbadar," fig. 7). The unfortunate Indian valet suffers not only from the cold but also from his master's vanity: "That oriental menial had a wretched life under the tyranny of Jos Sedley" (517; ch. 57). Even before driving to London, Jos must collect his baggage from India at Southampton, including "his boxes, his books, which he never read; his chests of mangoes, chutney, and currie-powders; his shawls for presents to people whom he didn't know as yet; and the rest of his *Persicos apparatus,*" the latter of which Harden translates as "oriental luxury" (533; ch. 59).[19] Although the influences on Jos are Indian rather than Near Eastern, like Clarence Bulbul in *Our Street* Jos is giving himself what Thackeray would have perceived as "Oriental" airs. However, in the context of Thackeray's stereotypical acceptance of (in Said's words) "the association between the Orient and sex," Jos's uneasiness in the presence of women and "dread lest they should make love to him" (532; ch. 59) only make his "Oriental" posturing in chapters 57–59 more ridiculous.

Fig. 7. "Mr. Jos's Hookahbadar" (Vanity Fair).

After Jos's reentry into English life, these exaggerated trappings of
"Oriental" splendor fade. He takes a house in a "comfortable Anglo-
Indian district" (539; ch. 60) of London and sends his Indian servant

"back to Calcutta" after the latter teaches "Jos's European [servant] the art of preparing curries, pilaws, and pipes" (535; ch. 59). Nevertheless, it is Jos's atmosphere of "Oriental" comfort that attracts Becky (compared here to a wandering Arab) when she encounters him at the end of the book at Pumpernickel, "as the most hardened Arab that ever careered across the Desert over the hump of a dromedary, likes to repose sometimes under the date-trees by the water; or to come into the cities, walk in the bazaars, refresh himself in the baths, and say his prayers in the Mosques, before he goes out again marauding. Jos's tents and pilau were pleasant to this little Ishmaelite" (611; ch. 67). Once again, Jos's and Becky's visions are antithetical—Jos seeing Becky as "the most virtuous . . . [and] one of the most fascinating of women" (594; ch. 65) who needs his help and Becky seeing Jos as someone whom she can use. Just as she fantasized about herself on an elephant before meeting Jos in chapter 3, so she is staying at the Elephant Hotel when she encounters him in Pumpernickel, and she uses a picture of Jos on an elephant to cement her hold upon him. Jos's eventual, ambiguous death suggests the ominousness of Becky's early fantasy, but his presence in the book as a whole underscores the significance in *Vanity Fair* of "Oriental" motifs. The most important of these motifs is that of "Oriental" slavery in terms of which the actions not only of Becky but also of Dobbin and Amelia can be explained.

(b)

IN CONNECTION WITH AMELIA, who marries George Osborne, it is helpful to begin by considering the woman whom George refuses to marry, Miss Swartz. This young woman has nothing to do with "Oriental" slavery and little to do with slavery of any sort. However, since she may be the first character who comes to a reader's mind in reference to slavery in this novel, a few words regarding Miss Swartz are in order. In fact, Miss Swartz, "the rich woolly-haired mulatto from St. Kitts" (4; ch. 1), is not a slave. Like Mr. Quadroon, she is on the receiving rather than the supplying end of slave-produced wealth. Along with the Sedleys' footman Sambo (a free black man), Miss Swartz, Mr. Swartz (her half-brother, mentioned fleetingly in chapter 56), and Mr. Quadroon contribute to the sense of actuality of the early nineteenth-century period in which the book is set—a time when wealthy English families occasionally employed black servants, and prosperous plantation owners who had begotten racially mixed children in the British West Indies occasionally made these children their heirs and/or arranged to have them educated in England. Although Miss Swartz and her brother, like Mr. Quadroon, presumably contain slave blood (Miss Swartz's "father was a German Jew—a slave-owner they say" [176; ch. 20]), all three of these racially mixed individuals are able to pay for their places in the social order of England with money evidently derived from slave labor. Moreover, just as Mr. Quadroon's implied voting record in Parliament suggests an ironic commentary on Mr. Crawley's pretensions, so to a somewhat greater extent Miss Swartz offers an ironic contrast to Amelia.

Whereas Amelia embodies all that might make her an eligible partner for George Osborne except money, Miss Swartz has little that might make her eligible except her wealth. An essay entitled "Waiting at the Station" (*Punch,* 9 March 1850), illustrates some of Thackeray's views on the subject of marital compatibility. In this essay, describing a group of young women about to emigrate to Australia in hopes of finding husbands and starting new lives, Thackeray allows his narrator to speculate about whether any of these "homely," lower-class women (all warranted as "honest" and "well-recommended") might appeal to a gentleman such as himself: "If you were an Australian Sultan, to which of these would you throw the handkerchief?" The answer is, "I am afraid not one of them" (8:253). The narrator explains further that, while women such as these might appeal to "a hardy colonist, a feeder of sheep, feller of trees, a hunter of kangaroos," they have no attraction for a Londoner of his background. In the essay's words:

> They are not like you, indeed. They have not your tastes and feelings: your education and refinements. They would not understand a hundred things which seem perfectly simple to you. They would shock you a hundred times a day by as many deficiencies of politeness, or by outrages upon the Queen's English—by practices entirely harmless, and yet in your eyes actually worse than crimes—they have large hard hands and clumsy feet. The woman you love must have pretty soft fingers that you may hold in yours: must speak her language properly, and at least when you offer her your heart, must return hers with its *h* in the right place, as she whispers that it is yours, or you will have none of it. (8:253–54)

The only motive that might bring a London gentleman to marry such a woman would be financial: "Between you, an educated Londoner, and that woman, is not the union absurd and impossible? Would it not be unbearable for either? Solitude would be incomparably pleasanter than such a companion.—You might take her with a handsome fortune perhaps, were you starving; but then it is because you want a house and carriage, let us say" (8:254). The narrator admits being "ashamed of" the "immense social distinction" that separates himself from these female emigrants (8:255). He also wishes them well in the new world to which they are going, far removed from "that Gothic society, with its ranks and hierarchies . . . in which we have been educated" (8:256). However, in the world as it is constituted in London in the early 1800s, Miss Swartz seems to be no better suited as a partner for an "educated Londoner" like George Osborne than one of the Australian emigrants whom Thackeray later described waiting at the railroad station.

The problem with George's attitude toward Miss Swartz is not that he does not wish to marry her, but that he repudiates her in such a snobbish way. Although Jack P. Rawlins suggests that Thackeray fails to indicate clearly whether Miss Swartz represents a "fit" or an "unfit partner" for George and that "what this means for Miss Swartz's dramatic role is confusion," the evidence offered by "Waiting for the Station" implies that Thackeray assumed his readers would automatically consider her unfit for George.[20] As Walter Besant pointed out in 1897, in many ways the compliant, sentimental Amelia represents the quintessential early Victorian young woman.[21] Her interests and aspirations are purely domestic. (The one subject that she fails to master satisfactorily at Miss Pinkerton's academy is geography, although her need for further "use of the backboard" [3; ch. 1] may also suggest that she is somewhat lacking in backbone.) While she is neither so clever nor so artistic as Becky Sharp, Amelia has perfected her penmanship and spelling. She also is able to sing and play the piano moderately well. She is not exceptionally beautiful, but when Ensign Stubble first sees her he exclaims spontaneously, "By Jove! what a pretty girl!" (234; ch. 27). In contrast, Miss Swartz seems not to have mastered even Miss Pinkerton's limited curriculum. She can play only two piano pieces and sing only three songs, including one that is also part of Amelia's repertoire—the song beginning "Fleuve du Tage," or as Miss Swartz pronounces the words, "Fluvy du Tajy" (182; ch. 21). George exclaims, "And you should see the hand she writes! Mrs. Colonel Haggistoun usually writes her letters, but in a moment of confidence, she put pen to paper for my sisters; she spelt satin satting, and Saint James's, Saint Jams" (176; ch. 20). In addition, George finds Miss Swartz as unattractive as the narrator of "Waiting at the Station" did the emigrants to Australia. As George thinks about Amelia, "The contrast of her manners and appearance with those of the heiress, made the idea of a union with the latter appear doubly ludicrous and odious" (180; ch. 21). Given Victorian standards, in preferring Amelia to Miss Swartz as a suitable partner for himself, George does not seem to be in the wrong. However, his vanity becomes evident in the manner in which he articulates his preference.

While the narrator presents Miss Swartz in chapter 21 as "that simple and good-natured young woman" and "honest Swartz" (181), George perceives her as "a Hottentot Venus" (185), one of the sights on public display in London in 1810.[22] The unfortunate African woman known as the Hottentot Venus was brought to England by an entrepreneur who subsequently exhibited her for a fee. Her most outstanding feature was her extremely large *derrière*—a natural bustle, as Mrs. Charles Mathews later described it, although in 1810 the bustle was not part of the costume of an English lady. In England, the Hottentot Venus was dressed so that her form was clearly revealed. In France, to which she was subsequently taken, Sartje, her South African name, was painted without any clothes at all. In England, she was the subject of newspaper articles, street ballads, and political cartoons. In France, where she was also exhibited, she was again the subject of jokes and even—after her death in 1815—of scientific dissection of her most intimate private parts. By likening Rhoda Swartz to the Hottentot Venus, George is scornfully dehumanizing her and revealing his own lack of humanity. Although Miss Swartz naively accepts the flattery of George's sisters as genuine and with the sisters' encouragement starts to allow George's "whiskers . . . to curl themselves round . . . [her] affections" (181), George is oblivious to what Miss Swartz herself may be feeling. When his father orders him to marry her, George falls back on racism: " 'Marry that mulatto woman?' George said, pulling up his shirt-collars. 'I don't like the colour, sir" (185). By limiting Rhoda Swartz to only one dimension—the color of her skin—George reveals his own limitations.

Furthermore, while Miss Swartz—despite her background—is literally a free woman, Amelia, whom George marries, figuratively becomes an "Oriental" slave. When George returns to Amelia to begin "his second courtship" (179; ch. 21), her response is one of humble adoration. George is aroused by her submissiveness: "He saw a slave before him in that simple yielding faithful creature, and his soul within him thrilled secretly somehow at the knowledge of his power" (170; ch. 20). Maria DiBattista has perceptively linked Amelia's slavishness in this scene with the Nubian slave and the slave girl in one of the charades acted at Gaunt House in chapter 51, although DiBattista incorrectly places this scene between George and Amelia on their wedding night. As she rightly argues, "The slave girl in the charades is only a public symbol of Amelia's private enslavement to a whole system of cultural imperatives."[23] In his reunion with Amelia, George perceives of himself as a "Sultan" (170; ch. 20). Elsewhere in the novel the idea of "Oriental" slavery is also invoked to describe Amelia's situation. In chapter 18, commenting on Amelia's inability to withdraw her love from George despite her recognition of his neglect prior to their marriage, the narrator observes: "We are Turks with the affections of our women; and have made them subscribe to our doctrine too. We let their bodies go abroad liberally enough, with smiles and ringlets and pink bonnets to disguise them instead of veils and yakmaks. But their souls must be seen by only one man, and they obey not unwillingly, and consent to remain at home as our slaves—ministering to us and doing drudgery for us" (153). Amelia "not unwillingly" obeys these cultural mandates to love one man only. After George's death, she carries this obedience to an extreme.

As a widow, Amelia meekly devotes herself to caring for her son and her aged parents, care made all the more difficult by their mutual poverty, as well as her parents' querulousness and physical decline. Her nursing of her terminally ill mother is described as "slavery" (510; ch. 56), a term Thackeray used in one of his own letters of 1841 to describe his care of his mentally ill wife before he could hire someone (a woman) to take his place.[24] After her mother's death, Amelia "slaved, toiled, patched and mended" on her father's behalf (515; ch. 57). Such self-sacrifice, the narrator suggests, is characteristic of the lot of many women: "O you poor women! O you poor secret martyrs and victims, whose life is a torture, who are stretched on racks in your bedrooms, and who lay your heads down on the block daily at the drawing-room table; every man who watches your pains, or peers into those dark places where the torture is administered to you, must pity you—and—and thank God that he has a beard" (514; ch. 57). While DiBattista suggests that the narrator's remark about his beard is simply an uneasy, humorous reference to "the sexual symbol of his difference and his exemption from such torture," it is also one more allusion to the motif of "Oriental" slavery.[25] In Thackeray's next novel, *Pendennis,* the narrator jokes at one point, "Does this . . . run a chance of being misinterpreted, and does any one dare to suppose that the writer would incite the women to revolt? Never, by the whiskers of the Prophet, again he says. He wears a beard, and he likes his women to be slaves" (P2:143).[26] Like the "large pair of Mahometan whiskers" that Robinson Crusoe grows while on his island, in Thackeray's thinking the beards that the narrators of *Vanity Fair* and *Pendennis* claim—with varying shades of humor—to wear in these passages are clearly an "Oriental" reference.

Some of Thackeray's remarks "On Love, Marriage, Men, and Women" (published in *Punch* on 14 July 1849 as part of "Mr. Brown's Letters to a Young Man about Town") offer further insights into both his view of "Oriental" slavery and certain complexities in his attitude toward Amelia in *Vanity Fair.* In this essay, Mr. Brown explains to his nephew what men want in a wife: "An exquisite slave is what we want for the most part, a humble, flattering, smiling, child-loving, tea-making, pianoforte-playing being, who laughs at our jokes however old they may be, coaxes and wheedles us in our humours, and fondly lies to us through life" (8:324). Nevertheless, Mr. Brown's assessment of female slavery is permeated with irony. He points out that the pretense of stupidity adopted by the typical nineteenth-century woman is nothing but socially induced duplicity:

> You see a demure-looking woman perfect in all her duties, constant in house-bills and shirt-buttons, obedient to her lord, and anxious to please him in all things; silent, when you and he talk politics, or literature, or balderdash together, and if referred to, saying, with a smile of perfect humility, 'Oh, women are not judges upon such and such matters; we leave learning and politics to men.' 'Yes, poor Polly,' says Jones, patting the back of Mrs. J.'s head good-naturedly, 'attend to the house, my dear; that's the best thing you can do, and leave the rest to us.' Benighted idiot! She has long ago taken your measure and your friends'. . . . Her smiles, her submission, her good humour, for all which we value her,—what are they but admirable duplicity? . . . Should he upbraid, I'll own that he prevail; say that he frown, I'll answer with a smile;—what are these but lies, that we exact from our slaves? lies, the dexterous performance of which we announce to be the female virtues: brutal Turks that we are! (8:325)

Just as Thackeray designated his 1846–47 *Punch* series on "The Snobs of England" as written "by one of themselves," so Mr. Brown admits his own participation in the male chauvinism that he describes. However, he also admits his own wife's refusal to conform to these patriarchal standards: "I do not say that Mrs. Brown ever obeyed me—on the contrary: but I should have liked it, for I am a Turk like my neighbour" (8:325). In other words, Mr. Brown's remarks suggest Thackeray's awareness that Amelia's "Oriental" slavishness may be encouraged by Victorian society and desired by Victorian men but that it is not universally practiced by Victorian women.

Even more important, Mr. Brown's argument indicates a consciousness on Thackeray's part that the socially induced docility exemplified by Amelia has serious shortcomings. In Mr. Brown's view, the limitations imposed by society on women may prove detrimental both to women and to society itself: "I hope the ladies will not take my remarks in ill part. If I die for it, I must own that I don't think they have fair play. In the bargain we make with them I don't think they get their rights. And as a labourer notoriously does more by the piece than he does by the day, and a free man works harder than a slave, so I doubt whether we get the most out of our women by enslaving them as we do by law and custom" (8:326). This remark offers an interesting commentary on Amelia's intellectual and psychological deficiencies in *Vanity Fair* and raises the possibility that much of the insipidity of her character, which modern readers find so troubling, may have been deliberately designed by Thackeray as a way of showing what a feeble person such an enfeebling environment can produce. Gordon N. Ray has observed that the series of essays—including this one—eventually collected as *Mr. Brown's Letters to His Nephew* "remains significant for its statement of Thackeray's general attitude towards society."[27] This piece in particular also seems significant for what it says about Thackeray's attitude toward women. Like most men of his day, he was in favor of what John Stuart Mill disapprovingly called "the subjection of women." Nevertheless, unlike many of his contemporaries, he was sensitive to the drawbacks associated with this subjection, although to a much lesser degree than Mill. As far as *Vanity Fair* is concerned, Mr. Brown's comments suggest that Thackeray generally approved of Amelia's submissiveness both to George and to the dictates of her culture but that Thackeray may have also stressed what he saw as the excessive "Oriental" slavishness inherent in Amelia's attitudes and actions as a way of showing the fundamental problems associated with such a pattern of behavior.

(c)

THE CONTRAST BETWEEN Amelia and Becky, of course, is at the heart of *Vanity Fair*.[28] While Thackeray calls attention to Amelia's slavishness, he also subtly points out Becky's antithetical tendency to enslave. Rawdon's marriage to Becky is initially described in terms of classical and Biblical examples of sexual subjugation: "Don't we see every day in the world many an honest Hercules at the apron-strings of Omphale, and great whiskered Samsons prostrate in Delilah's lap?" (138; ch. 16). Later, Becky looks upon her husband as "her errand-man and humble slave" (466; ch. 52). However, Rawdon is by no means Becky's only bondservant. In Brussels, General Tufto is "her slave and worshipper" (261; ch. 30). At the height of her success in London, as a result of her triumph in the charades at Gaunt House, "Lord Steyne was her slave" (461; ch. 51). Throughout her career, she insidiously fascinates numerous men, as Thackeray shows her fascinating Sir Pitt Crawley in an illustration near the end of chapter 45 (fig. 8). Even at the end of the

Fig. 8. Becky fascinating Sir Pitt Crawley (Vanity Fair).

novel, when her luck has almost run out but she fortuitously reencounters Joseph Sedley, "In the course of a week, the civilian was her sworn slave and frantic admirer" (611; ch. 67). As the novel stresses about Jos's subjection to Becky (two paragraphs before the scene illustrated by the ominous etching, "Becky's second appearance in the character of Clytemnestra"), "That infatuated man seemed to be entirely her slave" (622; ch. 67). Through such passages, Thackeray demonstrates the difference between Amelia's extreme submission and Becky's extreme urge to enslave others and implies that Becky's approach is just as undesirable as is Amelia's extreme passivity.[29]

As with Amelia's passivity, Becky's aggressiveness is presented in terms of the motif of "Oriental" slavery. The most conspicuous treatment of this motif in connection with Becky occurs in the charades at Gaunt House. DiBattista has provocatively analyzed Becky's role in these charades and what the charades suggest about Thackeray's view of women in Victorian society.[30] However, while DiBattista's comments about Amelia seem accurate, some of her remarks about Becky are more debatable. In particular, it appears a mistake to see Becky as "a figure of outraged womanhood" like Philomele and, to some extent, Clytemnestra, the legendary women Becky evokes with her parts in the charades.[31] She does resemble Philomele, who was changed into a nightingale in Ovid's version of the legend, in terms of her beautiful singing voice. She is like Clytemnestra in terms of her murderous propensities, suggested by the illustration depicting her "second appearance" in this role, as well as in her implied infidelity to her husband and willingness to dispense with his presence. For example, immediately after the party featuring the charades at Gaunt House, Rawdon is arrested for debt, and Becky fails to pay the money that will release him while she privately entertains Lord Steyne. Nevertheless, unlike Clytemnestra, who is motivated to take revenge on Agamemnon because of the sacrifice of her daughter Iphigenia, Becky cares nothing for her son: "She spurned children and children-lovers" (407; ch. 45). Unlike the raped and mutilated Philomele, Becky is a victimizer, not a victim. The only person actually mutilated in her experience is Lord Steyne, who until his death bears "a burning red mark" (587; ch. 64) where his forehead was cut by her diamond decoration thrown by Rawdon's hand. (The narrator also alludes obliquely to Becky-the-mermaid's underwater "wretched pickled victims" [578; ch. 64]). Moreover, in the context of the imagery of "Oriental" slavery both in the charade scenes and elsewhere in the novel, Thackeray seems to be subtly showing the limitations of Becky's attitude toward life.

One of the most insidious aspects of Becky's *modus operandi* is her willingness to play the role of slave when it suits her purposes. At the beginning of her marriage, in the style of the clever women Mr. Brown describes to his nephew, she caters to her husband's wishes and ministers to his comfort like a good-natured slave: "When he came home she was alert and happy: when he went out she pressed him to go: when he stayed at home, she played and sang for him, made him good drinks, superintended his dinner, warmed his slippers, and steeped his soul in comfort" (148; ch. 17). Through such "amiable slavishness," she converts her husband "into a very happy and submissive married man" (149; ch. 17), an arrangement that not only gives Becky control over the "heavy dragoon" (137; ch. 16) whom she has married but also allows her to continue her career of manipulating men without her husband's interference. Significantly, this description of Becky's "amiable slavishness," along with that of "your domestic models, and paragons of female virtue" (149), appears in chapter 17, paralleling the description already quoted from chapter 18 of Amelia's obedience to the supposedly Turkish principle that a woman's soul "must be seen by only one man" whom she will serve as a domestic slave. The similarity of these passages in successive chapters is only one example of Thackeray's patterning of material within the monthly numbers of his novel (in this case number five). The difference between the passages is that Amelia's slavish behavior is in earnest, while when Becky acts like a slave she is simply playing a role. This role-playing is particularly apparent late in the novel, in chapter 52, when Rawdon's suspicions about his wife are finally aroused and he refuses to leave her alone. Becky's reaction is to feign happiness at Rawdon's presence and once again concern herself with what might be pleasing or comfortable for her husband: "It was the early days of their marriage over again" (472). However, once Rawdon goes to sleep, her mask slips out of place: "He fell asleep after dinner in his chair; he did not see the face opposite to him, haggard, weary, and terrible; it lighted up with fresh candid smiles when he woke" (472). While Amelia's domestic slavery seems excessive, Becky's pretense of slavery regarding her husband is equally objectionable. The fundamental motive behind the pretense is simply Becky's desire to advance herself.

Just as Becky manipulates and deceives her husband by acting the role of domestic slave, so she frequently disguises her aggressiveness by playing the role of victim. Her pose of victim is most comical in conjunction with its effect on Jos Sedley. When she meets him near the beginning of the novel, she deliberately dresses to appear "the picture of gentle unprotected innocence, and humble virgin simplicity" (19; ch. 3), and she charms him by devices such as her song alluding to "her hapless orphan state" (30; ch. 4). Later, when she wants to secure a seat in Jos's carriage in case it might be necessary for her to flee from Brussels, she presents herself as a "victim to his attractions" (271; ch. 31) and fabricates a story of how she is suffering from Rawdon's jealousy of "the stout civilian" (265; ch. 31). Finally, when she meets Jos again in Pumpernickel and successfully enslaves him, she begins by portraying herself as "a white-robed angel escaped from heaven to be subject to the infernal machinations and villany of fiends here below" (594; ch. 65). Becky is also quite willing to abase herself in order to achieve her ends. After Waterloo, when Rawdon Crawley is severely reprimanded for gambling with and suspiciously winning money from other British officers in Paris, "If Rebecca had not gone on her knees to General Tufto, Crawley would have been sent back to England" (324; ch. 36). Eventually, the Crawleys do return to England, after Becky has settled her husband's pre-Waterloo debts, for which he would have otherwise been arrested. Back in London, she is rumored to cajole financial assistance from other men by the pretense of desperate helplessness that worked with General Tufto; reputedly "it was Becky's habit to levy contributions on all her husband's friends: going to this one in tears . . . falling on her knees to that one" (455; ch. 51). Similarly, in chapter 55, when urging Sir Pitt Crawley to help reconcile her with her husband (separation and scandal will destroy her social position), she again "flung herself down on her knees" (493), a scene highlighted in one of Thackeray's illustrations (fig. 9).

In such acts, Becky parodies Amelia's brand of submissiveness. However, the most striking example of Becky's role-playing of this type—and of its inherent eroticism—can be seen in her relationship with the Marquis of Steyne, the powerful master of Gaunt House. Lord Steyne embodies much of the imagery associated with "Oriental" slavery in *Vanity Fair*. It is no accident that the most extended representation of

Fig. 9. Becky on her knees to Sir Pitt Crawley (Vanity Fair).

this imagery occurs in one of the charades enacted at Gaunt House in chapter 51. As suggested by Thackeray's illustrated capital beginning chapter 52, depicting a leering "Oriental" potentate reclining against a cushion (fig. 10), Lord Steyne plays the part of sultan in his relationships with those whom he perceives as weaker than himself.[32] As sultan, Steyne wishes to obtain Becky as a slave, and the object of his "Oriental" display of seemingly absolute power in chapters 48 through 52 is the achievement of this end. He bullies his "Hareem" (435; ch. 49)—his wife and daughter-in-law—into inviting Becky to Gaunt House, and his "vizier" (454; ch. 51)—Mr. Wenham—treats Becky with polite but stealthy consideration. Chapter 52 (ironically entitled "In Which Lord Steyne Shows Himself in a Most Amiable Light") describes how Steyne exercises his influence to arrange a free education for little Rawdon at Whitefriars and an attractive position as housekeeper at Gauntly Hall for Becky's companion Briggs, arrangements that remove from Becky's household two major obstacles to Steyne's designs. The end of this chapter, describing Rawdon's imprisonment, which chapter 53 implies was also planned by Lord Steyne, offers yet another example of this sultan's use of power to remove all impediments to his goal. The first charade in chapter 51 visually foreshadows his arrangements in the next two chapters and implicitly conveys their sexual meaning.

As indicated by the "thrill of terror and delight [that] runs through

Fig. 10. Capital for chapter 52 of Vanity Fair, *suggesting Lord Steyne in the role of "Oriental" potentate.*

the assembly" (457) at Gaunt House when this charade begins, its content is intended to titillate its viewers. Its opening scene depicts a "Turkish voluptuary," an Ottoman "Aga" or potentate, "couched on a divan" (457), the position assumed by the figure representing Lord Steyne in the illustrated capital at the beginning of the next chapter and approximated by Steyne himself in chapter 53 when he is found by Rawdon "hanging over the sofa on which Becky sate" (478). As these parallels indicate, details of this first charade are echoed in Lord Steyne's designs. In the opening episode, the Turkish potentate purchases a lavishly bejeweled slave, just as in chapter 53 when Steyne is discovered with Becky, who is decked with jewels, he claims that he has purchased her from Rawdon. Moreover, just as the slave girl in this charade weeps in the first scene at her separation from her "Circassian bridegroom" but is then "perfectly reconciled" to her owner in the second (457), so Steyne (if he is indeed masterminding Rawdon's removal from Becky as the next few chapters suggest) may anticipate some objection on Becky's part, followed by her eventual submission. The part of the slave girl in this charade is not played by Becky, who instead subsequently enacts the more aggressive role of Clytemnestra. However, the illustration captioned "The Triumph of Clytemnestra" (but showing Becky, with her head bowed and her eyes cast down, next to the costumed individuals who played the slave girl and the potentate) creates the illusion that this seemingly submissive Clytemnestra is also somehow part of the "Oriental" tableau (fig. 11). Her dealings with Lord Steyne in the rest of this chapter and the two succeeding ones capitalize on this illusion.

Becky's relationship with the Marquis of Steyne is fundamentally a power struggle in which each of these two aggressive figures seeks to enslave the other. The events following the Turkish tableau at Gaunt House bring this power struggle to its climax. What Becky wants from Lord Steyne is as much money and social position as she can get—in particular, as she reminds him in chapter 48, "a place" (431) such as the colonial governorship that Steyne eventually arranges for Rawdon, giving him an income and clear social standing. To achieve this goal, Becky feigns submissiveness and implies that she is willing to play the role of slave. Twice, in conversations with Lord Steyne described in chapters 48 and 52, she pretends to be a victim of her husband's greed. As she fabricates her story in chapter 52, "It was my husband, by threats and the most savage treatment, forced me to ask for that sum about which I deceived you" (470). Her pretense of victimization is calculated for its effect on Steyne: "Persecuted virtue never looked more bewitchingly wretched" (470). Her role as Philomèle in the sec-

Fig. 11. "The Triumph of Clytemnestra" (Vanity Fair).

ond charade also suggests this message of victimization as DiBattista has accurately pointed out.[33] Nonetheless, it is important to remember that Becky is simply play-acting here, as in so many other places, and that her actions in the charades are calculated for their impact on the powerful man whom she is attempting to manipulate. Through Thackeray's familiar device of circling back, the charades in chapter 51 chronologically follow Becky's role-playing as victim in chapter 52.[34] Like a Houri (such as the slave girl whom Becky eclipses in the first charade) or an odalisque (of the type which Bedwin Sands's "black slave" is reputed to have "sown up . . . in sacks and tilted . . . into the Nile" [457; ch. 51]), Becky excites the admiration of Lord Steyne and his guests, including the Turkish Ambassador, Papoosh Pasha, by her singing and dancing. When Rawdon finds her alone with Lord Steyne in the great discovery scene in chapter 53, she is engaged in a private performance for the sultan who has elevated her to fortune, playing her part "in a brilliant full toilette" and "singing a snatch of the song of the night before" (478). Whether Lord Steyne is just now about to claim the sexual satisfaction implicit in his role as sultan and Becky's role as slave or whether he has previously received this satisfaction and is simply about to exact further sexual favors remains unclear and ultimately unimportant. As Rawdon says in chapter 55, "If she's not guilty . . . she's as bad as guilty" (500).

The scene of discovery in chapter 53 reveals not only the truth about Becky's nature to Rawdon's disillusioned eyes but also the truth about the power relationships that define her world. In order to enslave Lord Steyne, she is obliged to act like a slave herself. These two domineering characters cannot coexist in a nonenslaving relationship, as is later shown in chapter 64 by Becky's "little, timid, imploring curtsey" (588) when she sees him again and Steyne's sultanic threat of death unless Becky departs from the city where he is staying. Indeed, Becky is so sensitive to power and so attracted to powerful men that when her heretofore disregarded husband strikes Steyne and throws him to the floor Becky "stood there trembling. . . . She admired her husband, strong, brave, and victorious" (479; ch. 53). The fact that Thackeray himself called this description of Becky's unexpected admiration of Rawdon "a touch of genius" underscores the way in which the drama of power relationships associated with the enslaving imagery in this novel reaches a climax in this scene.[35] At this moment, Becky is temporarily the passive victim she has so often pretended to be. Steyne and Rawdon depart. Her maid robs her and leaves her lying on her bed, ironically like the helpless sexual object Becky has frequently personified in her pretenses with Lord Steyne.

(d)

FOR THACKERAY, BECKY'S urge to enslave others ultimately seems as self-defeating as Amelia's slavishness. Yet a third approach to human relationships, and sadly still an unsatisfactory one in the world of *Vanity Fair,* is exemplified by Dobbin in his attitude toward Amelia. As Bernard J. Paris has pointed out, both Dobbin and Amelia are fundamentally compliant persons.[36] Like Amelia, Dobbin appears excessively submissive in his relationship with George Osborne. Moreover, just as George perceives Amelia as a slave yielding to him as sultan at the time of their reunion in chapter 20, so Dobbin is presented as a slave at an equally critical moment in his friendship with George—the aftermath of his schoolboy fight with Cuff on George's behalf in chapter 5. After winning this fight with Cuff, "the unquestioned king of the school" (34) who has been bullying little George, Dobbin defies logic by worshipping the boy whom he has defended and "to whom henceforth he vowed such a love and affection as is only felt by children—such an affection as we read in the charming fairy-book Uncouth Orson had for splendid young Valentine his conqueror. He flung himself down at little Osborne's feet and loved him. Even before they were acquainted, he had admired Osborne in secret. Now he was his valet, his dog, his man-Friday" (39). The story of Valentine and Orson, popular in collections of nursery tales and chapbooks in Thackeray's youth, describes the adventures of twin brothers. One of these twins (Valentine) is found in a forest as an infant and raised at court where he becomes a knight. The other (Orson) is carried off into the woods by a bear and brought up there in a savage state. Valentine eventually captures and civilizes Orson.[37] As a reference in one of Thackeray's letters indicates, the version of the story with which he was familiar may have presented Orson as having been "enslaved" by the agent of civilization, Valentine.[38] At any rate, as indicated by the allusion to "man-Friday," the devoted native servant acquired by Robinson Crusoe when shipwrecked on a slave-trading expedition to the Guinea coast, the narrator evidently intends to present Dobbin as having figuratively enslaved himself in his subsequent relationship with his friend. In the novel as a whole, Dobbin's underestimate of his own worth in relation to the worthless George is clearly as wrongheaded as the excessive value that Amelia places on the fiancé who neglects her and the husband who engages in "a desperate flirtation" with another woman within six weeks of their marriage (252; ch. 29).

As U. C. Knoepflmacher has observed about Dobbin, "The man with the horselike name is a Houyhnhnm among the Yahoos."[39] Not surprisingly, in his attitude toward Amelia this fundamentally decent man strives for a relationship that avoids the extremes embodied by Amelia's servile submissiveness to George and Becky's aggressive enslavement of her male admirers. While George prepared for his marriage by taking a Turkish bath, Dobbin goes on vacation with Amelia (accompanied by Jos and young Georgy) to Pumpernickel where, as mentioned earlier, the bridge is adorned by a statue of a "prostrate Turk." The emblem of the defeated Turk is appropriate, for in his treatment of Amelia, Dobbin is no "Oriental" sultan. Unlike Dobbin, George condescendingly agrees to marry Amelia and then not only neglects his wife but, soon after their marriage, also bullies her in a manner worthy of his overbearing father. George becomes "angry . . . at finding his wife up on his return from the parties which he frequented" (255; ch. 29), and he scolds her "violently" in Brussels for her reluctance to visit Becky (251; ch. 29). This imperious attitude toward Amelia is ironically countered by George's own submission to Becky's charms when he becomes "caught in the little Circe's toils" (601; ch. 66). In contrast to the master-slave dynamics that permeate George's view of Amelia and Becky's view of George, Dobbin has no desire to see Amelia in a state of abject submission. The image of Amelia that Dobbin carries before his mind's eye is not that of Amelia as a "kneeling Esther," as George sees her at the start of their renewed courtship in chapter 20. Rather—in England, Europe, and India, as he tells her twelve years after Waterloo—Dobbin remembers Amelia as "a girl, in white, with large ringlets; . . . [who] came down[stairs] singing" (538; ch. 59). As indicated by this shift in position of mental images, Dobbin thinks of Amelia not as a slave at his feet but as a superior, almost angelic being descending towards him. Other variations on the Amelia-image in Dobbin's mind also suggest his sense of her superiority to ordinary life. He thinks of her (388; ch. 43) in mourning as "A gentle little woman in black, with large eyes and brown hair, seldom speaking, save when spoken to" (i.e., like a nun); as "a soft young mother tending an infant" (i.e., like a Madonna and Child); and as "a rosy-cheeked lass . . . hanging on George Osborne's arm" (i.e., the partner of his admired George).[40] In the years after George's death, Dobbin woos Amelia. He apparently wishes her to descend to his level but to do so voluntarily. Throughout most of the novel, he has no desire to coerce her in any way.

The exception—and the event that precipitates Dobbin's and Amelia's ultimate union—is Dobbin's attempt in Pumpernickel to force Amelia to repudiate Rebecca. For the first time in his dealings with Amelia, in an effort to protect her from the now thoroughly disreputable Becky, whom Amelia and Jos have naively befriended, Dobbin tries to exert himself like a stereotypical "Oriental" male. He begins his attempt to rid Amelia of Becky's company with what is for Dobbin an atypical remark, "If I have any authority in this house—" (607). The word "authority" lies at the heart of this scene between Amelia and Dobbin in chapter 66, in which Dobbin "suddenly broke the chain by which she held him, and declared his independence and superiority" (608). Earlier, the narrator has made it clear that, if Dobbin had only acted more assertively, he could have won Amelia long ago: "Why did he not take her in his arms, and swear that he would never leave her? She must have yielded: she could not but have obeyed him" (527; ch.

58). Instead, Dobbin customarily treats Amelia with courteous deference. He allows her to tyrannize him and make "him fetch and carry just as if he was a great Newfoundland dog" (602; ch. 66). Like Dickens's later Joe Gargery in *Great Expectations* (1860–61), who is so determined to avoid any kind of abuse of his wife that he passively allows her to "ram-page" over him, Dobbin lets himself behave as "a spooney" (602; ch. 66) partly because he consciously wishes to avoid the opposite extreme. In the heat of his disagreement with Amelia in chapter 66, Dobbin can honestly say that he is not "guilty of habitual harshness to women" (606–7). When Amelia challenges his use of the term "authority," Dobbin freely admits that "I misused the word" (607). At the same time, Dobbin also admits that Amelia is unable to reciprocate the rare kind of considerate, noncoercive love that he has offered her. As Dobbin declares truly, in a devastating indictment of Amelia's inadequacies: "You couldn't reach up to the height of the attachment which I bore you, and which a loftier soul than yours might have been proud to share" (608). With this recognition of Amelia's inability to respond to his non-"Oriental" love, Dobbin picks himself up from the position in which he has so long "placed himself at her feet" (608).

Ironically, however, Dobbin's assertion of his independence and authority in chapter 66 ultimately leads in the next chapter to his reconciliation with and marriage to Amelia, "the prize he has been trying for all his life" (620; ch. 67). In the passion of their quarrel, Dobbin has uncharacteristically allowed himself to act in a masterful way. As Paris has observed, this "masterful" behavior unexpectedly makes Dobbin more attractive to Amelia.[41] To be sure, after Dobbin's departure, Amelia's recollection of what Dobbin has done for her "rebuked her day and night" (616; ch. 67), and she quickly recognizes the need for his protection. Nevertheless, she also is acutely aware that the nature of their relationship has changed: "She had lost her power over him" (615; ch. 67). Hence, even before Becky provides her with tangible evidence of the folly of her idolatry of the long-dead George, Amelia takes steps to bring back Dobbin.

The imagery describing Dobbin's reunion with Amelia in chapter 67 recalls George's fantasy of the kneeling slave in his view of Amelia in chapter 20 and reveals the inherently incompatible terms in which this new relationship between Dobbin and Amelia will be constituted. As the ship bearing Dobbin approaches the quay at Ostend, Amelia feels an urge to kneel: "Emmy's knees trembled so that she scarcely could run. She would have liked to kneel down and say her prayers of thanks there" (620). While Amelia consciously directs her kneeling urge to God, the person to whom she actually abases herself as soon as the boat docks is Dobbin. She asks his forgiveness and hangs her head in response to his silent look of reproach, just as in her earlier make-believe with George she had groundlessly acted like "a guilty and unworthy person needing every favour and grace from him" (170; ch. 20). Despite Amelia's impulse to abase herself, Dobbin keeps her on her feet. As she disappears under his cloak, one of his hands "was engaged in holding her to his heart . . . and in preventing her from tumbling down" (620). Yet, while Dobbin has achieved the goal for which he has so long been striving, there still exists a fundamental discrepancy between the kind of love that he wants from Amelia and that which she is able to offer him. As indicated by his effort to keep Amelia standing at their moment of reconciliation, what Dobbin wants is an emotionally equal partner who (despite her literally short stature) can "reach up to the height of the attachment" that he bears. What the slavish and parasitical Amelia wants is an "oak to which . . . [she can] cling" (621). Consequently, it is not remarkable that, at the end of the novel, Dobbin seems happier in his relationship with his daughter by Amelia than with Amelia herself. Dobbin's only recourse is to turn to a younger generation in his effort to find the sort of love without master/slave ingredients that eludes him in the present world of Vanity Fair.

V

ULTIMATELY, THROUGH HIS figurative use of the idea of slavery, especially "Oriental" slavery, as it relates to his three central characters in *Vanity Fair,* Thackeray reveals his insight into the essential dehumanization of enslavement. As the British and Foreign Anti-Slavery Society defined this condition in 1842, "Enslaving men is reducing them to articles of property—making free agents chattels—converting *persons* into *things.*"[42] This definition anticipates David Brion Davis's formulation of slavery "as that condition in which man most closely approximates the status of a thing."[43] Characteristically, in his relationship with Amelia, George treats her like an object. He says of her to Dobbin, without realizing the implications of his remark, "There's no fun in winning a thing unless you play for it" (106; ch. 13). In a similar vein, with his suspicions about Mr. Sedley's financial status aroused, George's father coarsely refers to Amelia as "that little thing up stairs," a dehumanization of her to which George "with a self satisfied grin" does not object (111; ch. 13). George's general indifference to Amelia as a person with, in George Eliot's words, "an equivalent centre of self" is reflected in his materialism.[44] When Dobbin lends him money to buy a present for

Amelia, he buys a diamond shirt-pin for himself, forgetting or never knowing the lesson learned by Samuel Titmarsh in *The Great Hoggarty Diamond* "That a Good Wife Is the Best Diamond a Man Can Wear in His Bosom" (*Works* 4:128; from chapter title).

In contrast to George, Dobbin consistently views Amelia as a person, albeit, as he finally is forced to admit, a person unworthy of his love. Just as George's view of Amelia as a slave and thus a thing is paralleled by his materialistic acquisition of other things, so Dobbin's refusal to treat the woman of his dreams like a slave is paralleled by his generosity. Before Amelia's first marriage, he repeatedly bestows gifts upon her indirectly. He lends George money, which George misspends, to purchase her a present. He buys her old piano at the bankruptcy sale and anonymously sends it to her; ironically, when the piano arrives, Amelia mistakenly assumes that the gift comes from George, "the only one which she had received from her lover, as she thought" (537; ch. 59). Indeed, George himself is Dobbin's greatest gift to the woman whom he loves. When old Osborne breaks off George's engagement to Amelia, Dobbin reestablishes it and brings about the marriage, "having made up his mind completely, that if Miss Sedley was balked of her husband she would die of the disappointment" (170; ch. 20).

After George's death, Dobbin redoubles his generosity. He pays for George's funeral expenses as well as the expenses related to Amelia's care in Brussels and return to England. He also surreptitiously contributes most of the money on which the widow and her child are maintained for many years and gives so many presents to everyone in Amelia's household (including comically inappropriate gifts for her infant son, as shown in one of the illustrations) that he earns the nickname "Major Sugarplums." This type of generosity is symptomatic in *Vanity Fair* of how slaves show their allegiance to those who have enslaved them. When the young medical assistant Mr. Linton becomes enamored of the widowed Amelia, he "openly declared himself the slave of Mrs. Osborne" and "would abstract lozenges, tamarinds, and other produce from the surgery drawers for little Georgy's benefit" (347; ch. 38). At a time when old Sedley's speculations have again plunged his family into distress, Amelia herself quarrels with her mother over the issue of some Christmas presents (purchased by selling one of her gifts from Dobbin) that she wishes to give to young Georgy, to whom she has transferred many of her attitudes toward the older George. Dobbin's gifts to Amelia are thus a tangible sign of his willingness to let her tyrannize him as well as a sign of his recognition of her needs and his refusal to see her as simply the sexual object that she is for George.

Far removed from Dobbin's generosity, the link between enslavement of individuals and acquisition of things is most apparent in Becky's behavior. Relatively early in her career of ensnaring men, she acquires "many very handsome presents" from General Tufto "her slave and worshipper" (261; ch. 30). In chapter 30, as the army departs for what will eventually be the decisive battle of Waterloo, we see Becky coolly calculating the value of these objects, along with what Rawdon, another of her slaves, has previously given her or left in her care in the event of his demise. After Waterloo, Becky's materialism is equally pronounced. Her motivation for returning to England with Rawdon is her desire to replace the transitory pleasures of Paris with more substantial things: "Opera-boxes and restaurateur-dinners palled upon her: nosegays could not be laid by as a provision for future years: and she could not live upon knick-knacks, laced handkerchiefs, and kid gloves. She felt the frivolity of pleasure, and longed for more substantial benefits" (325; ch. 36). The specific tangible benefit that Becky wants is "a place or appointment at home or in the colonies" for her husband, from which she can reap the advantage (325; ch. 36). Even after she successfully establishes herself and Rawdon back in London, living "Well on Nothing a-Year," as described in the title of chapter 36, she continues to value objects more than people. She thinks to herself in a rare moment of introspection, "I wish I could exchange my position in society, and all my relations for a snug sum in the Three per Cent. Consols" (377; ch. 41).

Not only is Becky acquisitive, she is also remarkably tenacious in holding on to the things that she acquires. Her retentiveness can be seen in the fact that, near the end of the book, she is able to produce the note given to her by George Osborne fifteen years before, as well as the picture of Jos riding an elephant that she bought as a joke, early in her marriage, at the auction in Russell Square. Just as she aggressively strives to turn her male admirers into slaves—i.e., mere objects that she can manipulate—so, wherever possible, she maintains her hold on the objects that have come into her hands, including the enslaved Jos and ultimately her share of the money from his life insurance policy at the conclusion of the book.

What is revealed through this pattern of enslavement and debasement apparent in the most important human relationships of the three central characters in *Vanity Fair* is an obsession with power that seems to infect the most intimate personal dealings. In Amelia's case, the submissive mentality conditioned by her culture and exemplified in her relationship with George Osborne is so thoroughly ingrained that she appears unable to respond fully to any man who does not treat her like an "Oriental" slave. For Dobbin, who is able to win his wife only by acting in a dominant way that is out of keeping with his character,

Amelia's ingrained "Oriental" slavishness makes it impossible for him to achieve in his married life the kind of equality in love for which he yearns, that is, "such an attachment as mine deserves to mate with" (608; ch. 66). For Becky, love does not exist. Human relationships are merely a power struggle in which one tries to be an enslaver to avoid being a slave, and one may act like an "Oriental" slave to conceal enslaving designs. As Barbara Hardy has observed, things are "expressive" in Thackeray's fiction.[45] In each of the three cases examined here, attitudes toward slavery are reflected by attitudes toward things. Amelia allows George to treat her as one more pretty object that he acquires for himself. Dobbin does not wish to see Amelia as a thing and showers gifts upon her as a reflection of his impulse to view her as a person with needs and desires of her own. Becky accumulates as many things as possible as a manifestation of her urge to gain power over those around her. Her acquisitiveness seems compulsive, yet it may stem from an awareness of the essentially chaotic nature of the Vanity Fair world that Thackeray portrays. As the narrator comments when Becky contemplates exchanging her relatives for a sum of money invested in the Consols, "for so it was that Becky felt the Vanity of human affairs, and it was in those securities that she would have liked to cast anchor" (377; ch. 41). From this view "of human affairs," someone like Dobbin can only retreat, preoccupying himself finally with private domestic concerns and his book in progress about the "History of the Punjaub."

In the end, no real change in human nature occurs. Jos—with his appetite for pilaws and *"Persicos apparatus"*—is dead. Dobbin is married to the slavish Amelia, although not entirely compatible with her. Becky "chiefly hangs about Bath and Cheltenham" (623; ch. 67), reestablishing herself in genteel society with the help of the erroneous title "Lady Crawley," inaccurately appropriated from a bygone slave, her husband, and the insurance legacy left by a recent slave, the unfortunate Jos. However, it seems doubtful that Becky is actually happier in the life of convention and outward piety that she has now attained than she was in her Bohemian days, as, for example, on the morning when she waited for Jos's visit at the Elephant Hotel (591–92; ch. 65). Then, having revealed all he wishes to show or suggest about the lack of ultimate satisfaction in this world, the Manager of the Performance puts away his puppets and says *finis* to his story.

CHAPTER FOUR

Bondage and Freedom in
Pendennis

Shades of the prison-house begin to close
Upon the growing Boy,
—Wordsworth, "Ode: Intimations of Immortality
from Recollections of Early Childhood"

I

" **K**NOWING HOW MEAN the best of us is, let us give a hand of charity
to Arthur Pendennis, with all his faults and shortcomings, who
does not claim to be a hero, but only a man and a brother" (P2:372).[1]
Thus Thackeray concludes *The History of Pendennis,* a novel that Victorian readers commonly admired and modern readers commonly ignore.[2] According to George Saintsbury, who viewed the book as "from
first to last . . . prodigal of delights," at the time of creating *Pendennis* "Thackeray must have felt like Prometheus Unbound" in the sense
that the success of *Pendennis*'s predecessor, *Vanity Fair,* had finally brought
Thackeray professional recognition and a feeling of his full artistic
power.[3] Ironically, in light of Saintsbury's remark about Thackeray's
newfound sense of creative freedom, the closing words of the novel
echo a contemporary antislavery slogan, and the tension between freedom and bondage suggested by this echo is a dominant idea in the novel
as a whole.

The abolitionist slogan invoked at the end of *Pendennis* is "Am I Not
a Man and a Brother?" The words originally appeared as a motto on a
seal devised in 1787 by the Committee to Abolish the Slave Trade and
produced in its best-known form later that year as a cameo by one of
the committee's members, the distinguished potter Josiah Wedgwood

(fig. 12). Wedgwood also reproduced the design on seals and cameos that were distributed widely to promote the committee's cause; these particular cameos, which have been described as "early examples of campaign buttons,"[4] became popular and were frequently used in jewelry for both men and women. The Wedgwood design depicted a black man, in chains, with one knee bent to the ground and his bound hands upraised; the motto appeared around the upper border of the seal or cameo. At the time of the publication of *Pendennis* (1848–50), the picture of the bound and kneeling black man, along with the associated motto, had been commonly used in antislavery material for over half a century and had become a familiar part of the early and mid-Victorian scene. For example, the illustration by "Phiz" (Hablot Knight Browne) entitled "The Discovery of Jingle in the Fleet," for Dickens's *Pickwick*

Fig. 12. Wedgwood medallion, "Am I Not a Man and a Brother?" [Courtesy Smithsonian Institution.]

Papers (1836–37) contains a placard in the background that Michael Steig identifies as "the famous antislavery poster, 'Am I Not a Man and a Brother?,' " although the words are not legible in the Phiz engraving.[5] No allusion to this poster appears in Dickens's text; however, Phiz evidently felt that Victorian readers would recognize the design as a familiar emblem. Although Dickens did not refer to the slogan in this particular context, he echoed it frequently elsewhere. For instance in chapter 14 of *Bleak House* (1852–53), Caddy Jellyby complains of her enforced drudgery as her mother's amanuensis: "Talk of Africa! I couldn't be worse off if I was a what's-his-name—man and a brother!" Although Mrs. Jellyby's eyes are so fixed on Borrioboola-Gha that she cannot perceive her daughter's misery, Caddy insists, "I won't be a slave all my life."[6]

Thackeray's own familiarity with this antislavery slogan before *Pendennis* is evident in his paper "On Some Political Snobs," published in *Punch,* 4 July 1846, as part of "The Snobs of England" series. In this paper, Thackeray's persona protests about the outrageous costume of the typical footman: "We can't be men and brothers as long as that poor devil is made to antic before us in his present fashion—as long as the unfortunate wretch is not allowed to see the insult passed upon him by that ridiculous splendour. This reform must be done. We have abolished negro slavery. John must now be *emancipated from plush.* "[7] The note by John Sutherland to the phrase "men and brothers" in his edition of *The Book of Snobs* explains that " 'Am I not a man and a brother?' was the abolitionist's motto, and a favourite catchphrase of Thackeray's."[8] In an article dealing with Thackeray's use of this slogan in some of his other writings, Sutherland remarks that the reference in *Pendennis* "is wittily appropriate. As literary men . . . Arthur and Thackeray are slaves to the pen, and the writing man's emancipation from the indignity of the literary profession was one of Thackeray's lifelong campaigns."[9] Sutherland does not develop the implications of this allusion in the context of *Pendennis,* but these implications warrant more attention. Clearly Thackeray's use of the words "a man and a brother" at the end of *Pendennis* is an overt allusion to the popular antislavery slogan, just as his remark about the need of "a hand of charity" for Arthur Pendennis suggests the upraised hands of the kneeling slave in the abolitionist emblem. However, Thackeray's play of wit here is not confined simply to Arthur Pendennis's writing career or to his own. This concluding evocation of the idea of slavery in particular and bondage in general is the culmination of a motif that runs throughout the previous portions of the book.

II

THE MOST EXPLICIT—and explicitly pejorative—use of the idea of slavery in the novel is evident in the subplot. Within the overall subject of the development of Arthur Pendennis as a young man and as a writer is an intricate subplot dealing with the affairs of Sir Francis Clavering and his family, who impinge upon the life of young Pen in connection with his possible marriage to Sir Francis's stepdaughter, Blanche Amory. Blanche is affected and hypocritical. As Saintsbury writes, she "is extremely nice—one would not, I think, marry her, except in polygamous and cloistral countries, but that is about all that can be said against her" (12:xxiii–xxiv). Her stepfather is a dissolute reprobate who married Blanche's mother for the latter's money and is now squandering her fortune. Her mother, Lady Clavering—nicknamed the Begum—is the good-natured and well-meaning daughter of a deceased wealthy English lawyer in Calcutta, whose fortune, according to the valet of Arthur Pendennis's uncle, was probably "wrung out of the pore starving blacks" (P2:222). The antecedents of the Begum's money and thus the Claverings' current wealth are definitely shady. However, the emphasis of the latter portion of the novel lies on the schemes of young Pendennis's uncle, Major Pendennis, to wring some of this money out of Sir Francis Clavering's clutches to benefit the Pendennis family instead.

On the fringe of the Clavering entourage is a mysterious, somewhat melodramatic individual who goes by the name of Colonel Altamont and possesses some kind of secret influence over Sir Francis. The hidden reason for this influence is that Altamont is actually Lady Clavering's first husband, John Amory, the father of Blanche Amory. (More precisely, he is assumed to be Lady Clavering's first husband until the end of the novel reveals that he was married before he met the woman who has become Lady Clavering.) John Amory is believed to have died—although the circumstances were hushed up—after being sentenced to a penal colony for forging his father-in-law's name. Now in England, he extorts money from Sir Francis by threatening to reveal that the Clavering marriage is no marriage. Altamont's power over the wretched Sir Francis is a form of slavery. As Major Pendennis—a former officer in India and New South Wales who recognizes Amory and guesses the secret—thinks to himself, Clavering, "who would lose everything by Amory's appearance, would be a slave in the hands of the person who knew so fatal a secret" (P2:239). The Major's pragmatic conclusion is that Clavering should be a slave not in Altamont's hands but in the Major's own. With the power of this secret and without his nephew's knowledge, he blackmails Clavering into agreeing to give up his seat in Parliament in favor of young Arthur Pendennis, who is to marry Blanche and who will be further advanced by an exceptionally large dowry. Young Pen is thus to be enriched by a type of slave trade, a situation in which he somewhat naively acquiesces when, without knowing the reason for the Major's bargain with Clavering, Pen laughingly agrees with his friend Warrington's objection: "You're going to sell yourself, and Heaven help you!" (P2:238). As the narrator points out, this kind of traffic in human bodies is the way of the world: "And if every woman and man in this kingdom, who has sold her or himself for money or position, as Mr. Pendennis was about to do, would but purchase a copy of his memoirs, what tons of volumes Messrs. Bradbury and Evans would sell!" (P2:267).

The despicable nature of slavery in this sense of human exploitation for money or self-advancement is even more obvious in yet another, smaller episode enclosed within the subplot. While the Major is planning to profit from Clavering's secret, the Major's valet, Morgan, resolves to turn the secret to his own advantage. Like his longtime employer, whose pragmatism he mirrors, Morgan has a thoroughly selfish attitude, without the veneer of the Major's gentlemanly conduct and the slightly tempering effect provided by the Major's wider concern for the Pendennis name. Thus, when he overhears the conversation in which the Major confronts and masters Clavering, Morgan concludes to himself that everyone affected by the transaction would be willing to pay him to keep it quiet: "It may be a reg'lar enewity to me. Every one of 'em must susscribe" (P2:290).

From the Major's point of view, the valet is simply a convenient "animal" (P2:296). At the start of a sequence of events that leads to the dissolution of their master-servant relationship, the Major takes out his ill temper on Morgan at the end of a somewhat unsatisfactory holiday:

> In all his dealings with Morgan, his valet, he had been exceedingly sulky and discontented. He had sworn at him and abused him for many days past. He had scalded his mouth with bad soup at Swindon. He had left his umbrella in the rail-road carriage: at which piece of forgetfulness, he was in such a rage, that he cursed Morgan more freely than ever. Both the chimneys smoked furiously in his lodgings; and when he caused the windows to be flung open, he swore so acrimoniously, that Morgan was inclined to fling him out of window, too, through that opened casement. (P2:293)

In reality, through various shady speculations, Morgan has gradually become more wealthy than his employer. The valet has acquired a great deal of money and has quietly purchased the house in which the Major has his lodging. However, the Major is too entrenched in the traditional distinction between servants and gentlemen to see Morgan's wealth, when it is brought to the Major's attention, as anything more than a surprising aberration. The employer continues to view the valet as simply a creature intended to serve his master's needs. Like an abused child who vents his unhappiness by abusing a lowlier person than himself, at the end of the passage just quoted, Morgan takes out his feelings on his unfortunate landlady, Mrs. Brixham:

> Whilst the Major was absent from his lodgings, Morgan had been seated in the landlady's parlour, drinking freely of hot brandy-and-water, and pouring out on Mrs. Brixham some of the abuse which he had received from his master up-stairs. Mrs. Brixham was Morgan's slave. He was his landlady's landlord. He had bought the lease of the house which she rented; he had got her name and her son's to acceptances, and a bill of sale which made him master of the luckless widow's furniture. The young Brixham was a clerk in an insurance office, and Morgan could put him into what he called quod any day. Mrs. Brixham was a clergyman's widow, and Mr. Morgan, after performing his duties on the first floor, had a pleasure in making the old lady fetch him his boot-jack and his slippers. She was his slave. (P2:294)

Mrs. Brixham's forced servitude here is underscored by Thackeray's illustration, entitled "Mr. Morgan at his ease" (fig. 13), showing Mrs. Brixham kneeling before Morgan and undoing his boots. Not only does Morgan treat Mrs. Brixham as a slave, but he openly calls her housemaid "Slavey" (P2:301). The valet's unpleasant treatment of these women manifests the element of slavery inherent in his own treatment by the Major.

Ultimately, the relationship between Morgan and the Major becomes a power struggle, as each of these two self-seeking and self-protective individuals seeks to force the other to his knees. The term "knees" is not just a figure of speech, for the scene of Mrs. Brixham on her knees to Morgan is echoed in various guises through the subsequent sequence of events. When the Major returns home and summons Morgan, the latter grudgingly assumes the position into which he has just forced Mrs. Brixham and "knelt down to take his [the Major's] boots off with due subordination" (P2:294). As the scene progresses, Morgan reaches the point where he can no longer bear the Major's abuse and reacts by

Fig. 13. "Mr. Morgan at his ease" (Pendennis).

defying him. The Major discharges Morgan, but Morgan reveals his ownership of the house and states his defiance more emphatically: "I'll be your beast, and your brute, and your dog, no more, Major Pendennis Alf Pay" (P2:296). At this point, the reader's sympathies lie at least partly with Morgan, who has asserted himself against an old oppressor. Nonetheless, the subsequent elaboration about Morgan's exploitation of Mrs. Brixham—in contrast to the Major's more gentlemanly, although still self-protective conduct—makes clear that of these two worldlings, Morgan and the Major, Morgan is the more despicable.

After their confrontation, the former valet and the former master separate for the night, resolving to settle their accounts in the morning. Mrs. Brixham, who is in danger of financial ruin at the imminent departure of her lodger, the Major, then reveals to him her financial bondage to Morgan and the extent of the latter's lust for power. In Mrs. Brixham's words, "I—I must own to you, that I went down on my knees to him, sir; and he said, with a dreadful oath against you, that he would have you on your knees" (P2:298). As events ensue, however, the Major retains both his head and his footing. When Morgan demands payment for not revealing the Major's attempt at blackmail, the old officer pulls a pistol from his desk and threatens to shoot his former servant: "Kneel down and say your prayers, sir, for by the Lord you shall die" (P2:303). When Morgan, in terror, summons a policeman from the street, the Major calmly explains that the pistol is not loaded and accuses Morgan of theft, guessing correctly that Morgan must have appropriated items from the Major's wardrobe. To prevent a formal charge of theft and a public search of his trunks, which contain not only minor items of the Major's property but more serious evidence of Morgan's other disreputable transactions, Morgan reluctantly writes and signs a document, dictated by the Major, in which the ex-servant not only admits to robbing the Major and uttering "falsehoods regarding his and other honourable families" (P2:306) but also frees Mrs. Brixham of Morgan's financial claims on her. Thus the Major puts Morgan in a position in which he dares not try to damage the Major's reputation since the Major, by holding the valet's signed confession, is equally able to damage Morgan. The Major also incidentally frees himself from any pleas for charity by Mrs. Brixham, who had earlier begged him for financial help.

The episode of Morgan and Mrs. Brixham presents the idea of slavery in its most reprehensible and exploitive light. In this context, the Major's mistreatment of Morgan is not so bad as the latter's abuse of Mrs. Brixham since Morgan, as a hired servant, is potentially free to leave the Major's service and eventually does so.[10] However, the Major's blackmail of Clavering is presented as a kind of inescapable bondage, and the Major's plans for his nephew involve permanent bondage as well. As Pen says painfully to his uncle, after Morgan in turn reveals the full dimensions of the Major's scheme to the young man who is to profit by it, "If you had told me this tale sooner . . . I should not have found myself tied to an engagement from which I can't, in honour, recede" (P2:319). The Major's initial response is one of self-congratulation: "No begad, we've fixed you—and a man who's fixed to a seat in Parliament, and a pretty girl, with a couple of thousand a year, is fixed to no bad thing, let me tell you" (P2:319). Pen quickly makes clear, however, that he has no desire to profit from the Major's scheme once he understands its sordid roots. When Morgan attempts to sell the secret to him, assuming that Pen like his uncle is "trafficking with this wretched old Begum's misfortune; and would extort a seat in Parliament out of that miserable Clavering," Pen indignantly resolves to have nothing to do with the trade (P2:315). He also sees the consequences of his decision to withdraw from this kind of traffic as fitting punishment for his earlier worldly willingness to sell himself. As he declares to his uncle, "I am rightly punished by the event, and having sold myself for money and a seat in Parliament, by losing both" (P2:319).

To his uncle's dismay, Pen's decision is to renounce his seat in Parliament as well as Blanche's extra dowry and to reaffirm his commitment to marry Blanche with nothing except the original, modest dowry from her maternal grandfather's wealth. Only at this point, seeing the failure of his plans to improve the worldly standing of the Pendennises and echoing the words of another mistaken meddler in marital transactions, Cardinal Wolsey in *Henry VIII,* does the Major actually fall to his knees as he vainly begs Pen not to throw away his chance of worldly gain: "And—and Shakspeare was right—and Cardinal Wolsey—begad—'and had I but served my God as I've served you'—yes, on my knees, by Jove, to my own nephew" (P2:320). This image of kneeling, emphasized in chapters 29, 30, and 32 of volume 2, may reflect the pose of the kneeling slave in the antislavery emblem. At any rate, the image is a sign of subordination, evoking the suggestion of slavery and indicating the ugliness inherent in the Major's scheme to have Pen "sell" himself for worldly advantage. The motif of slavery, in turn, links the novel's diverse secondary strands dealing with Altamont, Clavering, Morgan, Mrs. Brixham, and the Major's interactions with these characters. Traffic in human beings, Thackeray seems to be indicating, is one of the activities of the kind of world that is Vanity Fair. In Bunyan's words in *Pilgrim's Progress,* "at this Fair are all such merchandise sold as houses, lands, trades, places, honors, preferments, titles, countries, kingdoms, lusts, pleasures, and delights of all sorts, as whores, bawds, wives, husbands, children, masters, servants, lives, blood, bodies, souls, silver, gold, pearls, precious stones, and what not."[11] In this context, in *Pendennis,* Thackeray depicts the idea of slavery in a negative light.

III

NONETHELESS, THACKERAY'S VIEW OF SLAVERY both in *Pendennis* and elsewhere is complex. As discussed in earlier chapters of this study, the image of slavery occupied an important role in Thackeray's thinking, although his feelings regarding human bondage were not entirely consistent. Indeed, by the late 1840s, a decade after the termination of British West Indian apprenticeship, controversy as to the rights, wrongs, and relevance to Britons of the subject of slavery was a familiar aspect of the mid-Victorian world. During the months in which *Pendennis* was serialized (November 1848–December 1850), the *Times* of London printed a number of leading articles calling for an end to the current British blockade of part of the coast of Africa in an effort to stop the slave trade and commenting on the intensifying disagreement over slavery in the United States.[12] In such articles, the *Times* attempted to treat the topic of slavery somewhat evenhandedly as a social evil but also as a problem with no simple or immediate solution.[13] More one-sidedly in *Fraser's Magazine,* December 1849, referring to the recent emancipation of blacks in the British West Indies, Carlyle declared that "Quashee, if he will not help in bringing out the spices, will get himself made a slave again (which state will be a little less ugly than his present one), and with beneficent whip, since other methods avail not, will be compelled to work"—a position that received a strong rebuttal from John Stuart Mill in the subsequent issue of *Fraser's.*[14] In the context of this current attention to "the Negro Question," it does not seem remarkable that what was to Thackeray the perennially interesting subject of slavery was much in his mind while working on *Pendennis.* Moreover, given the contemporary British awareness of the problematic nature of the topic as well as Thackeray's own characteristic tendency to try to see both sides of an issue whenever possible, it does not appear surprising that Thackeray's treatment of the idea of slavery in *Pendennis* is double-edged.

While Thackeray gives an obviously negative view of the subject of slavery in the subplot, in the main plot—dealing with the development of Arthur Pendennis from youth to maturity—he presents the concept of slavery in an ambiguously positive light. In the household in which the protagonist is raised, the most important individuals who care for him are his mother, Helen, and his informally adopted sister, Laura. These well-meaning but foolish women have allowed Pen to treat them as slaves: "What had made Pen at home such a dandy and such a despot? The women had spoiled him, as we like them and as they like to do. They had cloyed him with obedience, and surfeited him with sweet respect and submission, until he grew weary of the slaves who waited upon him, and their caresses and cajoleries excited him no more" (P2:143). The narrator is then quick to joke that his analysis of the reason for Pen's problem should not be construed as a manifesto for women's independence. Nonetheless, Thackeray seems to be perceptively suggesting that, however much one may desire the submission of others, the consequences of satisfying this desire, when carried to an extreme, can adversely affect the despot. In Pen's case, the consequences on his character of this early spoiling by "the slaves who waited upon him" form the central subject of *The History of Pendennis,* whose subtitle alludes to *His Fortunes and Misfortunes, His Friends and His Greatest Enemy.* As the narrator explains, part way through the novel, "Pen's greatest enemy was himself: and as he had been pampering, and coaxing, and indulging that individual all his life, the rogue grew insolent, as all spoiled servants will be; and at the slightest attempt to coerce him, or make him do that which was unpleasant to him, became frantically rude and unruly" (P2:119). The novel shows Pen's belated and reluctant development of self-discipline. His psyche must be taught to become a useful servant rather than a "spoiled" one. Thus, by the end of the novel, Pen has become "a man and a brother," i.e., a slave, in the relatively positive sense that he has outgrown his self-centered dandyism and accepted his bondage to the responsibilities of adult life. The shift is not a simple one, however. Throughout the book, Thackeray maintains a tension between Pen's movement toward bondage and his impulse toward freedom.

Evidence of this conflict between bondage and freedom is apparent in two literary allusions near the beginning of the novel. In volume 1, chapter 2, referring obliquely to knowledge that would make a woman blush, acquired by boys in public schools, the narrator remarks, "I don't say that the boy is lost, or that the innocence has left him which he had from 'Heaven, which is our home,' but that the shades of the prison-house are closing very fast over him, and that we are helping as much as possible to corrupt him" (16). The allusion is to Wordsworth's familiar "Ode: Intimations of Immortality," describing the "growing Boy" whose heavenly recollections gradually "fade into the light of common day." Wordsworth's view of human development as a process of gradual accommodation to "the light of common day" parallels much of the course of *The History of Pendennis.* In Wordsworth's terms, the novel shows the "earnest pains" with which the growing child (Arthur Pendennis) "dost . . . provoke / The years to bring the inevitable yoke."

At the same time, while the allusion to Wordsworth's poem suggests the idea of the movement from freedom to bondage, the motto of the Pendennises suggests the urge to move from captivity to freedom. The motto, "*nec tenui pennâ,*" also first mentioned in volume 1, chapter·2, comes from the opening lines of book 2, ode 20, of Horace's *Odes:* "Non usitata nec tenui ferar / penna" (freely translated "Mine are no weak or borrowed wings").[15] In the passage from which this quotation comes, the poet imagines himself being transformed into a bird:

> Mine are no weak or borrowed wings: they'll bear
> Me, bard made bird, through the compliant air,
> Earthbound no longer, leaving far behind
> The cities and the envy of mankind.
> Dearest Maecenas, I who was the child
> Of a poor family, I who have been styled
> Your shadow, need not as a shadow lie
> Penned by the Styx, or die as others die.
> Already the rough skin is forming on
> My ankles; metamorphosis into swan
> Moves up my body; downy plumage springs
> On arms and elbows; shoulder-blades sprout wings.
> And now I rise, singing, a portent more
> Talked of than Icarus was, ready to soar
> Over the roaring Bosphorus, the quicksands
> Of Syrtes and the Hyperborean lands.
> In Colchis and in Dacia, where they feign
> Scorn of our Marsian troops, in ignorant Spain,
> In farthest Thrace my verses shall be known:
> Gauls shall drink Horace as they do the Rhone.[16]

The motto appears in the second chapter of *Pendennis* as part of "the Pendennis coat of arms, and crest, an eagle looking towards the sun" (21), on Pen's father's memorial slab. Nevertheless, the motto, in many ways, appropriately suggests the career of young Arthur Pendennis, who repeatedly struggles to soar out of his "mother's nest" (P1:143), and who ultimately achieves fame as a writer. Ironically, however, Pen eventually returns to his "home-nest" (P1:160) by returning to his childhood home and marrying his adopted sister Laura. Similarly, Horace's allusion to Icarus ironically suggests that in the end Pen cannot successfully escape what he early perceives as the "captivity" (P1:208) of home. Thus, while this echo of Horace superficially implies Pen's struggles toward freedom, like the echo of Wordsworth it also implies Pen's ultimate movement into bondage by the ordinary obligations of life. This progression into a form of slavery is apparent in Pen's attitude toward the three major aspects of his life on which the novel concentrates: his marriage, his work, and his mother.

As Pen's good friend Warrington declares in chapter 53, evidently thinking of the misguided marriage that has blighted his own life, "We are the slaves of destiny. Our lots are shaped for us, and mine is ordained long ago" (P2:149). A major theme in the novel is the danger that Pen may be trapped by Warrington's kind of unfortunate marital commitment. The novel's comically striking first chapter focuses directly on this sort of marital mistake as young Pendennis (heir to the family's modest estate of Fairoaks) proudly announces his engagement to an actress almost a decade older than himself, and his uncle, Major Pendennis, prepares to rush to the scene of the potential disaster to prevent the marriage from taking place. The actress, Emily Costigan (professionally known as "Miss Fotheringay"), is ill-educated and unintelligent, but prudent. As the narrator comments about her three cautious letters to young Pen, letters actually written by someone else: "The young wiseacre had pledged away his all for this: signed his name to endless promissory notes, conferring his heart upon the bearer: bound himself for life, and got back twopence as an equivalent" (P1:83). Later, as a beginning student at the University of Oxbridge, Pen recalls Miss Fotheringay with embarrassment: "To think that he, Pendennis, had been enslaved by such a woman" (P1:169). However, other characters in the book are not so lucky, and Pen subsequently has two more narrow escapes.

As Dickens demonstrates with the examples of Stephen Blackpool and Louisa Bounderby in *Hard Times* (1854), divorce was virtually unobtainable for ordinary men and women in the mid-Victorian period, and marriage "for better for worse" could lead to lifelong misery if "worse" or worst ensued. The experience of Warrington shows the negative results of the kind of misalliance from which the Major rescued Pen. As Warrington remarks about Pen's aborted relationship with Emily Fotheringay, prior to describing his own secret marriage, "What would have been Arthur's lot now had he been tied at nineteen to an illiterate woman older than himself, with no qualities in common between them" (P2:186). Warrington then reveals that as a younger man he made the mistake of actually contracting such a union, a revelation he provides at the height of an argument between Pen and the latter's mother, in order to prevent Pen's "threatened . . . similar union" (P2:186) with Fanny Bolton, a flirtatious lower-class young woman whom Pen has resisted and his mother has maligned. Much earlier, Pen's mother had her own unhappy love affair. As the narrator explains near the beginning of the novel, Helen was unable to marry her cousin, Francis Bell, despite their mutual love, since Bell had impetuously engaged himself previously "and his hand pledged to that bond in a thousand letters—to a coarse, ill-tempered, ill-favoured, ill-mannered, middle-aged woman" (P1:75). Unhappily but honorably, Francis Bell fulfilled his obligation of marriage, from which he was released by his wife's death only after Helen had become Mrs. Pendennis. Laura, whom Pen ultimately weds, is the child of Francis Bell's second marriage, informally adopted by Helen after both of Laura's parents die. The examples of George Warrington and Francis Bell function in the novel as cautionary tales. They reinforce the idea that Pen ought to marry a woman whom he genuinely loves and with whom he has, in Warrington's words, "qualities in common."

Because both mutual love and mutual qualities are lacking, it is evident that Major Pendennis's subsequent scheme to marry his nephew to Blanche Amory for worldly reasons is as inappropriate as Pen's adolescent near-marriage with "the Fotheringay." Luckily, Pen escapes by declining the money and the seat in Parliament, without which Blanche prefers a wealthier suitor. Other mismatches in the novel turn out badly, as revealed by the experiences of Lady Clavering (who marries two successive scoundrels, Amory and Clavering) and Mrs. Lightfoot (who marries a fellow servant many years her junior, uses her savings to establish him as an innkeeper, and endures his alcoholism in return). In the context of these actual and potential marital mistakes, Thackeray seems to be suggesting that Pen's decision to marry Laura is an intelligent exercise of free will. By the end of the book, Pen finally discovers his genuine love for Laura. She is not only his social equal but, as his semi-sister, she also has most in common with him of all the young women in the novel. Nonetheless, the conspicuous emphasis throughout the book on the potentially galling nature of marital ties suggests Thackeray's awareness that all marriage involves a loss of freedom and that the marriage of Laura and Pen will be no exception. (The comic discovery at the end of the novel of the disreputable John Armstrong/Amory/Altamont's multiple marriages serves as a parody of this notion of the normally restrictive nature of marital ties.) Indeed, unlike the conventional happily-ever-after ending of fairy tales, the narrator questions the future happiness of Pen and Laura and does not fully allay the doubts he raises in his final paragraph, concluding with his allusion to the antislavery motto. The implication is that Pen as a married person is "a man and a brother," i.e., in some sense a slave, as Laura is as well.[17] Thackeray's use of the idea of bondage is not confined to the subject of Pen's marriage, however; even more explicitly, Thackeray links the notion of slavery to the concept of Pen's work.

Like marriage, work in this book is perceived as a form of bondage which responsible adults inevitably accept. Initially, any kind of serious labor is something which young Pen is only too eager to avoid. Early in the novel, the reader sees Pen as a schoolboy, "in no ways remarkable either as a dunce or as a scholar" (P1:15). When his uncle arrives to take Pen home because his father is dying, Pen is being lectured by "the

Doctor" at school for errors in construing Greek. After his father's death, once Pen realizes his importance as the deceased man's only child and his new role as "chief . . . and lord" (P1:20) of his mother's household, his first decision is that he will never return to school: "In the midst of the general grief, and the corpse still lying above, he had leisure to conclude that he would have it *all* holidays for the future, that he wouldn't get up till he liked, or stand the bullying of the Doctor any more" (P1:20). After this "liberation from bondage" (P1:43), as the narrator later describes the leaving of school, Pen pursues his own course of study: "He had a natural taste for reading every possible kind of book which did not fall into his school-course. It was only when they forced his head into the waters of knowledge that he refused to drink" (P1:24). Pen's self-indulgent reading, reflecting his fondness for "novels, plays, and poetry" (P1:15), is unwitting but excellent preparation for his eventual career as a writer. In the context of Pen's adolescence, nevertheless, it simply reflects the young protagonist's inclination to shirk more disciplined study.

Once at Oxbridge, Pen's distaste for serious work continues, although his reputation for ability among his fellow students is large: " 'Ah, if Pendennis of Boniface would but try,' the men said, 'he might do anything' " (P1:179). According to the narrator, Pen's fame among the undergraduates is comparable to that held in "negro-gangs . . . [by] private black sovereigns . . . to whom they pay an occult obedience, besides that which they publicly profess for their owners and drivers" (P1:179). The problem for Pendennis at this point is that he has not learned to manage himself and is not willing to let wiser heads drive or lead him. His career at college is described in the title to one chapter as a "Rake's Progress." His return to Fairoaks, after failing his degree examinations, is characterized in the title of another chapter as the "Prodigal's Return." At Laura's urging, he goes back in a subdued mood to Oxbridge, where "He went into a second examination, and passed with perfect ease" (P1:208). Nevertheless, rather than making any effort to use his education and native talents at this point, Pen returns to mope at Fairoaks, an attitude that elicits Laura's proper Victorian scorn: "He wastes his life and energies away among us, tied to our apron-strings. He interests himself in nothing: he scarcely cares to go beyond the garden-gate. . . . Why is he not facing the world, and without a profession?" (P1:253). Laura continues her denunciation: "All men . . . must work. They must make themselves names and a place in the world" (P1:253). When Pen lackadaisically makes his first proposal of marriage to Laura, motivated by his mother's wishes rather than his own, Laura emphatically rejects him in words that link the obligations of marriage with the obligations of work: "What do you offer in exchange to a woman for her love, honour, and obedience? If ever I say these words, dear Pen, I hope to say them in earnest, and by the blessing of God to keep my vow. But you—what tie binds you? You do not care about many things which we poor women hold sacred. . . . Go and work; go and mend, dear Arthur, for I see your faults, and dare speak of them now" (P1:278). Only after Pen is propelled to London by Laura and discovers his true vocation as a writer, does he finally accept this Victorian ethic of work.

Dedication to one's profession can be overdone, as demonstrated in the chapter entitled "The Knights of the Temple" by the example of the "selfish" over-zealousness of the law student Mr. Paley (P1:292). In contrast, what Laura has in mind is altruistically oriented, energetic but not obsessive work, eventually taking the form of writing "good books . . . such as might do people good to read" (P2:285–86). By volume 2, chapter 6, Pen has finally become enthusiastic about the value of earnest labor. He observes to his friend George Warrington, "Who ordered toil as the condition of life, ordered weariness, ordered sickness, ordered poverty, failure, success—to this man a foremost place, to the other a nameless struggle with the crowd—to that a shameful fall, or paralysed limb, or sudden accident—to each some work upon the ground he stands on, until he is laid beneath it" (P2:64).

In Pen's case, as his name suggests, the work that he has found to do is writing—prompted by Warrington's example and Pen's own need of money on which to live. Immediately, to Warrington's delight, Pen begins to rail at the publisher Mr. Bungay as a "slave driver" (P1:327), but Pen eagerly enlists as a writer for Bungay's *Pall Mall Gazette*. Moreover, while still retaining too much integrity to write an unfavorable review of a good book, Pen is generally happy to accommodate his abilities to the needs of Bungay and whatever other publishers will accept his work. As the narrator explains, "When you want to make money by Pegasus, (as he must, perhaps, who has no other saleable property,) farewell poetry and aerial flights: Pegasus only rises now like Mr. Green's balloon, at periods advertised before-hand, and when the spectator's money has been paid. Pegasus trots in harness, over the stony pavement, and pulls a cart or a cab behind him. Often Pegasus does his work with panting sides and trembling knees, and not seldom gets a cut of the whip from his driver" (P1:353–54).

In Warrington's words, Pen has become a "literary hack" in the sense that his "Pegasus" has become a hired cab horse (P1:353). The profession of authorship is presented here as a form of servitude, although it is a servitude that Pen readily accepts and the narrator condones. As the latter explains, "Do not let us . . . be too prodigal of our pity upon Pegasus. . . . If he gets the whip, Pegasus very often deserves it, and I for one am quite ready to protest . . . against the doctrine which some poetical sympathisers are inclined to put forward, viz., that men of letters, and what is called genius, are to be exempt from the prose duties of this daily, bread-wanting, tax-paying life, and are not to be made to work and pay like their neighbours" (P1:354). The idea of authorship as servitude is carried even further when Warrington suggests that he and Pen sell Pen's autobiographical novel *Walter Lorraine* to one of the rival publishers, Mr. Bacon and Mr. Bungay. The terms that Warrington uses to describe this transaction metaphorically suggest that they are selling *Walter Lorraine* into slavery: "No, we won't burn him: we will carry him to the Egyptians, and sell him. We will exchange him away for money, yea, for silver and gold, and for beef and for liquors, and for tobacco and for raiment. This youth will fetch some price in the market; for he is a comely lad, though not over strong; but we will fatten him up, and give him the bath, and curl his hair, and we will sell him for a hundred piastres to Bacon or to Bungay" (P2:26–27). In this sense, as Sutherland observes in the comment quoted earlier, the remark about Pen as "a man and a brother" at the end of the novel refers to the protagonist's profession of authorship. The narrator's concluding comment, however, is not an isolated witticism. Rather, it evolves not only from the novel's general concern with the motif of bondage but from the particular emphasis on writing as servitude and/or slavery earlier in the book. In the novel as a whole, the narrator's attitude toward this form of slavery seems largely one of toleration while still recognizing the often difficult nature of the writer's life. The slavery here, of course, is not seriously exploitive. Pen is selling his writing, rather than his own person as he almost did in the Blanche Amory episode. Furthermore, he reserves the right (as in the instance of the review) not to compromise his integrity. These differences are important reasons why slavery in this context seems acceptable, while in the Major's plans concerning his nephew and Blanche, slavery was a negative concept. At any rate, by the end of the novel, Pen has generally accepted his bondage to the world of work.

Moreover, by the end of the book, Pen is bound not only by his marital responsibilities and his work but by his inescapable awareness of his mother's values. Robert Bledsoe has argued provocatively that Pen ultimately discovers that he can achieve psychological security only by ceasing any effort to dissociate himself from his mother's wishes: "Final freedom from the terrors of insecurity involves Pen's willing enslavement to the mindlessness of Helen's sentimentality." In this reading of the novel, "Helen is the most important character," and "Pendennis does not grow up and away from his mother, as in a more conventional *Bildungsroman.* On the contrary, he grows up and back to her, rejecting the great world for Laura, whose arms are 'as tender as Helen's.' "[18] To some extent, this interpretation of the novel is perceptive, although Pen's ultimate return after Helen's death to the simple values of duty, home, and religion—and his choice of a wife in whom Helen has instilled these values—does not seem so abnormal when one considers that they were popularly approved and strongly emphasized values of the Victorian period.[19] In addition, Laura seems more than just "the agent of Helen's will" as Bledsoe perceives her.[20] By the time Laura finally accepts Pen, she has developed into an independent young woman whom Warrington admires, to whom the aristocratically connected public official Pynsent has proposed, and who her patroness Lady Rockminster thinks is too good for Pen. As Juliet McMaster emphasizes, "Pen does not marry her until *he* wants to, and that is after his mother's death."[21] In the end, Pen remains the central character. By the conclusion of the novel, he is bound by obligations other than just his memory of his mother. Nonetheless, as Bledsoe has rightly pointed out, the pattern of the novel is circular rather than linear. Like the biblical Prodigal Son to whom he is frequently compared, Pen ultimately returns to "the home-nest" (P1:160) where he chafed as a boy. However, to some degree at least, at the end of the novel, there is evidence that Pen is "chafing" (P1:160) once again.

As a writer in London, Pen amply demonstrates his ability to see more than one side of a question. Pen declares to Warrington in volume 2, chapter 23, "The truth, friend! . . . where is the truth? Show it me. That is the question between us. I see it on both sides" (P2:237). In context, Warrington dismisses Pen's indifferent, relativist attitude as preparation for his worldly decision to marry Blanche. Nonetheless, even after Pen has returned to Helen's and Laura's simple values, he retains—or is plagued by—his ability to see the opposite side of every issue. He explains to Laura that he is still unable to rid himself of the nagging word that plagues the sceptic "But":

> But will come in spite of us. But is reflection. But is the sceptic's familiar, with whom he has made a compact; and if he forgets it, and indulges in happy day-dreams, or building of air-castles, or listens to sweet music let us say, or to the bells ringing to church, But taps at the door, and says, Master, I am here. You are my master; but I am yours. Go where you will you can't travel without me. I will whisper to you when you are on your knees at church. I will be at your marriage pillow. I will sit down at your table with your children. I will be behind your death-bed curtain. (P2:325)

Even in the last paragraph of the novel, which foreshadows his future life, Pen is still described as subject to "fits of moodiness and solitude" (P2:371). As Robert A. Colby has pointed out, the ambivalence in Pen's character is evident in the two successive forms of Thackeray's cover illustration, showing the protagonist pulled between a mermaidlike woman and small satyr (or satyrs) on one side and an idealized Victorian woman and youthful cherub (or cherubs), with a church in the background, on the other.[22] Colby explains, "In the monthly parts, Pen looks in the direction of the good woman; by the time the story is published in book form Pen's eyes have shifted toward the sea nymph."[23] Thus, by the end of the novel, Thackeray seems to be quietly implying that the protagonist may not be entirely content with what Bledsoe has described as "Pen's willing enslavement" to Helen's world view. Like many other adults, both in the Victorian period and our own, he has returned to the values inculcated in his youth, but remains fitfully conscious of their limitations. This consciousness of his chains makes his constraint all the more evident.

In terms of Pen's development, his eventual bondage to his marriage, his work, and the values of his mother is presented as a positive form of slavery, although it is one that Pen does not accept with total docility and for which at the end, according to the narrator, he deserves the reader's "hand of charity." None of us, the narrator suggests, is perfect, and fettered as he is, Pen is one of us. His chains are the intangible ones of marriage, work, and traditional values. He has eschewed the extortion, exploitation, and outright selling of human beings for tangible profit inherent in Major Pendennis's and Morgan's schemes. This emphasis in the main plot of the novel on limitation and restraint may explain why so many, less willingly inhibited, modern readers find this novel less appealing than our Victorian predecessors did. The emphasis on limitations certainly explains why Pen does not seduce Fanny Bolton, despite his obvious opportunity, a deliberately self-denying action that sometimes evokes incredulity among post-Victorian readers. Thackeray's point, however, is that Pendennis is never an entirely willing slave to the conventions he accepts. In a similar vein, Thackeray explains in the preface that he will accept contemporary conventions of the novel and refrain from giving all the details about his protagonist's development as a young man. Nevertheless, he will strain against the restriction as best he can:

> Since the author of Tom Jones was buried, no writer of fiction among us has been permitted to depict to his utmost power a MAN. We must drape him, and give him a certain conventional simper. Society will not tolerate the Natural in our Art. Many ladies have

remonstrated and subscribers left me, because, in the course of the story, I described a young man resisting and affected by temptation. My object was to say, that he had the passions to feel, and the manliness and generosity to overcome them. You will not hear—it is best to know it—what moves in the real world, what passes in society, in the clubs, colleges, news'-rooms,—what is the life and talk of your sons. A little more frankness than is customary has been attempted in this story. (P1:xvi-xvii)

The idea of bondage, and the impulse against bondage, is thus a dominant motif in the novel. At the end of the book, Arthur Pendennis is presented simply as a human being, limited in the same ways that Thackeray suggests other human beings are typically bound.

CHAPTER FIVE

Henry Esmond as Slave and Master

Shall I bend low and in a bondman's key,
With bated breath and whispering humbleness,
Say this . . .
—SHAKESPEARE, *THE MERCHANT OF VENICE*

I

IN MANY WAYS, *Henry Esmond* is Thackeray's least Thackerayean novel. Alone among his full-length works of fiction, this one was not serialized. Instead, with *The History of Henry Esmond, Esq. A Colonel in the Service of Her Majesty Q. Anne. Written by Himself.*, the complete title under which the book first appeared in 1852, Thackeray embarked on a daring stylistic experiment. The work recounts the career of a man who is a boy during what came to be known (in the Whig view of history) as the Glorious Revolution of 1688 and who later achieves military distinction during the reign of Queen Anne. In this novel, Thackeray set out to produce a book that could masquerade—not only by its content but also through such devices as diction, tone, and even, in the first edition, typography—as an eighteenth-century, three-volume set of memoirs. For the most part, critics have agreed that he succeeded in his experiment.[1] They have also frequently seen the book as somehow set apart from Thackeray's other fiction. For Trollope, *Henry Esmond* is simply "the greatest work that Thackeray did," while Ray similarly describes it as "Thackeray's most careful and consummate work of art."[2] For Barbara Hardy, who discusses it largely in the context of *Vanity Fair, Pendennis,* and *The Newcomes*, "*Esmond* is the only novel which is primarily a psychological novel, rather than a social satire."[3]

Nonetheless, certain underlying similarities between *Henry Esmond* and Thackeray's other novels remain, such as the *bildungsroman* method of development that links *Esmond* with its predecessor, *Pendennis,* as well as with much of Thackeray's later fiction.[4] A further element of connection between *Esmond* and most of Thackeray's other novels is his concern once again in this book with the image of slavery.

II

As Ray has observed, one way of reading *Henry Esmond* is as a "domestic novel," a genre in vogue at the time of the book's first publication. It was in this way, so Ray contends, that readers of the 1850s viewed *Esmond,* an approach to the novel reinforced by the tendency of contemporary reviewers to give particular attention to passages dealing with the unhappy marriage between Rachel and Lord Castlewood.[5] An immediate source for such concern with marital distress in the novel was undoubtedly Thackeray's observation of the problems between his friend the Reverend William Brookfield and the latter's wife, Jane. However, Thackeray (whose own wife had long been hopelessly insane) was hardly an impartial observer, for by the end of October 1848 he had fallen seriously in love with Jane Brookfield. Mrs. Brookfield seems to have encouraged Thackeray's affection but never allowed him any sexual intimacy. In September 1851, at her husband's insistence, she terminated her relationship with Thackeray. Devastated by the loss of this relationship, which had grown increasingly important in his emotional life, Thackeray channeled his energies into the writing of *Esmond.* His penetrating analysis of marital discontent in book 1 of the novel, as well as his sensitivity to love and the pains of love throughout the book, surely derives much of its power from this experience with the Brookfields, as Ray has shown.[6] What has not been specifically pointed out, however, is the way in which the concept of slavery recurs in Thackeray's treatment of the conventional role of women, especially in marriage, in the world of *Henry Esmond.*

As explained by the narrator (Esmond himself in old age around 1740), slavery is an appropriate figure of speech for the customary condition of women in this novel. Esmond observes in book 1, chapter 11, "There's not a writer of my time of any note, with the exception of poor Dick Steele, that does not speak of a woman as of a slave, and scorn and use her as such" (93).[7] While Steele, with a number of his *Tatler* sketches, offered an antidote to the usual low opinion of women during this period, a far more negative stereotype commonly prevailed. Two of Thackeray's running headlines for the first edition indicate that men at the time at which this book supposedly occurs—as well as at the time at which it was being read—typically viewed women as "Our Slaves" (see the shoulder notes, 77, 92; bk. 1, chs. 9, 11). Writing this eighteenth-century novel in the nineteenth century, Thackeray operates with a dual perspective. As a mid-Victorian author looking back on events approximately one hundred and fifty years earlier, he is able to explore what are to him contemporary attitudes as well as attitudes of the past. For Thackeray, human nature in all epochs is fundamentally the same. As Andrew Sanders observes about the underlying similarity between Thackeray's novels that occur in the eighteenth century and those set in the nineteenth century, "His criticism does not extend over two different societies, but over an England which is substantially unchanged despite shifts in political and social fashions."[8] Hence in *Esmond,* Thackeray offers a scathing critique of the domestic slavery whose limitations he had previously shown in connection with Amelia in *Vanity Fair* and discussed in Mr. Brown's letter "On Love, Marriage, Men, and Women." The critique offered in *Henry Esmond* is relevant not only to the society depicted in the novel but to Thackeray's own.

In the unhappiness of her first marriage, Rachel Esmond voices a declaration of the wrongs of women that might appropriately be uttered by Chaucer's Wife of Bath. Unlike Chaucer's dame Alis, however, Rachel carefully expresses her complaint only to her two young children and the adolescent Henry Esmond. She says to Henry, who is at this time acting as tutor to her children and thus also to herself: " 'The men who wrote your books,' . . . 'your Horaces and Ovids and Virgils, as far as I know of them, all thought ill of us, as all the heroes they wrote about used us basely. We were bred to be slaves always; and even of our own times, as you are still the only lawgivers, I think our sermons seem to say that the best woman is she who bears her master's chains most gracefully' " (77; bk. 1, ch. 9). As Viscountess Castlewood, Rachel's personal unhappiness results not simply from the loss of the affections of her husband, a man who ceases to love her once her physical beauty has been spoiled by smallpox. Her misery is also heightened by the realization that her once idolized husband is not worthy of her reverence and respect. Worst of all, her domestic distress is compounded by her concealed, erotic attraction to youthful Henry Esmond, of which the young man himself is largely oblivious. In this situation, Rachel Esmond struggles to do what she perceives to be her duty. She tries to suppress the nonmaternal aspect of her love for Henry; although emotionally estranged from her husband, she continues to live in the same household with him and concentrates on car-

ing for her children. Nonetheless, her unhappiness is only intensified
by an awareness of the degree to which she and the children are help-
lessly dependent on her irresponsible husband's actions. In recounting
Rachel's fears as Lord Castlewood's gambling dissipates the family
estate, Henry the narrator observes:

> For his rule over his family, and for his conduct to wife and chil-
> dren, subjects over whom his power is monarchical, any one who
> watches the world must think with trembling sometimes of the
> account which many a man will have to render. For in our society
> there's no law to control the King of the Fireside. He is master of
> property, happiness,—life almost. He is free to punish; to make
> happy or unhappy; to ruin or to torture. He may kill a wife grad-
> ually, and be no more questioned than the Grand Seignior who
> drowns a slave at midnight. (109; bk. 1, ch. 13)

For Thackeray, this kind of domestic tyranny, whether practiced in the
Orient or in England, is clearly to be repudiated.

As always, of course, Thackeray makes an effort to consider both
sides of the issue. While the narrating Henry Esmond clearly sympa-
thizes with Rachel, he also tries to do justice to her husband's point of
view. Henry is quick to note that, as "King of the Fireside," Lord Castlewood errs "from a disposition rather self-indulgent than cruel"
(109; bk. 1, ch. 13). Henry also understands that part of Lord Castlewood's dissatisfaction with his wife is culturally induced by the discovery that their respective levels of intelligence do not coincide with
their society's stereotypes of masculine and feminine abilities. In writing his memoirs, the mature Esmond remarks, "Much of the quarrels
and hatred which arise between married people come in my mind from
the husband's rage and revolt at discovering that his slave and bed-
fellow—who is to minister to all his wishes and is church-sworn to honour and obey him—is his superior; and that *he* and not she ought to be
the subordinate of the twain—and in this consciousness, I think, lay the
cause of my lord's anger against his lady" (93; bk. 1, ch. 11). Although
Lord Castlewood is reckless, sensual, and self-indulgent, he is not a
fundamentally evil man. In analyzing the relationship between Francis
and Rachel Esmond, Henry makes a conscious effort to present not
only the lady's but also the lord's aspect of the case: "And if it be pain-
ful to a woman to find herself mated for life to a boor, and ordered to
love and honor a dullard: it is worse still for the man himself, perhaps,
whenever in his dim comprehension the idea dawns that his slave and
drudge yonder is in truth his superior: that the woman who does his
bidding and submits to his humour, should be his lord" (93). Ulti-

mately, however, it remains clear that in this kind of situation Henry's—and Thackeray's—sympathies lie with the lady. Whether she be Rachel Esmond or any woman mated with a husband significantly less intelligent than herself, her "treasures of love [are] doomed to perish without a hand to gather them; sweet fancies and images of beauty that would grow and unfold themselves into flower; bright wit that would shine like diamonds could it be brought into the sun" (93). As Henry explains, "The tyrant in possession crushes the outbreak of all these, drives them back like slaves into the dungeon and darkness, and chafes without that his prisoner is rebellious and his sworn subject undutiful and refractory" (93). For a woman, such a marriage is slavery indeed.

III

NEVERTHELESS, domestic slavery of wives to overbearing husbands is by no means the only form of slavery in *Henry Esmond*. Throughout much of the novel, Thackeray perceptively shows the way in which Henry's own status approximates that of a slave. This servile feature of Henry's situation is most apparent in book 1, where the young Henry is seen as an outsider, without any assured identity of his own. In *Slavery and Social Death*, Orlando Patterson has perceptively argued that an important component of slavery is "natal alienation."[9] What he means by this formulation is that slavery involves alienation from one's own kinship system. In other words, a slave is someone who has been isolated from any true connection not only with living relatives but also with ancestors and even with descendants. Hence the slave must accept whatever identity is chosen for him or her by the master. Moreover, in societies based on kinship, the only such system available to the slave is that of the master; thus the slave must become a fictive part of the master's kinship system. According to Patterson, "Slaves differed from other human beings in that they were not allowed freely to integrate the experience of their ancestors into their lives, to inform their understanding of social reality with the inherited meanings of their natural forebears, or to anchor the living present in any conscious community of memory."[10] Patterson's analysis of slavery is provocative and far-reaching. When applied to *Henry Esmond*, his argument concerning "natal alienation" seems especially illuminating. Numerous readers have remarked about the significance of memory in *Esmond*. In a sense, the entire novel can be seen as—to use Patterson's phrase—a "struggle to reclaim the past" by a mature Henry Esmond, finally aware of his identity and determined to pass on this knowledge to his descendants.[11] More specifically, the initial part of the novel demonstrates the way in which an alienated Henry Esmond exists in a slave-like role first in the household of the third Viscount Castlewood and then in that of the fourth Viscount, while the last part of the novel explores Henry's compulsive slavery to the fourth Viscount's daughter Beatrix.

(a)

AS THE TITLE of chapter 3 of book 1 explains, Henry first comes to Castlewood, the family estate of the Esmonds, "as page to Isabella." Abandoned in infancy by his father, Thomas Esmond, Henry has been raised in obscurity by a family of Huguenot silk-weavers, relatives of his mother who have been forced to emigrate to England from French Flanders because of their religion. While Henry eventually learns these details and others about his background (bk. 2, ch. 13), as a young boy he is simply conscious of his alienation. In the Pastoureau household, where he first becomes aware of his surroundings, his dominant experience is one of loss. Although in this household "he had a dear, dear friend . . . whom he called aunt" (18; bk. 1, ch.3), the "aunt" (actually his mother's cousin), soon dies. The household also contains an Uncle George (another cousin and unrequited lover of Henry's mother), who tells the little boy that "his mother [was] an angel,"—praise that is promptly negated by the head of the household, old Pastoureau, who says, "Angel! she belongs to the Babylonish scarlet woman" (18). After the aunt's death, Bon Papa Pastoureau marries a woman who not only calls little Henry "ill-names" (18) and neglects him in favor of her own two children but also drives Uncle George away. It is not surprising, then, that the young boy is both eager to leave when Father Holt comes to remove him from the Pastoureau family and willing to accommodate himself in a servile capacity in the new household to which Holt brings him. It is also not surprising that, in response to Father Holt's kindness and attention, the lonely child "gave himself up with an entire confidence and attachment to the good Father and became his willing slave almost from the first moment he saw him" (23).

In the household of Thomas Esmond, third Viscount Castlewood, Henry's position for the most part remains lowly. His first sight of his new master is as "a grand languid nobleman in a great cap and flowered morning-gown, sucking oranges" (20; bk. 1, ch. 3), an appearance which, as John Loofbourow points out, "recalls the story-book panoply of an oriental potentate."[12] During the rest of the third Viscount's lifetime, Henry's status resembles that of an ambiguously favored yet still dependent slave. Patterson observes that, upon acquiring a slave, a master commonly enacts certain "rituals of enslavement," such as changing the slave's name or religion.[13] Upon entering the third Viscount's entourage, Henry goes through both of these rituals; his name is changed from Henry Thomas to Henry Esmond (his true name although he does not yet know this fact), and his religion is changed from Huguenot Protestant to Roman Catholic. He is also initiated into his duties as page to Thomas Esmond's wife, "waiting at her chair—bringing her scented water and the silver basin after dinner—sitting on her carriage step on state occasions, or on public days introducing her company to her" (25; bk. 1, ch. 3).

In reality, of course, Henry is the third Viscount's legitimate son and heir, although Henry does not discover this fact until many years later when he hears the fourth Viscount's deathbed confession. As a youth in Thomas Esmond's household, the boy soon comes to a knowledge of his apparent illegitimacy, a circumstance that fills him "with no small feeling of shame". (21; bk. 1, ch. 3). For Patterson, illegitimacy is an appropriate model for the role of even the most benevolently treated slave within a master's family: "At best, the slave was either viewed as an illegitimate quasi-kinsman or as a permanent minor who never grew up. He might be 'of the lineage,' but . . . he was never *in* it."[14] " 'Of the lineage,' but . . . never *in* it" is at the heart of Henry Esmond's problem until the point much later in his life when the "bar-sinister was removed from Esmond's thoughts" (151; bk. 2, ch. 3). As a boy in his father's family, his position remains marginal. He receives kindness from Thomas Esmond when the latter's wife, Lady Isabel (or Isabella), is absent and roughness when she is present. Like a good slave, he is docilely eager to accept the identity that the Viscount, Viscountess, and Father Holt have chosen for him. As the old Viscountess later explains, "Our intention was to make a priest of him" (277; bk. 3, ch. 2), a role that would not only provide for Henry but also (in Patterson's terms) complete his alienation from his own kinship system by denying him descendants. What Thackeray is perceptively suggesting in these details about Henry's childhood is the way in which his protagonist's early upbringing resembles the life of a slave.

(b)

IN THE HOUSEHOLD of Francis Esmond, who succeeds his cousin Thomas to become the fourth Viscount Castlewood, Henry's servile status continues. News of his father's death intensifies his sense of alienation:

> He was in the hands of Heaven and Fate; but more lonely now, as
> it seemed to him, than he had been all the rest of his life: and that

night as he lay in his little room, which he still occupied, the boy
thought with many a pang of shame and grief of his strange and
solitary condition: how he had a father and no father; a nameless
mother that had been brought to ruin, perhaps, by that very father whom Harry could only acknowledge in secret and with a
blush, and whom he could neither love nor revere. And he sick-
ened to think how Father Holt, a stranger, and two or three soldiers, his acquaintances of the last six weeks, were the only friends
he had in the great wide world, where he was now quite alone.
(52; bk. 1, ch. 6)

His feelings at this moment focus on his lack of supporting kindred: "Is
there any child in the whole world so unprotected as I am?" (52). Not
surprisingly, then, he eagerly subordinates himself to the new Viscountess Castlewood when she offers him the kinship system for which he
yearns: " 'And this is our kinsman,' she said; 'and what is your name,
kinsman?' " (6; bk. 1, ch. 1). To Henry, the woman who welcomes him
as an authentic Esmond seems like a goddess ("a *Dea certè,*" [6; bk. 1,
ch. 1]), and her subsequent actions in this scene make clear that she is
willing to overlook what seems to be Henry's lack of legal connection
with the family. When the old housekeeper alludes to Henry's illegitimacy, Rachel Esmond, the new Viscountess, blushes and then returns
to place her hand on the boy's head in a gesture of protective kindness.
Henry's response is a corresponding gesture of abasement: "The boy
. . . felt as if the touch of a superior being or angel smote him down
to the ground, and kissed the fair protecting hand as he knelt on one
knee" (7; bk. 1, ch. 1).

Nevertheless, despite Rachel's kindness in this initial scene, the fundamental ambiguities in Henry's position remain. As the mature Esmond describes the equivocal position of his former self while waiting
for the new lord and lady of Castlewood: "Henry Esmond was no servant though a dependent, no relative though he bore the name and inherited the blood of the house" (8; bk. 1, ch. 1). Indeed, in terms of his
status at Castlewood, the young Henry Esmond can be viewed as a
slave-like dependent whom the fourth Viscount has inherited along
with the rest of the estate. Once again, the lonely boy eagerly adopts a
new religion—in this case Anglican—in order to accommodate himself to the values of his protectors. Again, the dominant agent in his
conversion (previously Father Holt and now Rachel Esmond) values
him more highly as a result of the readiness of this change of faith. To
an even greater degree than with the former Viscountess, young Henry
devotes himself to waiting upon his new mistress: "It cannot be called
love, that a lad of twelve years of age, little more than a menial, felt

for an exalted lady, his mistress: but it was worship. To catch her glance, to divine her errand and run on it before she had spoken it, to watch, follow, adore her became the business of his life" (55; bk. 1, ch. 7). Again, the boy acquiesces in the identity that has been chosen for him. Instead of being a Roman Catholic priest, he will become an Anglican one, although it is not until after Rachel repudiates him following her husband's death that Henry allows himself to articulate the sense of slavery that he perceived in this destiny: "Had it been a mitre and Lambeth which his friends offered him, and not a small living and a country parsonage, he would have felt as much a slave in one case as in the other, and was quite happy and thankful to be free" (164; bk. 2, ch. 5).

For the most part, Rachel treats Henry with kindness and views him as one of her family during his youth at Castlewood. Nevertheless, as her maternal affection for him develops into a suppressed, adulterous love, she is capable of rejecting him in a way that confuses the adolescent boy at the same time that it reawakens his fundamental feelings of alienation. When the sixteen-year-old Henry admits visiting the blacksmith's house and thus unwittingly exposing himself to smallpox, Rachel responds with a fit of poorly concealed, jealous rage at this evidence of his interest in the blacksmith's daughter, Nancy Sievewright. Significantly, Rachel focuses her tirade against Henry on a denial of any kinship between him and herself:

> "My lord," she said, "this young man—your dependent—told me just now in French—he was ashamed to speak in his own language—that he had been at the ale-house all day, where he has had that little wretch who is now ill of the small-pox on his knee. And he comes home reeking from that place—yes, reeking from it—and takes my boy into his lap without shame, and sits down by me, yes, by *me*. He may have killed Frank for what I know— killed our child. Why was he brought in to disgrace our house? Why is he here? Let him go—let him go, I say, to-night, and pollute the place no more." (65; bk. 1, ch. 8)

In these remarks to her husband, Henry is explicitly "your dependent," who is excluded from the family circle.

Eventually, after Henry's illness and her own (and after learning of Nancy's death), Rachel apologizes to the teen-age boy, who apparently fails to discern her true feelings. She then reestablishes her former quasi-maternal relationship with the youth. However, a few years later, in her mental turmoil after her husband's death, Rachel again inflicts emotional pain on Henry by insisting on his alien status. When she visits him in prison after the duel in which Lord Castlewood is killed by Mohun, Rachel not only wildly accuses Henry of responsibility for her husband's death but also again insists that the young man has no real connection with her household. She says about her husband: "He would have had you sent away, but like a foolish woman, I besought him to let you stay. . . . Why did he not send you from among us? 'Twas only his kindness that could refuse me nothing then" (137; bk. 2, ch. 1). Although Rachel's underlying passion for Henry motivates her secretly to steal his sleeve-button during this visit, she seems to be consciously trying to deny this passion for him by her harsh behavior toward the bewildered young man. Subsequently, she sends him a cold letter (written by the clergyman whom she names to the living intended for Henry) in which she alludes to Henry as her kinsman but treats him as just the opposite. Responding to this letter's indication of Rachel's altered attitude toward the kinship for which he yearns—and knowing by now the secret of his birth—Henry thinks bitterly, "he had endowed her family with all they had, and she talked about giving him alms as to a menial!" (140; bk. 2, ch. 1).

In his treatment of the alternations in Rachel's behavior, Thackeray is as usual a perceptive psychologist. While her vacillation between acceptance of Henry as a member of her family and her denial of him as a true kinsman confuses and hurts the young man in question, her actions can be seen as compulsive manifestations of her own inner uncertainties. Since the time of the novel's first publication, readers have been troubled by the incestuous implications of the relationship between Rachel and Henry. As John E. Tilford, Jr., has pointed out, it seems likely Thackeray intended to show that Rachel herself was distressed by these implications.[15] Hence, in her denials of Henry's kinship with her, at moments when she is obviously disturbed by the nature of her feelings for him, Rachel can be seen as attempting to negate the incestuous aspect of their relationship. In a sense, throughout book 1 and in part of book 2, Henry's and Rachel's inner drives are antithetical. While Henry yearns for an affirmation of his kinship with Rachel and her family as a way of overcoming his long-standing sense, in Patterson's terms, of "natal alienation," Rachel feels, whenever her true attitude toward Henry threatens to surface, that she must deny their kinship in order to assuage her sense of guilt.

Implicit in the details of the Rachel-Henry love story lies the biblical story of Joseph and Potiphar's wife. Although Thackeray does not explicitly refer to this story in *Henry Esmond,* he does so in his previous novel, *Pendennis.*[16] This familiar tale from chapter 39 of Genesis—along with the Jacob-Esau and Jacob-Rachel tales from the same biblical book, which are significantly mentioned in *Esmond*—was undoubtedly in Thackeray's thoughts as he was working on this novel in 1851–52.[17] (Perhaps the story about Joseph is also intended to be present in the devout Rachel's mind as, after her husband's death, she struggles with the thought of what she perceives to have been her "Sin" [177; bk. 2, ch. 6]). In the biblical account of Potiphar's wife and Joseph, the former attempts to persuade Joseph to have sexual relations with her while he is an Egyptian slave of her husband. When Joseph, a trusted overseer of Potiphar's household, refuses the advances of his master's wife, she falsely accuses Joseph of attempted adultery with her and causes him to be thrown into prison. The analogies with Henry's situation are striking. He is trusted by his master, Lord Castlewood, and loved by his master's wife. He eventually is confined in prison, and his master's wife accuses him falsely, although unlike Potiphar's wife, Rachel conceals the true nature of her feelings from the young man whom she loves, accuses Henry of what readers might see as a violation of the sixth commandment rather than the seventh, and makes her false accusation after Henry is imprisoned rather than before.

The tale about Potiphar's wife and Joseph also suggests some of the incestuous dimensions of Rachel's relationship with Henry. According to Davis's interpretation of this story in *Slavery and Human Progress,* "In Egypt, Joseph was regarded as an alien and outsider, as the accusation of Potiphar's wife makes clear (she seems to have held the common assumption that a household slave was fair game for sexual exploitation, whereas Joseph seems to have regarded the overture as in some sense incestuous, or oedipal)."[18] As in Davis's view of the slave Joseph, Henry feels so closely bound to his master's family that his attitude toward this family is one of kinship. Thus—consciously at least—Henry cannot conceive of any kind of nonmaternal relationship with his master's wife and is even singularly unenthusiastic in his two proposals of marriage to her after his master's death (bk. 2, ch. 6, and bk. 3, ch. 13). In contrast, like Potiphar's wife with Joseph, Rachel insists on Henry's servile dependency—hence his lack of true kinship with her—when her covert sexual feelings toward him verge on showing themselves during her emotional upheaval after her husband's death or her earlier rage about Nancy Sievewright.

However, the aspect of his youth and young manhood with Rachel and Francis Esmond that most clearly epitomizes Henry's slave-like status is the matter of his profession. After his release from prison, Henry opts to enter the army. He looks back bitterly on the clerical life for which he had been "bred" (124; bk. 1, ch. 14) but from which he has now been liberated by Rachel's apparent hostility toward him in the aftermath of her husband's tragic death: "A discontent with his former bookish life and quietude—a bitter feeling of revolt at that slavery in which he had chosen to confine himself for the sake of those whose hardness towards him made his heart bleed—a restless wish to see men and the world—led him to think of the military profession" (154; bk. 2, ch. 3). Henry's reason for perceiving the clerical profession as "slavery" is that, once he has lost "that first fervour of simple devotion, which his beloved Jesuit priest had inspired in him," he does not really have a religious vocation (79; bk. 1, ch. 9). He thinks of the ministry as that "profession to which worldly prudence rather than inclination called him" (88, bk. 1, ch. 10) and prepares to take religious orders because Rachel has promised to provide for him by giving him the living at Castlewood when the present incumbent dies.

An equally important factor in Henry's acquiescence in Rachel's plan is simply the fact that it is her plan. At Cambridge, he becomes convinced "that his own calling was in no way the pulpit. But as he was bound, before all things in the world, to his dear mistress at home, and knew that a refusal on his part would grieve her, he determined to give her no hint of his unwillingness to the clerical office" (89; bk. 1, ch. 10). As he thinks elsewhere about her determination to settle him as a clergyman at Castlewood, "his mistress had told him that she would not have him leave her: and whatever she commanded was will to him" (121; bk. 1, ch. 14). When Rachel herself repudiates this scheme, Henry is distressed at her irrational anger but eventually pleased at his freedom from what had previously seemed to be his destined life: "Young Esmond of the army was quite a different being to the sad little dependent of the kind Castlewood household and the melancholy student of Trinity Walks—discontented with his fate, and with the vocation into which that drove him: and thinking with a secret indignation that the cassock and bands, and the very sacred office with which he had once proposed to invest himself, were in fact but marks of a servitude which was to continue all his life long" (164; bk. 2, ch. 5). As Henry clearly sees, looking back on his career, this intended perpetual servitude was a slavery from which he has fortunately escaped.

A brief comparison with some of Thackeray's impressions of the life of Swift further illuminates this novel's presentation of young Esmond as a slave. In his lecture on Swift, which he delivered as part of his series on *The English Humourists of the Eighteenth Century* while working on *Henry Esmond,* Thackeray saw young Swift as occupying a slave-like position in the household of his patron Sir William Temple. In Thackeray's words in *The English Humourists,* concerning an obsequious letter from Swift to Temple: "I don't know anything more melancholy than the letter to Temple, in which, after having broke from his bondage, the poor wretch crouches piteously towards his cage again, and deprecates his master's anger. He asks for testimonials for [religious] orders. . . . Can prostration fall deeper? Could a slave bow lower?" (13:485). Unlike Thackeray's fictitious character at Castlewood, Swift had no Rachel to alleviate the unpleasant features of his servitude. In addition, according to Thackeray, Swift made the mistake, which Esmond managed to avoid, of becoming a clergyman without a genuine vocation: "Having put that cassock on, it poisoned him: he was strangled in his bands. He goes through life, tearing, like a man possessed with a devil" (13:490). In Thackeray's view, Swift was a man who revered God but, because of his skepticism, should not have become a clergyman. Hence, once committed to this erroneous profession, Swift could no more find peace than the hag-haunted central character of the first of James Ridley's *Tales of the Genii* (1764): "Like Abudah in the Arabian story, he is always looking out for the Fury, and knows that the night will come and the inevitable hag with it" (13:490).[19] In his treatment of Henry's youthful career, Thackeray seems to be consciously showing a young man whose early servile status resembled Swift's. Nevertheless, in Thackeray's view, Swift's early career differed from that of the fictional Esmond in certain significant ways, one of which in particular— the choice of profession—Thackerary felt had seriously embittered an author whom he disliked.

(c)

THE FINAL PORTION of *Henry Esmond*, dealing with Henry's obsessive love for Rachel's daughter, Beatrix, gathers together these suggestions of slavery that proliferate in the early sections of the novel. Loofbourow has noted that "motifs of compulsion dominate Book III."[20] As demonstrated above, however, such motifs are present throughout book 1 and book 2 until Henry's liberation from prison and adoption of the military life, "secretly glad to have escaped from that fond but ignoble bondage at home" (164; bk. 2, ch. 5). Unfortunately, Esmond's freedom is short-lived, for he returns from his first campaign to fall under Beatrix's spell. After being reconciled with Rachel, Henry proposes that they emigrate together to the land that the Esmond family holds in Virginia. Nevertheless, when Rachel declines this proposal (apparently still experiencing guilt for falling in love with Henry before her husband's death), the young man makes little attempt to overcome her objections. Instead, almost immediately after his overture to Rachel, Henry becomes dazzled by the appearance of her daughter,

Beatrix, now grown to be a woman. Like Dobbin's recollection of Amelia coming downstairs when he first sees her as an adult in *Vanity Fair,* Esmond's sight of Beatrix descending the stair at Walcote remains imprinted on his memory. Decades later, as he narrates his story, Henry still vividly remembers the scene: "Esmond had left a child and found a woman grown beyond the common height, and arrived at such a dazzling completeness of beauty, that his eyes might well show surprise and delight at beholding her" (178–79; bk. 2, ch. 7). As Rachel warns him, eyes like those of Beatrix have the power to captivate a man, but even before the mother's warning, the daughter's glances have begun their work: "A pair of bright eyes with a dozen glances suffice to subdue a man, to enslave him and inflame him" (182; bk. 2, ch. 7). Indeed, even most of Henry's military career in book 2 can be seen as a manifestation of the slavery to Beatrix that replaces the slavery, as a dependent at Castlewood, of his early life. Henry thinks at the beginning of book 3, chapter 1, "His desire for military honor was that it might raise him in Beatrix's eyes" (263).

Nevertheless, despite his rapid promotion, Esmond fails to win the love of the young woman with whom he has become obsessed. Not only does Esmond, recounting this experience in old age, repeatedly present himself as Beatrix's slave, but his imagery emphasizes the demeaning quality of this enslavement. As he writes about his feelings when Beatrix ignores him in order to flirt with other men:

> When the writer's descendants come to read this Memoir, I wonder will they have lived to experience a similar defeat and shame? Will they ever have knelt to a woman, who has listened to them, and played with them, and laughed at them,—who, beckoning them with lures and caresses, and with "Yes," smiling from her eyes, has tricked them on to their knees; and turned her back, and left them? All this shame, Mr. Esmond had to undergo; and he submitted, and revolted, and presently came crouching back for more. (258; bk. 2, ch. 15)

Thackeray's language here is strikingly similar to that which he used in his lecture on Swift in the passage quoted earlier, to describe the way in which he envisioned Swift prostrating himself and crouching before Temple. The analogy underscores Henry's miserably servile condition in relationship to Beatrix. However, numerous descriptions after Henry becomes "enthralled" (205; bk. 2, ch. 10) by her also corroborate this point. He says about himself and Beatrix, "She was a Princess . . . and one of her subjects—the most abject and devoted wretch, sure, that ever drivelled at a woman's knees—was this unlucky gentleman; who bound his good sense, and reason, and independence hand and foot; and submitted them to her" (283; bk. 3, ch. 2).

Despite his awareness of the senseless nature of his infatuation, Henry is unable for at least a decade to shake himself free from his emotional bondage to Beatrix. Many years after the memorable sight of Beatrix at Walcote, he says to Rachel about her daughter (apparently oblivious of the fact that Rachel herself still loves him in a nonmaternal way): "Far or near she knows I'm her slave. I have sold myself for nothing, it may be. Well, 'tis the price I choose to take" (251, bk. 2, ch. 15). Even after Beatrix's unfulfilled betrothals first to Lord Ashburnham and then to the Duke of Hamilton, Esmond continues to yearn after this young woman with whom he is "besotted" (293; bk. 3, ch. 3). The underlying purpose of his intrigue near the end of the novel to place the Stuart claimant, the Prince of Wales, on the English throne after the death of Queen Anne is to lift himself in Beatrix's eyes. Only when Beatrix herself subordinates this momentous political scheme to her own amorous intrigue with the Prince, is Henry able to free himself from his slavery to her. When he finds the note with which she directed the foolish Prince to a private assignation at Castlewood (at the point when the latter should have remained in London to assert his claim to the throne), Henry's "love of ten years was over; it fell down dead on the spot" (386; bk. 3, ch. 13). While Beatrix deserts her family and flees to France, presumably as mistress of the Prince, Henry marries Rachel and moves with her to Virginia. This marriage, at the close of *Henry Esmond,* is unobtrusively foreshadowed throughout the novel, yet seems surprisingly unexciting when it occurs. Without Beatrix and with Rachel, the placid "Indian summer" (389; bk. 3, ch. 13) of Esmond's life begins.

IV

IN VIEW OF THE emphasis on Esmond himself as the victim of slavery during the book, it comes as a bit of a shock to realize that, in the course of his memoirs, he reveals himself as a slavemaster as well as a former slave. In Virginia, the famous diamonds that he inherited from the old Dowager Viscountess are used to buy supplies for the new estate: "Our diamonds are turned into ploughs and axes for our plantations, and into negroes, the happiest and merriest, I think, in all this country" (389; bk. 3, ch. 13). Earlier in book 3, Henry had given these diamonds to Beatrix on the occasion of her engagement to the Duke of Hamilton. Henry had then urged her to keep them when pressing his own suit for her hand after the Duke's death, only to have Beatrix return the diamonds when spurning their giver in favor of the Prince of Wales. In other words, the jewels that failed to obtain Beatrix are now used to buy slaves. While Esmond's "negroes" are specifically described as happy, the fact remains that they are slaves. The somewhat equivocal description of Esmond in the preface, by Rachel Esmond Warrington, underscores his position at the end of his life as a slaveowner in Virginia: "Though I never heard my father use a rough word, 'twas extraordinary with how much awe his people regarded him; and the servants on our plantation, both those assigned from England and the purchased negroes, obeyed him with an eagerness such as the most severe task-masters round about us could never get from their people" (xxvii). Of course, slavery was a fact of life in eighteenth-century Virginia, and in the middle of the eighteenth century and earlier, even affluent people in England occasionally owned black servants.[21] For example, at the height of her career as a Maid of Honour, Beatrix has a little black servant—apparently a slave—named Pompey who has been given to her by one of her admirers (286; bk. 3, ch. 3). Similarly, the old Viscountess—Henry's father's widow—is waited on by "a blackamoor in a Turkish habit, with red boots and a silver collar on which the Viscountess's arms were engraven" (151; bk. 2, ch. 3). However, to cite two important exceptions to attitudes prevailing not long after Esmond's day, no less notable an eighteenth-century Englishman than Samuel Johnson adamantly condemned black slavery, and an equally notable eighteenth-century Virginian, George Washington, made provision, after his own death and that of his wife, to liberate his slaves.[22] The fact that Henry, as slaveowner, feels no such scruples, and apparently takes his blacks as much for granted as Beatrix and old Lady Isabel did theirs suggests that—in the picture of him at the end of his career—at least a faint element of irony may be at work. The contrast between his role as a slaveholder at the end of his life and his earlier servile status corroborates this suggestion of irony.

Henry's ultimate relationship with Rachel also contains ironic dimensions. Despite his compulsive servility during the courtship of Beatrix, the woman whom he finally marries is only too eager to abase herself to him. When Rachel learns both the truth about Henry's birth and his refusal to claim his title so that her son may inherit it, she throws herself to her knees: " 'Don't raise me,' she said, in a wild way, to Esmond, who would have lifted her. 'Let me kneel—Let me kneel and—and—worship you' " (278; bk. 3, ch. 2). Out of gratitude for the way in which Rachel and her late husband treated him as one of the family when he apparently had no legitimate claim on their bounty, Henry is now willing to forgo his title, estate, and legitimate name. However, he is not willing to forgo submissive idolatry in a wife. Beatrix remarks perceptively, "I won't worship you, and you'll never be happy except with a woman who will" (304; bk. 3, ch. 4). While Beatrix does not realize Henry's sacrifice at this point and thus remains unaware of her mother's intensified motives for worshipping Henry, Beatrix sensitively recognizes that Rachel is the kind of woman Henry truly wants: "You want a woman to bring your slippers and cap, and to sit at your feet and cry 'O caro! O bravo!' whilst you read your Shakespeares, and Miltons, and stuff. Mamma would have been the wife for you had you been a little older, though you look ten years older than she does" (304–5; bk. 3, ch. 4). Just as she had once been her first husband's "chief slave and blind worshipper" (76; bk. 1, ch. 9), so Rachel comes to idolize Henry, an attitude the latter complacently accepts when he describes in his last sentence the talisman that she cherishes: "The only jewel by which my wife sets any store, and from which she hath never parted, is that gold button she took from my arm on the day when she visited me in prison, and which she wore ever after, as she told me, on the tenderest heart in the world" (389; bk. 3, ch. 13). While Henry began their relationship by worshipping Rachel as if she were a goddess, she ends by adoring him as if he were a god.

Other readers have occasionally pointed out the capacity for irony inherent in Esmond's memoirs. While most critics have seen Henry as, in John Sutherland's words, "a gentleman, ethically noble . . . an ideal Everyman," J. Hillis Miller has argued on the contrary that this narrative by Henry himself "is an obstinately blind self-justification."[23] Probably, the truth lies somewhere in between. As Esmond himself observes, "We have but to change the point of view, and greatest action looks mean; as we turn the perspective-glass, and a giant appears a pigmy" (202; bk. 2, ch. 10). It seems likely, as Juliet McMaster, Lionel Stevenson, and Ina Ferris have suggested in varying ways, that Thackeray intends us to see Esmond as potentially both selfless and selfish, to recognize his acts of selflessness as well as the inevitable personal bias of his words.[24] Like Conrad's Lord Jim, Thackeray's Henry Esmond appears deliberately designed to remain ambiguous.[25] In his presentation of Esmond, Thackeray evokes questions that he refuses to put to rest.

What this resulting dual vision means as far as the motif of slavery is concerned is an underlying tension between Esmond as slave and Esmond as master. Like Othello in the work that Beatrix calls Henry's "favorite play" (306; bk. 3, ch. 4), Henry is both slave-like and domineering. Just as—especially for eighteenth and nineteenth-century viewers of Shakespeare's play—Othello resembles a slave in terms of the color of his skin, so Esmond is "a black man" (153; bk. 2, ch. 3). Literally, in eighteenth-century terminology, this latter phrase simply indicates that Henry has a dark complexion.[26] However, it also figuratively suggests the way in which his role is that of a slave in terms of his youthful relationship with his protectors and his later relationship with Beatrix. Moreover, just as Othello murders his wife in the belief that she has committed adultery, so Esmond too eventually becomes a virtually omnipotent "King of the Fireside." Indeed Beatrix, only half in jest, cites Othello as an illustration of domestic tyranny and claims that if married to her Henry would eventually follow Othello's example:

> "Why, after I belonged to you, and after one of my tantrums, you would have put the pillow over my head some night and smothered me, as the black man does the woman in the play that you're so fond of—What's the creature's name?—Desdemona. You would, you little black-eyed Othello!"
> "I think I should, Beatrix," says the Colonel. (304; bk. 3, ch. 4)

The domineering streak that Esmond humorously admits to possessing here is corroborated by the novel's preface, written by his daughter and describing the older Esmond in Virginia: "They say he liked to be the first in his company; but what company was there in which he would not be first?" (xxvii). While Esmond's daughter intends to praise her father, here and elsewhere in the preface she ironically reveals details that suggest a negative side to his character, and both sides must be considered in order to understand the full complexity of the character that Thackeray is depicting.

Although Thackeray claimed that work on *Esmond* occupied him "to the exclusion of the 19th. century,"[27] he has clearly used the potent nineteenth-century image of slavery in this novel to achieve his own artistic ends. In terms of the slave/slavemaster dichotomy in his depiction of Henry Esmond, Thackeray seems to be showing a more subtle version of the dynamics of enslavement evident in *Barry Lyndon*. Just as Barry treats others as slaves after being treated as a slave himself, so Henry evidently enjoys being a master after so many years of being a kind of slave. However, unlike Barry, Esmond refrains from bullying his dependents and treats his wife with the consideration that generally ensures a contented marriage. While much of Barry's behavior appears pathological, Esmond's (at least apart from his obsession with Beatrix) is much closer to what one might consider normal. Nevertheless, the more one examines *Henry Esmond*, the more one realizes that this novel is the triumphant presentation by Thackeray of a fascinating and ultimately enigmatic character. Thackeray's use of the idea of slavery in the book contributes to the richness of this presentation.

CHAPTER SIX

"Selling of Virgins" in The Newcomes

What is any respectable girl brought up to do but to catch some
rich man's fancy and get the benefit of his money by marrying
him?

—SHAW, *MRS. WARREN'S PROFESSION*

I

WITH THE NEWCOMES (1853–55), Thackeray returned to his own
nineteenth century from the eighteenth-century world of *Henry
Esmond.* Moreover, to a much greater degree than his previous novels
set in the nineteenth century, *The Newcomes* anatomizes the Victorian
world that Thackeray knew. While *Vanity Fair* occurs in large part during the Regency and *Pendennis* concentrates primarily on the individual
history of its central character, *The Newcomes* offers a panoramic view
of well-bred society of the 1830s and 1840s, where characters amuse
themselves by reading Dickens's recently published *Oliver Twist.* The
world of *The Newcomes* also takes on many aspects of the 1850s, whose
widespread bigoted conformism, as Gordon N. Ray has noted, "urgent-
ly required" the satiric treatment given to it by this vast yet skillfully
crafted book.[1] As one contemporary reviewer wrote, *The Newcomes*
appeared so true to life that it hardly seemed a novel at all: "This is
Mr. Thackeray's masterpiece, as it is undoubtedly one of the master-
pieces of English fiction, if fiction is the proper term to apply to the
most minute and faithful transcript of actual life which is anywhere to
be found."[2] For George Saintsbury, *The Newcomes* was "scarcely even a
microcosm; it is almost the world itself" (14:xxvi). In this vast web,

the idea of slavery is one small strand, yet it is an integral strand that warrants careful attention.

The impression of copiousness produced by this book stems in part from its cultural, as well as its satiric, scope. Of all Thackeray's novels, *The Newcomes* has perhaps the broadest cultural base, encompassing material drawn not only from England but also from the continent of Europe (where Thackeray was travelling while he wrote part of the book), from India (where he spent his early childhood), and from America (which he had recently visited). For Thackeray, exposure to different cultures led to a conviction of their underlying similarity. As the narrator observes at the beginning of *The Newcomes,* "Since last he besought good-natured friends to listen once a month to his talking, a friend of the writer has seen the New World, and found the (feather-less) birds there exceedingly like their brethren of Europe" (14:5). Also for Thackeray, because of his belief in unchanging human nature, this similarity existed not only from culture to culture but also from age to age. Hence the biblical story of Joseph and the brothers who sell him into slavery but grovel to him later when they find him rich and powerful in Egypt is used in *The Newcomes* to illustrate Thackeray's point about the similarity between people in the time of Genesis and in Victorian England: "We would not thrust brother Joseph down a well and sell him bodily, but—if he has scrambled out of a well of his own digging, and got out of his early bondage into renown and credit, at least we applaud him and respect him" (14:62). In all times and places, the novel suggests, whoever is rich becomes respected.

Subtitled *Memoirs of a Most Respectable Family, The Newcomes* satirizes the heartlessness of what commonly passes as "respectability." A ma-jor motif in the novel is the marriage market in which "respectable" upper-class English women are routinely "sold" into loveless mar-riages arranged for economic reasons. Critics have often discussed the satiric examination of respectability in this novel and the book's pre-occupation with the idea of mercenary marriage, as well as the role of Colonel Thomas Newcome (an unworldly misfit in the world of *The Newcomes*) as an illustration of Thackeray's ideal of the gentleman.[3] What has not been explored in depth is the relevance of Thackeray's thoughts about American slavery to his treatment of the marriage market in this book.[4] Nonetheless, although Thackeray makes few overt remarks concerning American slavery in this novel, his recent experience with and reaction to this contentious contemporary subject form a significant part of the background of *The Newcomes.* Written soon after his return from his first visit to America, the book indirectly bears at least some of the fruit of his observations of American slavery. A summary of these impressions offers a useful introduction to the novel.

II

WHILE THACKERAY HAD LONG been fascinated by the image of slavery, his feelings about slavery in real life crystallized during his lecture tours to the United States in 1852–53 and 1855–56. To be sure, he had witnessed slave markets on his trip to the Near East in 1844. However, his personal contacts with Islamic slavery had been brief, and he seems to have viewed it as simply one more exotic characteristic of "Oriental" culture. In America in the 1850s, the subject of slavery was of far greater current interest, and Thackeray's interest in the topic was correspondingly heightened. In Boston, he sought out the liberal clergyman Theodore Parker, a noted antislavery lecturer.[5] As a lecturer himself in a number of large cities of the Southern United States, Thackeray was hospitably entertained by wealthy slaveowners. In the homes of these slaveholders—as well as on the streets, in hotels, and even on an arranged visit to at least one plantation—he saw enough of American slavery to allow him to form what he felt was an accurate assessment.[6] Modern readers, who have the advantage of today's historical perspective, may disagree with his remarks. Thackeray insisted to an English correspondent, "I don't know what may happen in far off rice and cotton fields. I tell you only what I saw."[7] For good or bad, an inability to see beyond immediate data was one of Thackeray's characteristics. He freely declared, "I have no head above my eyes."[8] Hence, his comments about American slavery in his letters must be understood in the context of his desire to describe to distant friends and relatives what he had observed with his own eyes, primarily in such cities as Richmond, Charleston, and Savannah.

As John Sutherland has observed, many of Thackeray's remarks throughout his career about black men and women reflect Victorian assumptions that we would today repudiate as racist.[9] Firsthand observation of blacks in the American South readily convinced him of their inherent difference from whites. He wrote to his mother in February 1853, from Washington:

> They are not my men & brethren, these strange people with retreating foreheads, with great obtruding lips & jaws: with capacities for thought, pleasure, endurance quite different to mine.
> . . . they don't seem to me to be the same as white men, any

more than asses are the same animals as horses; I don't mean this disrespectfully, but simply that there is such a difference of colour, habits, conformation of brains, that we must acknowledge it, & can't by any rhetorical phrase get it over; Sambo is not my man & my brother; the very aspect of his face is grotesque & inferior. I can't help seeing & owning this; at the same time of course deny-ing any white man's right to hold this fellow-creature in bondage & make goods & chattels of him & his issue; but where the two races meet this weaker one must knock under; if it is to improve it must be on its own soil, away from the domineering whites.[10]

Thackeray's position here is complex. His humanitarian impulses need to be separated from both his racial preconceptions and his objection to clichés. In this passage, he is partly satirizing the common antislavery slogan "Am I Not a Man and a Brother?" which he had earlier used at the end of *Pendennis*. More important, the passage reveals that, while Thackeray viewed blacks as both unlike and inferior to whites, he also viewed slavery as inherently wrong and denied "any white man's right to hold this fellow-creature in bondage." Despite his assumptions re-garding racial differences (common in the thinking of writers on both sides of the slavery issue in the 1850s), Thackeray firmly believed that slavery was unjustified.

As his travels in America continued, Thackeray continued to be in-trigued by the black people whom he saw. He wrote to one of his daughters in March 1853 from Charleston: "What interests me in this place is the negro-children I think. I am never tired of watching their little queer half pretty half funny faces—It's a great error to suppose they are unhappy, they are the merriest race ever seen—they are tended by their masters with uncommon care—They have the best of food, of doctors when they are ill, of comfortable provision in old age. Slaves they are and that's wrong: but admitting that sad fact, they are the best cared for poor that the world knows of."[11] This theme about "the best cared for poor that the world knows of" was continued in other letters from America, where Thackeray observed that the slaves whom he witnessed seemed better treated on the whole than many domestic servants and industrial workers in England.[12]

The reasons for Thackeray's repeated emphasis on what seemed to him to be the acceptable aspects of slavery are manifold. His remarks can partly be explained by noting that he was a kindly man whose be-havior toward his own servants was exemplary, and that he saw in America only what was shown to him.[13] His Southern hosts were ex-tremely gracious.[14] Presumably, like anyone trying graciously to enter-tain a distinguished visitor, they made an effort to show him the best that they had to offer. In addition, just as the sights and sounds of the East on his journey to Cairo in 1844 probably appealed so strongly to Thackeray because they evoked memories of his early Indian childhood, so the sight of black slaves in the American South may have been less abhorrent to Thackeray than to many visiting Englishmen (such as Dickens) because these black slaves unconsciously reminded Thackeray of the native servants who had cared for him as a child in India. Furthermore, as an adult, a habit of trying to look at both sides of a complex issue was one of his basic characteristics. As Geoffrey Tillotson has said about Thackeray, "He sees things too completely to want to attack them complete."[15]

In addition, some of Thackeray's remarks about the South should be understood in light of his dislike of stereotypes. Just as he took care to avoid conventional stereotypes in his treatment of characters like Dobbin and Beatrix, so Thackeray seems to be consciously determined in his comments about slavery not to fall into the negative stereotype of slaveholding societies that had become popular in England (which in the 1850s prided itself on having abolished slavery in its West Indian colonies in the 1830s while the United States had still not followed this example). As Davis explains about the formation of this widespread stereotype, "As early as the mid-eighteenth century . . . slave societies were acquiring the image of social and cultural wastelands blighted by an obsessive pursuit of private profit. The negative image was popularized by Anglo-American magazines, newspapers, poetry, plays, and treatises on political economy."[16] By the third decade of the nineteenth century, according to Davis, "British and American abolitionists were coming to view black slavery as a Dantean inferno, a microcosm of the sinful human condition. Enticed by every temptation, deprived of the redeeming discipline of labor and self-improvement, the planters—whether in the West Indies or the American South—were exhibited as living representations of every human vice."[17] Thackeray appears to be deliberately reacting against this kind of negative stereotype when he wrote, for example, from Charleston to Dr. John Brown: "It's all exaggeration about this country—barbarism, eccentricities, nigger cruelties, and all."[18] Ironically, while Thackeray successfully avoided falling into negative stereotypes of the white society of the South, he succumbed to many prevailing views of blacks now recognized as stereotypical.

Apart from the issue of stereotyping, the accuracy of Thackeray's remarks concerning the American slaves' quality of life is debatable. According to the historian Eugene D. Genovese, in the period between 1831 and 1861 "the condition of the slaves worsened with respect to access to freedom and the promise of eventual emancipation; it got better with respect to material conditions of life."[19] As far as such material living conditions as diet and hours of labor are concerned, Genovese also presents evidence to corroborate the nineteenth-century American slaveholders' contention "that their slaves lived better than the great mass of peasants and industrial workers of the world."[20] The basic problem, to contradict the Party slogan in Orwell's *Nineteen Eighty-Four,* was simply that slavery is not the same as freedom. In Genovese's words, "A good master might give his slaves breaks to rest or go swimming, but he could not give them that sense of controlling their own time and labor which might have made even the longest hours and most arduous work seem reasonable and pleasant."[21] It seems likely that Thackeray noticed the humanity with which the slaveowners whom he visited generally treated their slaves and failed to recognize the prevailing cultural commitment to an anti-emancipation policy behind this humane behavior.

In any case, although this conclusion is also debatable, what Thackeray witnessed in America led him to the conviction that the institution of slavery was inevitably doomed for economic reasons.[22] Thackeray observed, "In many of the States slavery will die from its deadness— four blacks do the work of one white, and these four have their families; piccaninnies bed-ridden parents, and all of whom the Master has on his hands."[23] In another letter he remarked, "I don't think it's of long duration . . . unless perhaps in the cotton-growing countries where the whites can't live and the negroes can."[24] To a third correspondent he wrote, "It is the worst economy, slavery, that can be, the clumsiest and most costly domestic and agricultural machine that ever was devised. 'Uncle Tom's Cabin' and the tirades of the Abolitionists may not destroy it, but common sense infallibly will before long."[25] Since the slaves whom he saw were generally uneducated and ill prepared for freedom, Thackeray concluded that immediate emancipation would be a catastrophe: "They are no more fit for freedom than a child of 10 years old is fit to compete in the struggle of life with grown up folks."[26]

Hence, on the basis of his first visit to the United States, Thackeray came to believe that American slavery was a social wrong, with no easy solution except that which time and progress would eventually provide. In the meantime, he felt impelled to explain to his relatives and friends back in England that the slaveowners who hosted and entertained him during his travels in the American South were far more humane than abolitionist propaganda depicted them as being:

> The outcry against the practice has done this good perhaps that it
> has piqued the slave-holders into being *extra*-good to their ser-

vants. And for freeing them—Bon Dieu it is an awful measure to contemplate—there are three millions of them. You must indemnify not only the master but the slave whom you set free. The practice of the country (not the law) is strongly against separating families, and a man is held infamous who does such a crime. The people are no worse than we are whom they taunt about the frightful state and tyranny exercised over our poor—We acquiesce perforce in the state of things so do they—And until Nature affords some outlet for the evil, as with us when the Colonies have carried off multitudes of our poor and raised the wages of those who remain at home,—slaves these poor dark folks must remain: as slaves they have been ever since their race (for what we know) began.[27]

While Thackeray's conjectures about black history in Africa were uninformed, his descriptions of the master-slave relationship that he saw demonstrated by his hosts in the American South were as true to his own observation as possible. It seems not to have occurred to him, however, that these hosts were apt to be exceptionally well read and enlightened and not necessarily typical members of their communities.

On Thackeray's second visit, in 1855–56, when his health had worsened and he took a somewhat more jaundiced view of American ways, he continued to view slavery as an acceptable institution under the current circumstances, but he also clearly perceived that institution's negative side. He wrote to his daughters in February 1856:

How fond you would both be of the little blackies—they are the dearest little imps—I have been watching them all day, about pumps, crawling in gutters, playing in sunshine—I think I shall buy one and bring it home—and happy they unquestionably are—but but—I remember telling you of a pretty little child scratching my elbow and holding up a plate to me at dinner when I was here before, and now—now my friend has tired of Charleston and his beautiful luxurious house gardens and establishment, and has sold his house and his wines—and I dont like to ask abt. the ebony child whom he tickled and nursed and brought up in luxury, and who I fear may be sold too.[28]

From Savannah, in the same month he wrote, "Slavery no where repulsive—the black faces invariably happy and plump, the white ones eager and hard; 'We never use that word which you have just employed' says a gentleman to me at Augusta—'We respect our servants Sir—'Yes Sir but a boot is a boot, and a slave is a slave, whatever else you call him.' "[29] While Thackeray felt that the slaves whom he saw were contented and generally well treated, he also believed slavery was fundamentally wrong and that its reality should not be disguised by rhetoric. In Thackeray's view, in the current imperfect situation, a measure of a slaveowner's decency was his degree of care for the human possessions for whom he had become responsible.

Fundamentally, after witnessing American slavery, Thackeray decided that it was hypocritical for Englishmen to condemn slavery in the United States while British society itself was so deeply flawed. Ray argues that Thackeray "subdued his conscience" with the "quietist" conclusion that the slaveholding American South was no worse than contemporary industrial England.[30] This conclusion does seem to have satisfied him, and he certainly refrained from public comments on the slavery issue both in the United States and after his visits. In his fiction, however, Thackeray was not so quiet on this topic as he was in public life. The theme that runs through his treatment of the idea of slavery in *The Newcomes* is related to his belief in the transatlantic similarities of social imperfection. He wrote in 1853 from Richmond, Virginia, to his friend Albany Fonblanque, owner and former editor of the liberal *Examiner,* concerning the material prosperity of American slaves: "This to be sure leaves the great question untouched that Slavery is a wrong. But if you could decree the Abolition tomorrow, by the Lord it would be the most awful curse and ruin to the black wh. Fate ever yet sent him. Of course we feel the cruelty of flogging and enslaving a negro— Of course they feel here the cruelty of starving an English laborer, or of driving an English child to a mine—Brother, Brother we are kin."[31] The concept that is central to Thackeray's view of American slavery is one of kinship with English social injustice.

III

AS A NOVELIST, Thackeray was undoubtedly sensitive to the fact that the controversy over slavery in 1852 gained impetus from a novel, Harriet Beecher Stowe's rapidly famous *Uncle Tom's Cabin.* This passionately antislavery, religiously permeated work appeared in book form in March 1852. By the end of the year, according to Ann Douglas, "it was apparent that the little lady from Maine had written the bestseller of the nineteenth century."[32] When Thackeray arrived in the United States in November 1852 for his first lecture tour, *Uncle Tom's Cabin* was one of the major topics of conversation—a topic that Thackeray studiously avoided, just as he avoided reading the novel, since friends had warned him that taking a public position on this subject would quickly lead to controversy and jeopardize the success of his tour.[33] His secretary, Eyre Crowe, later explained, when describing their selection of material to read on the trip by railroad from Boston to New York:

> I expended twenty-five cents in the purchase of "Uncle Tom's Cabin," and was properly harrowed by the tale told by Mrs. Beecher-Stowe. But Thackeray declined to plunge into its tale of woe; his opinion expressed upon it being that stories founded upon such painful themes were scarcely within the legitimate purview of storytelling. Besides, judicious friends had dinned well into his ears the propriety of his not committing himself to either side of the Slavery Question, then a burning one, if he wished his career as a lecturer not to become a burthen to him.[34]

However, although Thackeray eschewed public comment both on the issue of slavery and on Mrs. Stowe's book, his private opinion was clear. He observed in a letter to his mother in January 1853, from New York, "I want to see slaves & slave-countries with my own eyes. I dont believe Blacky *is* my man & my brother, though God forbid I should own him or flog him, or part him from his wife & children. But the question is a much longer [one than] is set forth in Mrs. Stowe's philosophy."[35] In this letter, Thackeray continued, "I shant speak about it, till I know it, or till its my business, or I think I can do good." Although Thackeray never did speak out directly on "the Slavery Question," *The Newcomes* in 1853–55 and later *The Virginians* in 1857–59 offered him an opportunity indirectly to express at least some of his thinking on this subject.

Whether Thackeray eventually read *Uncle Tom's Cabin* remains unclear. In June 1853, once Thackeray had returned to England, he finally met Harriet Beecher Stowe and found her quite different in appearance and manner from what he had expected—a reversal that he potentially extended to her book. As he wrote to Mrs. Baxter, "In place of the woman I had imagined to myself after the hideous daguerreotype I found a gentle almost pretty person with a very great sweetness in her eyes and smile. I am sure she must be good and truth-telling from her face and behavior: and when I get a country place and a leisure hour shall buckle to Uncle Tom and really try to read it."[36] There is no definitive evidence that Thackeray ever did find "a leisure hour" in which to "buckle to Uncle Tom." The book did not appear among the contents of his library sold after his death.[37] His caricature of "Legree whipping 'Uncle Tom,' with little Eva as a spectator," included in a letter of 1856 to an American friend, indicates unfamiliarity with specific details of the novel, in which Eva is dead long before Tom is fatally flogged, and the fatal beating is primarily performed by two of Legree's black subordinates.[38] Nonetheless, either through Crowe's description or that of other readers, Thackeray was evidently familiar with the outline of Stowe's story. Moreover, once out of sight of Stowe's "truth-telling" face, his complaint about the one-sidedness of her book returned. He wrote to William Bradford Reed on 21 July 1853, "I keep back some of the truth: but the great point to try and ding into the ears of the great stupid virtue-proud English public, is that there are folks as good as they in America. Thats where Mrs. Stowe's book has done harm, by inflaming us with an idea of our own superior virtue in freeing our blacks whereas you keep your's. Comparisons are always odorous Mrs. Malaprop says."[39] In dealing with the concept of slavery in the two novels (*The Newcomes* and *The Virginians*) that immediately followed his two American visits, Thackeray clearly seems to have determined to take a route different from that exemplified by Stowe.

The heart of Thackeray's objection to Stowe's novel may be suggested by Crowe's remark about what Thackeray considered "the legitimate purview of storytelling." As Charles Mauskopf has demonstrated, "In keeping with . . . [his] ideals of historical objectivity, Thackeray opposed the use of the novel for the display of any sort of prejudice or the advocacy of any cause, as not the proper sphere of interest of the novel nor the proper function of the novelist."[40] For example, in an 1845 review of Charles Lever's *St. Patrick's Eve,* Thackeray declared, "You can't allow an author to invent incidents, motives, and characters, in order that he may attack them subsequently. How many Puseyite novels, Evangelical novels, Roman Catholic novels have we had, and how absurd and unsatisfactory are they."[41] In other words, Thackeray not only believed that fiction should be realistic (i.e., tell the "truth") but that it should achieve this goal by practicing a Keatsian kind of Negative Capability—by presenting different aspects of any issue and refraining from taking sides.[42] It is precisely this kind of open-mindedness that is lacking in Stowe's powerful work of propaganda. In contrast, in his treatment of "the selling of virgins" in *The Newcomes,* Thackeray achieves the kind of untendentious balance that he sought in a work of fiction.

IV

(a)

ALTHOUGH THACKERAY MAKES only a few explicit references to America or American slavery in *The Newcomes,* his recent contact with the United States clearly underlies much of his thinking in this book. Near the beginning of chapter 2, in an effort to establish the climate of opinion in England at the time the founder of the Newcome family arrived in London, the narrator alludes in passing to "when Mr. Washington was heading the American rebels with a courage, it must be confessed, worthy of a better cause" (14:14–17)—an unlucky remark that evoked such an uproar in the United States, following publication of the first installment, that Thackeray was obliged to defend himself in a letter to the London *Times* (23 November 1853). After this experience, it is not surprising that Thackeray was cautious about his comments concerning the United States in the rest of *The Newcomes*. Nonetheless, significant evidence of his recent American trip remains. As scholars have pointed out, the character of the book's heroine, Ethel Newcome, appears to derive, at least to some degree, from that of Sally Baxter, the lively New York girl with whom Thackeray platonically fell partly in love while in America and whom he advised on matters of the heart.[43] A more explicit American allusion also suggests some of Thackeray's own deepest feelings. In chapter 5 of the novel, the narrator comments about the similarity between breaking up a relationship between an enslaved parent and child and sending an English child home from India, as Thackeray himself had been sent at the age of five: "In America it is from the breast of a poor slave that a child is taken: in India it is from the wife, and from under the palace, of a splendid proconsul" (14:66). The principle behind this remark concerning the analogy between Anglo-Indian children and slave children wrenched from their mothers is one of cross-cultural parallel. Another, thematically more significant, example of this kind of parallel is the ironic observation that Thackeray allows himself to make in chapter 28 concerning the recent "address to Mrs. Stowe." In both English society and the American South, Thackeray suggests, similar betrayals of affection occur. An examination of the novel in light of the "address" to which Thackeray is referring demonstrates this point.

Chapter 28, entitled "In which Clive Begins to See the World," takes place in Baden, where young Clive Newcome becomes acquainted with the gambling, merrymaking, and matchmaking that occupy visitors to this "prettiest town of all places where Pleasure has set up her tents" (14:349). For the upwardly mobile, mercantile family of Clive's cousin Ethel Newcome, the primary business of the day is matchmaking. In particular, Ethel's family encourages the long-standing engagement between Ethel and Lord Kew and arranges an engagement between Ethel's brother Barnes and Lady Clara, the daughter of the impoverished Earl of Dorking. Both of these impending mercenary marriages—especially the latter between the helpless Clara and the heartless Barnes—prompt the narrator to allude ironically to Harriet

Beecher Stowe: "So that the diatribe wherein we lately indulged, about the selling of virgins, by no means applies to Lady Ann Newcome, who signed the address to Mrs. Stowe, the other day, along with thousands more virtuous British matrons; but should the reader haply say, 'Is thy fable, O Poet, narrated concerning Tancred Pulleyn, Earl of Dorking, and Sigismunda, his wife?' the reluctant moralist is obliged to own that the cap *does* fit those noble personages" (14:363). Despite the narrator's tongue-in-cheek distinction between the families of Edith and Clara, his remarks about "the selling of virgins" are relevant to both young women. In Ethel's case, as the novel elsewhere makes clear, her mother Lady Ann is quite prepared to sell her daughter into a mercenary marriage as she herself was sold. The results of such a sale, as Clara's case illustrates, can resemble some of the circumstances deplored in the contemporary antislavery document that the narrator here invokes.

This document was a notable public letter entitled "An Affectionate and Christian Address of Many Thousands of Women of Great Britain and Ireland to Their Sisters, the Women of the United States of America." Circulated in late 1852 and early 1853, the "Affectionate and Christian Address" was a remarkable public relations feat. The text is worth quoting in its entirety:

> A common origin, a common faith, and, we sincerely believe, a common cause, urge us, at the present moment, to address you on the subject of that system of negro slavery which still prevails so extensively, and, even under kindly disposed masters, with such frightful results, in many of the vast regions of the western world.
>
> We will not dwell on the ordinary topics,—on the progress of civilization, on the advance of freedom everywhere, on the rights and requirements of the nineteenth century,—but we appeal to you very seriously to reflect, and to ask counsel of God how far such a state of things is in accordance with His holy word, the inalienable rights of immortal souls, and the pure and merciful spirit of the Christian religion.
>
> We do not shut our eyes to the difficulties, nay, the dangers, that might beset the immediate abolition of that long established system: we see and admit the necessity of preparation for so great an event: but, in speaking of indispensable preliminaries, we cannot be silent on those laws of your country which, in direct contravention of God's own law, 'instituted in the time of man's innocency,' deny in effect to the slave the sanctity of marriage, with all its joys, rights, and obligations; which separate, at the will of the master, the wife from the husband, and the children from the parents. Nor can we be silent on that awful system

which, either by statute or by custom, interdicts to any race of man, or any portion of the human family, education in the truths of the Gospel and the ordinances of Christianity.

A remedy applied to these two evils alone would commence the amelioration of their sad condition. We appeal to you, then, as sisters, as wives, and as mothers, to raise your voices to your fellow-citizens, and your prayers to God, for the removal of this affliction from the Christian world. We do not say these things in a spirit of self-complacency, as though our nation were free from the guilt it perceives in others. We acknowledge, with grief and shame, our heavy share in this great sin. We acknowledge that our forefathers introduced, nay, compelled, the adoption of slavery in those mighty colonies. We humbly confess it before Almighty God, and it is because we so deeply feel, and so unfeignedly avow, our own complicity, that we now venture to implore your aid to wipe away our common crime and our common dishonour.[44]

The stimulus behind the address was the recent appearance of *Uncle Tom's Cabin*. The document was sponsored by the Duchess of Sutherland, who began her campaign on its behalf with a meeting on 26 November 1852 at her London home known as Stafford House.[45] Eventually, the Stafford House Address, as it was sometimes called, gained the signatures of over half a million women—including many in the highest ranks of British society. Bound into twenty-six volumes and enclosed in a case made of oak, the document and its signatures were presented to Harriet Beecher Stowe.

Not surprisingly, a public activity of such magnitude evoked controversy. Prominent supporters like the Earl of Shaftesbury (who had composed it) lobbied on its behalf.[46] Wives of prominent men—including Charles Dickens, Alfred Tennyson, Viscount Palmerston, and Lord John Russell—allowed their names to be used in support of the document. Eventually, 562,848 women signed the address.[47] The statement also generated opposition, however. Some hard-line abolitionists objected to the document's gradualist approach to emancipation. For example, the writer Mary Howitt joined the committee endorsing the address and was then visited by representatives of the British and Foreign Anti-Slavery Society who asked her to withdraw her support of the statement.[48] Despite reservations by committed abolitionists, who found the address too tame, most complaints about the address came from the opposite direction, from individuals who found the document extreme, intemperate, or misguided. One of the many negative letters that appeared in the London *Times* regarding the address provides a good summary of some of the objections (expressed in earlier letters to this newspaper) that the document had aroused:

> One writer talks of the insufficiency of women to manage a subject
> which requires the most experienced legislation; another tells
> them to look at home, and redress the grievances and abuses under
> their own eyes; a third laughs at the active sympathy excited by
> the perusal of an American novel, whereas no authentic history
> had ever moved any of these ladies into action before; a fourth
> upbraids them with buying cheap sugar, and insinuates a doubt of
> their sincerity so long as they assist in keeping up the immense
> demand for slave-cultivated cotton by wearing raiments of that
> material; while a fifth, with very fair irony, asks whether she may
> not become a party to an untruth with a clear conscience for the
> sake of signing her name with duchesses and marchionesses.[49]

Another contributor of a letter to the London *Times* compared the
women promoting the address to Mrs. Jellyby (in Dickens's currently
serialized *Bleak House*).[50] From Virginia, the wife of former President
John Tyler wrote to tell the English ladies to stop meddling in American
affairs and to confine their sympathies to British problems (such as
the situation in Ireland). In Mrs. Tyler's words, "The golden rule of
life is for each to attend to his own business and let his neighbour's
alone! This means peace, love, friendship. The opposite means hatred,
ill-will, contention; it destroys the peace of neighbourhoods, and is the
fruitful cause of discord among nations."[51] Thackeray's own view of
what he described as "the Sutherland House Womanifesto" was negative.[52] He felt that the address was based on ignorance of America and
the actual conditions of American slavery as he had seen it. In addition,
as he wrote from Philadelphia to his friend Lady Stanley concerning
the address, before visiting the South but perhaps thinking of objections
like those raised by Mrs. Tyler, "It only makes ill blood."[53]

. As Thackeray's facetious allusion to the "Womanifesto" indicates,
one striking feature of the address was its female constituency. An
equally notable feature was the high social status of some of the document's female supporters. As the attendant publicity emphasized, the
address was signed by "three duchesses, one marchioness, fifteen coun-
tesses, seven viscountesses, [and] seven ladies of baronets."[54] Clearly,
at this point in the fall of 1852 and the spring of 1853, shortly before
Thackeray began *The Newcomes,* the issue of slavery was one that the
"ladies" of England seemed to have taken under their particular juris-
diction. When Stowe herself arrived in London in May 1853 (where
she met Thackeray, just home from America and about to embark on
his new novel), she was eagerly welcomed by the Duchess of Sutherland and other aristocratic women. In view of his disapproval of the
Stafford House Address, it is not surprising that Thackeray was moved
to write a private parody, focusing on the ladies' aspect of the enter-

prise. Ray points out in a footnote to his edition of Thackeray's letters,

> In a Sotheby catalogue of July 27, 1928, the following fragment is
> quoted from a two page manuscript in Thackeray's hand entitled
> "A Womanifesto": "An Army of five hundred thousand ladies
> with tasteful banners on wch. poor Gumbo is displayed kneeling
> in his chains and asking piteously whether he is not a man and a
> brother? . . . their Koran, their book of Mormon, the book of
> the Law—a novel. The Sage of Grosvenor Gate [Lord Shaftes-
> bury] bewailed the decline of Public Morals; and the Knebworth
> Apollo [Bulwer-Lytton] twanged his silver bow, and none seemed
> to heed the voice of the moralist, or even to be tickled by the ar-
> rows of the bard."[55]

The conclusion to which this fragment leads is that Thackeray perceived the Stafford House Address as not only misguided and ineffec-
tual but also conspicuously feminine and genteel.

(b)

IN *THE NEWCOMES,* Thackeray's negative reaction to the Stafford House
Address is apparent, not just in his explicit reference to the address in
chapter 28 but in the novel as a whole. More specifically, in this novel
Thackeray seems to be responding to what he perceived as the conspicuous association of upper-class British women with the cause of
antislavery in 1852–53. For Thackeray, who was familiar with the arranged marriages that characterized upper-class British society, the
emphasis of the address on the "sanctity of marriage, with all its joys,
rights, and obligations" must have appeared blatantly hypocritical. In
the summer of 1853, he wrote to Sally Baxter, cautioning her about an
English suitor who Thackeray believed was "spoiled by the heartlessness of London," which, he further explained,

> is awful to think of—the most godless respectable thing—thing's
> not the word but I can't get it—I mean that world is base and
> prosperous and content, not unkind—very well bred—very unaf-
> fected in manner, not dissolute—clean in person and raiment and
> going to church every Sunday—but in the eyes of the Great Judge
> of right & wrong what rank will those people have with all their
> fine manners and spotless characters and linen? They never feel
> love, but directly it's born, they throttle it and fling it under the
> sewer as poor girls do their unlawful children—they make up
> money-marriages and are content—then the father goes to the
> House of Commons or the Counting House, the mother to her
> balls and visits—the children lurk up stairs with their governess,

and when their turn comes are bought and sold, and respectable
and heartless as their parents before them. Hullo!—I say—Stop!—
where is this tirade a-going to and apropos of what?—Well I was
fancying my brave young Sarah (who has tried a little of the
pomps & vanities of her world) transplanted to ours and a London
woman of society—with a husband that she had taken as she
threatens to take one sometimes just because he is a good parti.
No—go and live in a clearing—marry a husband masticatory, ex-
pectoratory, dubious of linen, but with a heart below that rumpled
garment—let the children eat with their precious knives—help
the help, and give a hand to the dinner yourself—yea, it is better
than to be a woman of fashion in London, and sit down to a
French dinner where no love is.[56]

Thackeray's train of thought in this letter explicitly links his advice to
Sally with *The Newcomes* as he concludes, "Immense Moralist! I think
I'll call in Anny now, and give her a turn at the new novel. I see a chapter out of the above sermon and you know I must have an i to the main
chance—." In his depiction of "the selling of virgins" in *The Newcomes,*
Thackeray indirectly suggests that "respectable" British society—whose
marital practices he openly condemns in this letter—is just as flawed as
the slave-selling American South.

   Although the novel primarily conveys the motif of the marriage
market by concentrating on the experiences of two upper-class British
girls, Lady Clara and Ethel, the book makes clear that traffic in young
women is by no means confined to any single historical age or culture.
The narrator, Arthur Pendennis, dryly observes: "France is the country where that sweet Christian institution of *mariages de convenance*
(which so many folks of the family about which this story treats are
engaged in arranging) is most in vogue" (14:406). In the marriages of
Paul de Florac, his mother Mme. de Florac, and the elderly Duc d'Ivry,
the unfolding pages of *The Newcomes* demonstrate the unhappy consequences of this "sweet" French custom. In the case of the gentle Mme.
de Florac, who is forced to ignore her early love for Thomas Newcome
in order to wed someone older than her father at the latter's insistence,
the results of this arranged marriage are especially poignant. As she
says to Ethel: "Is it written eternally that men are to make slaves of us?
Here in France, above all, our fathers sell us every day. And what a society ours is! Thou wilt know this when thou art married. There are
some laws so cruel that nature revolts against them, and breaks them—
or we die in keeping them. . . . I have been nearly fifty years dying"
(14:629). Elsewhere, the novel alludes to Hogarth's *Marriage à la Mode*
(14:414, 720), showing that the problems associated with a *mariage
de convenance* are by no means confined to France or even to the

nineteenth century. The narrator remarks at the end of chapter 28 concerning contemporary marriages: "St. George of England may behold
virgin after virgin offered up to the devouring monster, Mammon
(with many most respectable female dragons looking on)—may see
virgin after virgin given away, just as in the Soldan of Babylon's time,
but with never a champion to come to the rescue!" (14:776). In *Vanity
Fair* and *Henry Esmond,* Thackeray had suggested that women were
treated like slaves in marriage. In *The Newcomes,* he indicates that they
are sold like slaves when their marriages are arranged.

Moreover, *The Newcomes* stresses that this kind of selling of women
is not limited to Europe. The narrator's "diatribe . . . about the selling of virgins" and his allusion to the Stafford House Address are followed by an extended comparison between the "sale" of an earl's
daughter in England and an Indian suttee:

> For though I would like to go into an Indian brahmin's house and
> see the punkahs and the purdahs and tattys, and the pretty brown
> maidens with great eyes, and great nose-rings, and painted fore-
> heads, and slim waists cased in cashmere shawls, kincob scarfs,
> curly slippers, gilt trousers, precious anklets and bangles; and
> have the mystery of Eastern existence revealed to me (as who
> would not who has read the *Arabian Nights* in his youth?) yet I
> would not choose the moment when the brahmin of the house was
> dead, his women howling, his priests doctoring his child of a
> widow, now frightening her with sermons, now drugging her
> with bhang, so as to push her on his funeral pile at last, and into
> the arms of that carcass, stupefied, but obedient and decorous.
> And though I like to walk, even in fancy, in an earl's house, splen-
> did, well ordered, where there are feasts and fine pictures and fair
> ladies and endless books and good company; yet there are times
> when the visit is not pleasant. And when the parents in that fine
> house are getting ready their daughter for sale, and frightening
> away her tears with threats, and stupefying her grief with narcot-
> ics, praying her and imploring her, and dramming her and coax-
> ing her, and blessing her, and cursing her, perhaps, till they have
> brought her into such a state as shall fit the poor young thing for
> that deadly couch upon which they are about to thrust her:—
> when my lord and lady are so engaged, I prefer not to call at their
> mansion, No. 1000 in Grosvenor Square, but to partake of a dinner
> of herbs rather than of that stalled ox which their cook is roasting
> whole. (14:363–64)

Both English and Indian customs involve deadening the natural feelings of women in order to satisfy the wishes of their families. As the
narrator continues about the marriage/funeral ceremony:

There are some people who are not so squeamish. The family
comes of course; the most reverend the Lord Arch-Brahmin of
Benares will attend the ceremony; there will be flowers and lights
and white favours; and quite a string of carriages up to the pago-
da; and such a breakfast afterwards; and music in the street and
little parish boys hurrahing; and no end of speeches within and
tears shed (no doubt), and his grace the Arch-Brahmin will make
a highly appropriate speech (just with a faint scent of incense
about it as such a speech ought to have), and the young person
will slip away unperceived, and take off her veils, wreaths, orange
flowers, bangles, and finery, and will put on a plain dress more
suited for the occasion, and the house-door will open—and there
comes the SUTTEE in company of the body: yonder the pile is
waiting on four wheels with four horses, the crowd hurrahs and
the deed is done. (14:364)

The Indian suttee results in the wife's literal death, while the *mariage de
convenance* can lead to the kind of psychological death that Mme. de
Florac has known.

Ultimately, the novel suggests, "selling of virgins" is a universal
custom. Once again, as in *Vanity Fair,* Thackeray invokes the idea of
"Oriental" slavery as an image of woman's traditional lot. As Ethel
remarks about the situation of girls like herself in the London marriage
market, "We are as much sold as Turkish women; the only difference
being that our masters may have but one Circassian at a time" (14:425).
Richard Doyle's illustrated capital for chapter 43, which shows three
figures in Eastern costume including a woman being sold to a leering
man, connects the ideas of both "Oriental" slavery and the "selling of
virgins" (fig. 14). In this chapter, while attempting to explain why the
socially insignificant and only moderately affluent young painter Clive
should not hope to marry his cousin Ethel, Pendennis observes: " 'The
Circassian beauties don't sell under so many thousand purses,' . . . 'If
there's a beauty in a well-regulated Georgian family, they fatten her:
they feed her with the best *Racahout des Arabes.* They give her silk robes,
and perfumed baths; have her taught to play on the dulcimer and dance
and sing; and when she is quite perfect, send her down to Constantinople for the Sultan's inspection. The rest of the family never think of
grumbling, but eat coarse meat, bathe in the river, wear old clothes,
and praise Allah for their sister's elevation.' " (14:568–69). Pendennis
asks rhetorically near the end of this oration for Clive's behalf, "Do
you suppose the Turkish system doesn't obtain all the world over?"
(14:569). The novel makes clear that the answer to this question should
be "Yes." An earlier lecture on the same theme from Pendennis to
Clive Newcome in chapter 41 draws an analogy between the marriage

Fig. 14. Capital for chapter 43 of The Newcomes, *suggesting the ideas of "Oriental" slavery and the "selling of virgins."*

market and a well-known London horse market, an analogy also suggested by Doyle's illustrated capital for chapter 54, showing Lady Kew auctioning Ethel as "Lot 1" before a group of men (fig. 15). Pendennis's remarks in chapter 41 further extend this analogy to encompass both "Oriental" and American slavery. In Pendennis's words, "You look astonished, my poor boy? You think it is wicked in me to talk in this brutal way about bargain and sale; and say that your heart's darling is, at this minute, being paced up and down the May Fair market to be taken away by the best bidder. . . . What I say is wicked and worldly, is it? So it is: but it is true, as true as Tattersall's—as true as Circassia or Virginia" (14:537). In other words, Thackeray suggests, not only the Turkish but also the Virginian system prevails throughout the world.

The novel depicts the similar yet diverging experiences of Ethel and Lady Clara against this background of the universal merchandizing of women, although the system more seriously harms the latter. As her maiden name suggests, Lady Clara Pulleyn has a vulnerable quality; like a pullet (a young hen), she seems doomed to be a victim. The names of other members of her family contribute to this metaphor of poultry. Her father is the Earl of Dorking (a type of chicken); her unmarried sisters include Hennie, Biddy, and Adelaide, while her oldest brother is Viscount Rooster. Appropriately, their family estate is

Fig. 15. Capital for chapter 54 of The Newcomes, *showing Lady Kew as auctioneer and Ethel as "Lot 1."*

Chanticlere. Since Chanticlere is heavily mortgaged, Lord and Lady Dorking must arrange financially advantageous marriages for their daughters. Thus, despite her love for Jack Belsize (younger son of Lord Highgate), Lady Clara is "sold" by her family to the rapacious Barnes Newcome, the eldest son of Sir Brian Newcome and partner in the prominent banking firm of Hobson Brothers and Newcome.

Not surprisingly, the marriage between Lady Clara and Barnes turns out badly. As the narrator comments a few years after the wedding, "You understand, the man to whom her parents sold her does not make her happy, though she has been bought with diamonds, two carriages, several large footmen, a fine country-house with delightful gardens and conservatories" (14:693). More surprisingly, Lady Clara becomes so desperate in her marriage to the cold-hearted and abusive Barnes that she violates Victorian convention and elopes with Jack Belsize, who has unexpectedly become Lord Highgate after the deaths of his elder brother and father. The elopement results in scandal, as well as Lady Clara's loss of her children, who remain in their father's custody. The eventual divorce proceedings contain echoes of the famous suit for damages, as part of an adultery action, brought against Lord Melbourne in 1836 by George Norton, husband of the talented and attractive Caroline Norton, granddaughter of the dramatist Richard Brinsley Sheridan. Because the evidence against him was flimsy, Melbourne was acquitted, and Caroline Norton's innocence was legally established. Hence, George Norton was unable to obtain the divorce that he had hoped to achieve as one of the outcomes of the trial. However, he and Caroline, whose initials, "C. N.," are the same as those of Clara Newcome, lived apart. As Robert A. Colby has pointed out, Mrs. Norton was again in the news not long before the appearance of the April 1855 installment of *The Newcomes* containing Lady Clara's divorce. In 1853, George and Caroline Norton were embroiled in a legal dispute concerning property rights. In 1854, as a result of this dispute, Mrs. Norton published a pamphlet entitled *English Laws for Women in the Nineteenth Century*, in which she compared the current legal situation of Englishwomen to that of American slaves.[57] Whether Thackeray read this pamphlet, which alludes to Harriet Beecher Stowe's recent visit, is unclear, although it is known that he conducted research into the Norton-Melbourne trial in preparation for this part of *The Newcomes*.[58] In any event, Thackeray shows that Lady Clara is still unhappy even after leaving Barnes because she is now ostracized by society: "So Lady Clara flies from the custody of her tyrant, but to what a rescue? The very man who loves her, and gives her asylum, pities and deplores her. She scarce dares to look out of the windows of her new home upon the world, lest it should know and reproach her. All the sisterhood of friendship is cut off from her. If she dares to go abroad she feels the sneer of the world as she goes through it; and knows that malice and scorn whisper behind her" (14:775). Because of his marriage to her, Lady Clara's new husband, Lord Highgate, also finds that his social equals avoid his home, with the result that he too eventually avoids the home that his wife has unintentionally blighted: "No wonder that her husband does not like home, except for a short while in the hunting season. No wonder that he is away all day; how can he like a home which she made so wretched?" (14:776). Once one has been sold into a mercenary marriage, Lady Clara's example suggests, even a subsequent marriage for love may not remedy the unhappiness resulting from the initial betrayal of affection.

Within the novel, Lady Clara's experience functions as a warning to Barnes's sister Ethel, who originally also seems destined as a commodity in the marriage market. However, unlike the feeble and (for the most part) passive girl who eventually becomes her sister-in-law, Ethel is an active, complex, and dynamic individual.[59] Although attracted to Clive and resentful of the way in which her family has arranged a marriage for her with Lord Kew, she still acquiesces—at least temporarily—in this arrangement, knowing that Kew's wife will become a countess. Nonetheless, she cannot resist making satiric comments about the fate that her family has prepared for her. For example, after witnessing a water-color exhibition, she compares women in the marriage market whose marriages have already been arranged to prepurchased paintings being exhibited until the end of the season. She underlines her point by taking a green ticket (indicating "sold") from one of the paintings and wearing it in her dress at a family dinner (14:361–62). Later, at a ball, she flirts outrageously with other men despite her fiancé's presence. When Lord Kew remonstrates with her the next day, she gives him an anonymous letter that she has just received detailing his own past escapades as a man of pleasure. Her giving him the letter terminates their engagement since Kew, a decent young man who has regretted his past, concludes that she would not have done so if she really loved him. The novel makes clear that Ethel's actions are prompted by rebellion against what she perceives as the slavery for which she is destined. Concerning the pivotal interview between Lord Kew and Ethel, the narrator remarks, "Her high spirit was in perpetual revolt, at this time, against the bondage in which her family strove to keep her" (14:442). Ethel herself declares angrily concerning Lord Kew's lecture, "I am not a lawful slave yet, and prefer to remain unmolested, at least as long as I am free" (14:441). Ethel's impulse toward freedom makes the chains that attempt to hold her more conspicuous.

The dissolution of Ethel's engagement to Lord Kew only prompts her family to try to arrange another match. Once again, Ethel chafes at the slavery in which she also partly acquiesces. She has heard nuns singing in the chapel of a convent adjacent to Mme. de Florac's quiet Parisian garden, and she comments to Clive, "I was thinking, that almost all women are made slaves one way or other, and that these poor nuns perhaps were better off than we are" (14:636). Nevertheless, she participates in the plan of her determined grandmother, Lady Kew, to arrange a marriage between Ethel and the Marquis of Farintosh. Eventually, Farintosh proposes, and the engagement is announced. In delight at the impending marriage, Lady Kew makes a will, leaving her fortune to Ethel. Lady Kew then unexpectedly dies, giving the not yet married Ethel the financial independence to follow her own desires. Not until Lady Clara's elopement, however, does Ethel realize her own potential freedom. As she explains to Pendennis's wife, Laura, "I lay awake, thinking of my own future life, and that I was going to marry, as poor Clara had married, but for an establishment and a position in life; I, my own mistress, and not obedient by nature, or a slave to others as that poor creature was—I thought to myself, why shall I do this?" (14:791). Even prior to their engagement, Ethel recognized and disliked Farintosh's condescending view that the girls who sought to marry him were slaves, an attitude similar to George Osborne's view of Amelia in *Vanity Fair*. Ethel explains to Laura: "Not that Lord Farintosh thinks me, or any one, of his rank. . . . He is the sultan, and we—every unmarried girl in society is his humblest slave. His Majesty's opinions upon this subject did not suit me, I can assure you: I have no notion of such pride!" (14:790). After their engagement, Ethel comes to understand her fiancé's character more fully and realizes that she does not respect him. Hence, she breaks off their engagement, recognizing that she is her "own mistress" and not a "slave" like Clara.

In his treatment of Ethel, Thackeray evidently seems to have had the Stafford House Address in mind. As already discussed, much of Ethel's history, like Clara's, focuses on the London marriage market, which denies the true meaning of marriage to the women "sold" just as, according to the Stafford House manifesto, slavery denies "the sanctity of marriage" to the slave. In addition, Ethel ironically illustrates at least part of the second negative feature of slavery against which the address protests. According to the document, slavery also "interdicts . . . education in the truths of the Gospel and the ordinances of Christianity," a charge which Mrs. Tyler, whose husband was a Virginia planter and slaveowner, vehemently denied in her letter in the *Times*.[60] Within this context, it is noteworthy that Thackeray stresses Ethel's faulty education in *The Newcomes*. Near the beginning of chapter 10, the narrator attributes this faulty education to her mother's habit of "constantly falling in love with her new acquaintances" and then just as regularly falling out of love (14:132). This kind of compulsive transient infatuation may be one of the emotional side effects of a social system in which true love is deliberately stifled, or throttled, to use the image that Thackeray employed in his letter to Sally Baxter about the London marriage market. At any rate, Lady Ann's flightiness results in a bewildering succession of governesses for her daughter. The narrator explains that Ethel

> had had so many governesses—all darlings during the first week, and monsters afterwards—that the poor child possessed none of the accomplishments of her age. She could not play on the piano; she could not speak French well; she could not tell you when gunpowder was invented; she had not the faintest idea of the date of the Norman Conquest, or whether the Earth went round the sun, or vice versa. She did not know the number of counties in England, Scotland, and Wales, let alone Ireland; she did not know the difference between latitude and longitude. She had had so many governesses: their accounts differed: poor Ethel was bewildered by a

multiplicity of teachers, and thought herself a monster of ignorance. (14:132)

Among the consequences of this poor training appears to be a deficiency in the very kind of Christian education that the Stafford House Address maintained was lacking in a state of slavery. When Ethel visits a parish Sunday School, she finds that girls much younger than herself are much more knowledgeable than she: "They gave her a book at a Sunday School, and little girls of eight years old answered questions of which she knew nothing. The place swam before her. She could not see the sun shining on their fair flaxen heads and pretty faces. The rosy little children holding up their eager hands, and crying the answer to this question and that, seemed mocking her. She seemed to read in the book, 'Ethel, you dunce, dunce, dunce!' " (14:132). When considered in light of the Stafford House Address, this passage suggests Thackeray's belief that American slavery has no monopoly on ignorance, just as it has no monopoly on the selling of women.

Much later in the book, Thackeray again picks up the theme of Ethel's ignorance, although the idea is now broadened to include her faulty emotional preparation for life. Laura explains to her husband about Ethel: "Life and experience force things upon her mind which others learn from their parents or those who educate them, but for which she has never had any teachers. Nobody has ever told her, Arthur, that it was wrong to marry without love, or pronounce lightly those awful vows which we utter before God at the altar" (14:786–87). Ethel's problem is that she has been deliberately trained to be worldly. Laura likens her to "dancing girls brought up by troops round about the temples, whose calling is to dance, and wear jewels, and look beautiful . . . in Pagoda-land. They perform before the priests in the pagodas; and the Brahmins and the Indian princes marry them" (14:787). The feature that sets Ethel apart from other "dancing girls" in the London marriage market is her ability to recognize what she has been programmed to do, along with her ultimate refusal to play her part. What makes her one of the most fascinating characters in Thackeray's fiction is her ability to change. Not only does she reject the worldliness in which she has been bred and break her engagement with Farintosh. She also resolves to become a mother to Clara's abandoned children and remedy the deficiencies in her own background in order to educate them. Her letters to Laura reveal the dedication with which she fulfills this resolution: "She educated herself in order to teach them. . . . She set herself to work like a schoolgirl" (14:812). The idea of Ethel's faulty education—perhaps suggested to Thackeray by the Stafford

House Address—ultimately becomes a vehicle for showing Ethel's eventual growth, as well as her personal determination to grow.

V

INDEED, ACCORDING TO Pendennis's friend George Warrington, the merchandizing of women in the London marriage market may be more brutal than any slave market in the American South. Warrington declares in chapter 43 in a cynical outburst about English women of fashion, "Rather than have such a creature I would take a savage woman, who should nurse my dusky brood; and rather than have a daughter brought up to the trade I would bring her down from the woods and sell her in Virginia" (14:573).[61] Thackeray's reason for singling out Virginia as a location for selling slaves may stem from the ill-fated excursion to a slave market in Richmond by his secretary, Eyre Crowe, during Thackeray's 1853 visit to that city. Crowe had gone to a slave auction and started to sketch but was forced to leave by angry whites.[62] As indicated by the account and sketch subsequently published by Crowe, one of the sights that he observed on this occasion was a group of young black women waiting to be sold (fig. 16).[63] While Thackeray disapproved of his secretary's trip to the slave auction because Thackeray feared that the incident might evoke Southern hostility toward himself and mar the success of the lecture tour, the evidence of *The*

Fig. 16. Eyre Crowe, "In the Richmond Slave Market," from With Thackeray in America.

Newcomes suggests his awareness and remembrance of what Crowe had seen. Warrington's remarks in chapter 43 of the novel are exaggerated, but Thackeray's analogy between the British marriage market and the American slave market is clear.

Thackeray's point in this comparison is that wrongdoing transcends national borders. As Pendennis observes about his own wife, whose opinions he generally admires, "Against all marriages of interest this sentimental Laura never failed to utter indignant protests" (14:882). Against marriages of interest *The Newcomes* as a whole protests as well. Wherever such marriages occur and people marry for reasons other than love—so the novel suggests—the partners involved are likely to feel unhappy and eventually enslaved. After marrying Rosey, who is pretty but completely unlike Ethel, to fulfill the dream of his father, Colonel Newcome, Clive thinks miserably, "With the best intentions in the world, what a slave's life it is that he has made for me!" (14:853). Fortunately for readers yearning for a romantic ending, Rosey dies in childbirth, leaving Thackeray's persona, in a postscript, to speculate that Ethel and Clive will eventually marry "in fable-land" where "Anything you like happens" and "the poet . . . [may make] the hero and heroine happy at last, and happy ever after" (14:1009). In the real world, however, about which this evocation of "fable-land" implicitly reminds us, unhappiness remains, and marital distress cannot be escaped with a wave of a poet's hand. "Brother, Brother we are kin," Thackeray wrote from the United States concerning the analogy between American slavery and British inhumanity. The example of *The Newcomes* extends this remark not just to brothers but to sisters.

CHAPTER SEVEN

Slavery as Touchstone in
The Virginians

If you put a chain around the neck of a slave, the other end fastens
itself around your own.
—PROVERB QUOTED BY EMERSON IN "COMPENSATION"

I

THACKERAY'S MOST EXPLICIT fictional description of American slavery
occurs in *The Virginians*. This book, which followed *The Newcomes*
as well as Thackeray's second visit to the United States, was conceived
as a sequel to *Henry Esmond* (1852) and set partly in colonial America.
Serialized from November 1857 to October 1859, *The Virginians* contains
numerous scenes involving black slaves and their white owners. However, virtually all modern critics have avoided detailed discussion of
this element of the book, perhaps because the black characters are
generally minor ones and perhaps also because the often stereotypical
traits of these characters can seem embarrassing to modern sensibilities.
Another possible reason for the paucity of critical comment on the
slavery scenes of *The Virginians* may be a feeling that there are enough
things wrong with this loosely constructed, awkwardly plotted, and
inconsistently narrated novel without adding the charge of racial in-
sensitivity to Thackeray's sins.[1] Yet Thackeray actually appears to
have given a significant amount of thought to the topic of slavery in
this work. In fact, the motif of slavery provides at least a small element
of order in an otherwise disorderly book.

In *The Virginians,* Thackeray's view of slavery is both more complex
and more negative than appears on the surface. Thackeray formed a

number of warm friendships with people in the American South; in addition, both in *The Virginians* and in his previous American letters, he did not vehemently denounce slavery or dwell on its horrors as an abolitionist writer would have, instead pointing out that the slaves whom he saw generally seemed happy. Thus he is sometimes mistakenly assumed to have supported the idea of slavery itself.[2] Thackeray was not an egalitarian, and regrettably—like many nineteenth-century British and American writers on both sides of the slavery issue—he made the racist assumption that blacks were inferior to whites. Nonetheless (see chapter 6 of this study), while he disliked the rhetoric, the one-sidedness, and the holier-than-thou tone of propaganda regarding American slavery and while he also felt that instant emancipation in the United States would have disastrous effects, he believed that slavery was inherently immoral.

In light of his complex opinion on the subject, Thackeray's refusal to sermonize about the pros or cons of slavery in *The Virginians* is not surprising. Part of this refusal is due to his habit of trying to see both sides of any issue. In addition, two controversial books that appeared prior to Thackeray's American tours undoubtedly contributed to his determination to avoid anything resembling a polemical approach. The first of these books was Charles Dickens's *American Notes* (1842), a book that, like the American scenes in *Martin Chuzzlewit,* reflected Dickens's disillusionment with the United States after his own initial tour in 1842. *American Notes* is filled with uncomplimentary pictures of American life. From Thackeray's point of view, it offered an example of what a well-bred English visitor—and thoughtful writer—ought not to write. Although Thackeray had originally toyed with the idea of publishing a travel book containing his impressions of the United States, as other English visitors besides Dickens had done, he soon dismissed the notion. He declared to his friend Albany Fonblanque in 1853 from Richmond, Virginia, "What could Dickens mean by writing that book of *American Notes*? No man should write about the country under 5 years of experience, and as many of previous reading. A visit to the Tombs, to Laura Bridgman and the Blind Asylum, a description of Broadway— O Lord is that describing America?"[3] In particular, Dickens's chapter concerning slavery, which emphasized the atrocities of the institution and contained material we now recognize was taken from an American abolitionist pamphlet, must have struck Thackeray as hasty and one-sided.[4] When the elderly Washington Irving heard that Thackeray had begun serializing a novel about the United States, Irving is reported to have contrasted Thackeray's general approach to a subject with that of Dickens. As one of Thackeray's American correspondents explained, " 'Oh!' said Irving to me the other day . . . 'What a fine book he will make of that!' 'Have you read it Mr. Irving?' I asked. 'No, I have so much to do, but I know Thackeray. I know what he is capable of doing, a man of great mind, far superior to Dickens. Dickens's prejudices are too limited to make such a book as Thackeray is capable of making of the 'Virginians.' "5 In his handling of slavery in *The Virginians,* Thackeray seems to have characteristically resolved to be as fair to all sides of the issue as possible.

The second book that undoubtedly affected Thackeray's treatment of this topic in *The Virginians* was Harriet Beecher Stowe's *Uncle Tom's Cabin* (serialized in 1851–52 and published as a book in 1852). From Thackeray's perspective, as discussed in chapter 6 of this study, Stowe's fervently antislavery novel offered another one-sided example of what not to write; a major reason for his objection to the book was his belief that fiction should not be a vehicle for propaganda. However, as Charles Mauskopf has noted, Thackeray also believed that a novel should have a moral purpose, a conviction that Mauskopf sees as ultimately irreconcilable with what he describes as Thackeray's goal of "historical objectivity."6 Some of the seeming inconsistencies in Thackeray's treatment of slavery in *The Virginians* may stem from his effort to satisfy these conflicting claims of "realism and morality."7 At any rate, in this novel Thackeray seems to be attempting to present what he considered an accurate picture of slavery as he envisioned it in eighteenth-century Virginia, along with his own ethical reaction to the institution of slavery, without falling into the pitfall of Stowe's kind of polemic.

II

As *THE VIRGINIANS* unfolds, the concept of slavery functions as a touchstone for judging the values of many of the individuals in the book. All three of the major white characters, Madam Esmond and her sons Harry and George Warrington, as well as a number of the minor ones can be evaluated in terms of their attitudes toward slavery. For example, after opening the action of the book in 1756, the omniscient narrator who presides over the first seventy-one chapters of this novel explains in chapter 3:

> The question of Slavery was not born at the time of which we write. To be the proprietor of black servants shocked the feelings of no Virginian gentleman; nor, in truth, was the despotism exercised over the negro race generally a savage one. The food was plenty; the poor black people lazy, and not unhappy. You might have preached negro emancipation to Madam Esmond of Castle-

wood as you might have told her to let the horses run loose out of her stables; she had no doubt but that the whip and the corn-bag were good for both.

Her father may have thought otherwise, being of a sceptical turn on very many points, but his doubts did not break forth in active denial, and he was rather disaffected than rebellious. (15:27–28)

Ostensibly, the narrator seems to suggest in this passage that "The question of Slavery" is not relevant to this novel. Implicitly, however, the passage indicates that the topic of slavery actually plays an important role in helping the reader evaluate the novel's characters. While Madam Esmond considers emancipation unthinkable, her father seems— in this novel at least—privately to hold a different view. When the reader considers that Madam Esmond gradually emerges in *The Virginians* as a major but far from admirable character and that her father is Henry Esmond, reappearing briefly from the earlier novel that bears his name, the significance of this implied difference of opinion becomes apparent.

In old age, as he appears in *The Virginians,* Henry Esmond is content to keep his opinions to himself and yield all matters of daily life to his daughter, who was introduced tangentially in the earlier book as the author of its preface. The result of this evasion of day-to-day responsibility is a diminished, virtually emasculated, ex-protagonist. Esmond of *Henry Esmond* was a complex individual who painfully experienced figurative slavery in his own life yet at the end of his career purchased actual slaves for his American plantation. In contrast, Esmond of *The Virginians* is a far more simple, less interesting person. This shadowy, latter-day Henry Esmond has doubts about the institution of slavery but lets his daughter overrule him. When one of his youthful grandsons remarks that Madam Esmond runs her father's life, saying "Why don't you stand up like a man?," the old man replies, "Because I like sitting down best, my dear. . . . I am an old gentleman, and standing fatigues me" (15:31). Nevertheless, the suggestion remains in *The Virginians* that, even though he is too feeble to oppose his daughter overtly, Esmond's covert questioning of slavery in this novel is morally correct.

The third chapter of *The Virginians,* "The Esmonds in Virginia," also shows a difference of opinion on the subject of slavery in the younger generation, paralleling the implicit difference of opinion between Madam Esmond and her father. As briefly explained in the similarly titled preface to *Henry Esmond,* "The Esmonds of Virginia," the result of Colonel Henry Esmond's marriage to Rachel Castlewood was a daughter, also named Rachel, who in turn married a Mr. Warrington. The latter died shortly after his marriage, and his widow, Rachel Esmond Warrington, then gave birth to twin sons who eventually fought on opposite sides in the American Revolution. Chapter 3 of *The Virginians* gives an inverted extension of this earlier preface by briefly summarizing some of the main events of *Henry Esmond* and then elaborating on the subsequent lives of the Esmond family in the New World—especially the lives of the Colonel's grandsons and their relationship with their mother, who is so obsessed with genealogical pride that, after her father's death, she commonly allows herself to be termed Madam Esmond. As the chapter also makes clear, the two sons of this prideful and imperious woman are temperamentally distinct.

One striking manifestation of the difference between these twin boys lies in their attitude toward the black slaves on the Esmond estate, "of whom," according to the narrator, "there was a large and happy family" (15:30). As the narrator explains in chapter 3, Harry, the younger twin, "was of a strong military turn, drilled the little negroes on the estate and caned them like a corporal, having many good boxing-matches with them, and never bearing malice if he was worsted" (15:30). In contrast, George "was sparing of blows and gentle with all about him," a frame of mind that the narrator demonstrates: "As the custom in all families was, each of the boys had a special little servant assigned him; and it was a known fact that George, finding his little wretch of a blackamoor asleep on his master's bed, sat down beside it and brushed the flies off the child with a feather fan, to the horror of old Gumbo, the child's father, who found his young master so engaged, and to the indignation of Madam Esmond, who ordered the young negro off to the proper officer for a whipping" (15:30–31). This early episode provokes a "fierce quarrel" between young George Warrington and his mother. While little Harry is content to adopt a youthful version of the standard Virginian opinion about the role of slaves as inferiors to be "drilled" and potentially "caned," little George challenges the status quo, here represented by his mother's decision to punish the young slave whom George has treated as an equal: "Trembling with passionate rebellion against what he conceived the injustice of procedure, he vowed—actually shrieking out an oath, which shocked his fond mother and governor, who never before heard such language from the usually gentle child—that on the day he came of age he would set young Gumbo free—went to visit the child in the slave's quarters, and gave him one of his own toys" (15:31). The significance of this episode is underscored in the chapter's illustrated capital, which shows the black child asleep and solicitously tended by George, to the consternation of the young slave's father (fig. 17). In the novel as a whole, this early quarrel between George and his mother foreshadows

Fig. 17. Capital for chapter 3 of The Virginians, *showing young Gumbo asleep on young George's bed.*

his later acts of rebellion. It also makes clear that, though the attitude toward slaves on the Esmond estate is generally one of benevolent paternalism, the possibility of unfair treatment exists and that George Warrington's personal view of slavery differs significantly from the opinion that prevails around him.

As the novel progresses, the institution of slavery even more clearly becomes a criterion by which certain of the characters can be evaluated. For example, their differing treatment of their black servants by the end of the novel again underscores the difference between Harry and George. As a child, George is his elderly "grandfather's favourite and companion" (15:32). Thus it does not seem surprising that, in the course of the novel, as Gerald C. Sorensen has pointed out, "In both appearance and temperament . . . [George] is the incarnation of Henry Esmond."[8] On the contrary, Harry seems reminiscent of Francis, Lord Castlewood, in the earlier novel—whom Madam Esmond describes as "a fine tall stout animal" (15:9) and whom Sorensen terms "brave and noble, but hagridden and vaguely stupid."[9] This distinction between George's intelligent thoughtfulness, a quality reminiscent of his grandfather, and Harry's good-natured stupidity is evident at the conclusion of *The Virginians* when George, who has inherited an English title and estate after a period of great poverty, explains that he has emancipated his black valet, Gumbo, "as a reward for his admirable love and fidelity to me when times were hard" (15:934). Much earlier in the novel, however, in chapter 46—entitled "Chains and Slavery"— Harry experienced even more difficult times when he was imprisoned for debt in England and was comforted for a while solely by the same Gumbo. Yet, after his release, Harry seems not to have thought of the reward of emancipation for this faithful servant, whom he commends in a letter written to George on the occasion of Harry's volunteering for military service with the British army: "If any accident should happen, I know you will take care of poor Gumbo as belonging to my dearest best George's most affectionate brother" (15:672). As will be explained later, the text of the novel is actually a bit confusing concerning Gumbo's status in chapter 46. However, the fact that Harry refers to Gumbo as a possession in this letter in chapter 63—combined with George's subsequent explanation of why he ultimately gave the loyal black servant his freedom—indicates that, in Harry's service, Gumbo remains a slave.

Near the end of the book, George returns to visit his mother and brother in America on the brink of the American Revolution. Although war has not yet been declared, Harry has become a proponent of the American cause, while Madam Esmond remains fiercely loyal to England. In contrast to Harry, George finds himself on the British side of the quarrel, although his loyalty is less fanatical than that of his mother. As George explains, having become the novel's first-person narrator by this point:

> Theoretically my opinions were very much more liberal than those of my brother, who, especially after his marriage, became what our Indian nabobs call a Bahadoor—a person ceremonious, stately, and exacting respect. When my Lord Dunmore, for instance, talked about liberating the negroes, so as to induce them to join the king's standard, Hal was for hanging the governor and the Black Guards (as he called them) whom his excellency had crimped. 'If you gentlemen are fighting for freedom,' says I, 'sure the negroes may fight, too.' On which Harry roars out, shaking his fist, 'Infernal villains, if I meet any of 'em, they shall die by this hand!' (15:934)

The political ironies here are striking. In George's words, "Harry should have been the Tory, and I the Whig" (15:934). Equally striking, however, is the fact that Thackeray is once again using the idea of slave emancipation to suggest George's mental and moral superiority to his brother.

In addition, Madam Esmond's reaction to the concept of emancipation underscores the leading feature of her personality in the novel as a whole—her tendency to domineer. As George further explains in the passage just quoted: "And my mother agreed that this idea of a negro insurrection was the most abominable and parricidal notion which had ever sprung up in her unhappy country. She at least was more consistent than brother Hal. She would have black and white obedient to the powers that be: whereas Hal only could admit that freedom was the right of the latter colour" (15:934). On the Esmond estate, Madam Esmond herself embodies "the powers that be." The narrator observes early in the book: "The truth is, little Madam Esmond never came near man or woman but she tried to domineer over them. If people obeyed, she was their very good friend; if they resisted, she fought and fought until she or they gave in" (15:35). As the adult George remarks to his brother about their childhood in Virginia, "We were made little slaves" (15:719). Even Harry, as an adult in England, is able to perceive his degree of bondage to his mother. He explains to Hetty Lambert, when she scolds him for citing his submission to Madam Esmond as a reason for not volunteering for military service, "No negro on our estate is more a slave than I am" (15:648).

Ultimately, both George and Harry rebel against their mother. Goaded by Hetty, Harry enters the army without his mother's permission. Although Madam Esmond subsequently approves of his action and takes pride in his military achievements, she quarrels with him bitterly after his eventual return to America when he decides to marry a woman—raised as a dependent in the Esmond household—whom his mother deems inappropriate as a partner for her son. George's rebellion begins even earlier, starting with his youthful dispute with his mother over the punishment of little Gumbo. Moreover, George's adolescence and young manhood are likewise punctuated by similar disputes between mother and son. The culmination of this fight for independence is George's decision—even before that of his brother Harry—to marry against his mother's wishes. As Juliet McMaster has accurately pointed out, Madam Esmond's intense hostility to the marriages of her sons reflects Thackeray's "continuing concern with the sexual element in the parent-child relationship."[10] In addition, the battles between Madam Esmond and her children show Thackeray's continuing concern with the idea of slavery versus freedom as an informing metaphor of this book.

Ignored by his mother, who refuses to send money that is due him (in George's words, apparently "in order to starve me into a surrender" [15:900]), George manages to eke out a precarious existence by writing and tutoring in London. At this point, he has exchanged slavery to his mother for slavery to literary hackwork. As a footnote by Thackeray, in the role of editor, observes, one of George's descendants "says he remembers a book, containing his grandfather's book-plate, in which were pasted various extracts from reviews and newspapers in an old type, and lettered outside *Les Chaînes de l'Esclavage*" (15:864n). However, the successive deaths of his cousin and paternal uncle in England unexpectedly free George of his financial troubles, as well as any need to depend on his mother, by causing him to inherit the Warrington estate. In the context of the novel, the domestic wars between Madam Esmond and her children, exemplified by this protracted battle with George, serve as analogues of the eventual war of independence between America and its mother country.[11] In political as in personal affairs, the novel suggests, the rebellion was partly provoked by a maternal figure's "imperious domineering spirit" (15:890).

When the events of war temporarily threaten to make the abolition of slavery a reality, Madam Esmond characteristically refuses to accept the possibility. The occasion to which George alludes in his reference to "When my Lord Dunmore . . . talked about liberating the negroes, so as to induce them to join the king's standard" is part of history. At the outset of the revolution, Dunmore, the British governor of Virginia, issued a proclamation offering freedom to fugitive slaves who rallied to the British cause.[12] The proclamation was intended to apply only to slaves who deserted from masters fighting on the side of the rebels, although it undoubtedly also attracted some slaves who fled from loyalist owners, as Madam Esmond perceives the case to be: "The arming of the negroes was, in her opinion, the most cowardly blow of all. The loyal gentry were ruined, and robbed, many of them, of their only property" (15:952). In the context of this situation in the novel, even the liberal George considers Dunmore's policy ill-advised, just as George disapproves of Dunmore's flight from Williamsburg to the safety of the British fleet offshore. As George observes, in the example of Madam Esmond's estate, as well as her house in Richmond, the proclamation has attracted "A score of our worst hands [who] . . . fled to our courageous governor's fleet; not all of them, though some of them, were slain, and a couple hung by the enemy for plunder and robbery perpetrated whilst with his lordship's precious army" (15:952). George remonstrates with Dunmore in person, although George's objection to the proclamation seems to be simply that it is damaging the loyalist cause and contributing to a dangerous atmosphere of lawlessness. His mother's objection reflects the same attitude that she held in chapter 3, where she equated blacks with horses. Her domestic clergyman subsequently suggests, as the hostilities escalate, that one implication of the announcement that we now know as the American Declaration of Independence is "that all men being free, therefore Gumbo and Sady, and Nathan [black servants of the Esmond family], had assuredly a right to go to Congress." In response, Madam Esmond dismisses the idea: "Tut, tut! my good Mr. Hagan . . . let us hear no more of this nonsense" (15:963–64). Here, in chapter 90 near the end of the book, as in chapter 3 near the beginning, Thackeray is subtly using the question of slavery to emphasize Madam Esmond's chronic compulsion to domineer.

Additional, less important figures in the novel are also characterized in terms of their opinions on the subject of slavery. For example, in the episode that opens the novel, the person who first meets Harry Warrington on his arrival in England is Mr. Trail, partial owner of the ship that has brought the young man from Virginia. Upon hearing that, because of a shortage of labor, Madam Esmond raises and exports to him far less tobacco than she might otherwise produce, Mr. Trail promptly suggests, "I have lately engaged in the Guinea trade, and could supply her ladyship with any number of healthy young negroes before next fall" (15:4). However, Harry receives this suggestion "coldly," with the explanation that "We are averse to the purchase of negroes from Africa. . . . My grandfather and my mother have always objected to it, and I do not like to think of selling or buying the poor wretches" (15:4–5). In the minds of many eighteenth- and nineteenth-century humanitarians, the "Guinea trade" (i.e., the African slave trade) was one of the worst aspects of the institution of slavery. Great Britain abolished its lucrative slave trade from Africa in 1807 (twenty-six years before the 1833 act to abolish slavery itself in the British West Indies). Thus Mr. Trail's involvement in "the Guinea trade," though legal in 1756, clearly establishes him as a merchant in whom the profit motive is uppermost. Trail's rationalization that "It is for their [the slaves'] good, . . . for their temporal and their spiritual good! . . . And we purchase the poor creatures only for their benefit" (15:5) simply shows the hypocrisy of this self-announced Christian.

As first Harry and then George grow acquainted with England, other characters reveal themselves negatively in terms of their attitudes toward slavery. When Harry first arrives in England, George is believed to have been killed by American Indians. Hence, Harry is assumed to be the heir to Madam Esmond's wealth in Virginia, and some of the most disreputable members of aristocratic British society, including his own British relatives, go to work to fleece the young American of his money. When Harry is eventually rescued from confinement for debt by the unexpected appearance of George (the elder twin and true heir), Harry resolves to gamble no more. In response, two of his former gaming associates greet Harry's new abstention with derision:

> 'How do you mean, Mr. Warrington?' cries my Lord March.
> 'Have you lost Virginia, too? Who has won it? I always had a fancy to play you myself for that stake.'
> 'And grow an improved breed of slaves in the colony,' says another. (15:551)

This passing remark about growing "an improved breed of slaves" is presumably an oblique reference to the possibility of cohabitation between slave women and their male owners. Thus the remark indirectly suggests Lord March's licentiousness. However, British aristocrats have no premium on lack of ethics in this novel. The wily old American merchant, Mr. Van den Bosch, who arrives in England with his granddaughter near the end of the book, has made his fortune by the least humanitarian means: "Mr. Van d. B., for all he bragged so of his Dutch parentage, came from Albany, and was nobody's son at all. He had made his money by land speculation, or by privateering (which was uncommonly like piracy), and by the Guinea trade" (15:728). Again, "the Guinea trade" is mentioned as an important component of Mr. Van den Bosch's wealth. The fact that numerous Englishmen of different social stations are so willing to tolerate this man and woo his granddaughter, Lydia, demonstrates that money often outweighs all other concerns on both sides of the Atlantic ocean.

Little Lydia Van den Bosch proves to be just as calculating as her grandfather, and her indifference to humanitarian concerns is again presented in terms of what Thackeray's contemporaries sometimes called "the Negro question." While her grandfather was characterized through his involvement in "the Guinea trade," Lydia's character becomes clear in her proposed treatment of old Lockwood (Henry Esmond's faithful retainer from the earlier book). As the heir to old Van den Bosch's wealth, Lydia successfully achieves a loveless marriage of convenience with the decadent British Lord Castlewood. Thus she becomes mistress of the Castlewood estate in England, where she quickly establishes her supremacy over her new British relatives-in-law, including the formidable Baroness Bernstein (Beatrix Esmond in old age). As part of her new regime at Castlewood, Lydia—supported by her grandfather—suggests the idea of sending the elderly Lockwood to the workhouse, a proposal that amazes even Lord Castlewood and that George Warrington explains is contrary to British custom. As George ironically observes, "It is very hard on us, Mr. Van den Bosch, that we are obliged to keep our old negroes when they are past work. I shall sell that rascal Gumbo in eight or ten years" (15:776). Knowing his master's kindness, Gumbo comments with a grin, "Don't tink you will, master!"—a remark that George dismisses with more irony (15:776). The term "us," in this context, seems to refer to Americans, who Mr. Van den Bosch has just complained are forced to keep their old servants (i.e., slaves): "I am sure I wish we had such an asylum [workhouse] for our folks at home, and that we were eased of the expense of keeping our old hands" (15:775). In other words, with tongue in cheek, George is pretending agreement with Van den Bosch regarding the desired mode of dealing with elderly servants as a way of making the point that Lydia cannot be allowed to treat old Lockwood more callously than an aged slave would be treated in America. George's argument about "What will the county say if you banish old Lockwood?" (15:775) has its effect, and the elderly porter is kept. Later, when George falls upon financial hard times, Lydia visits him and his wife and suggests that they economize by selling Gumbo—a suggestion that George ignores. In both episodes, Thackeray uses the topic of slavery to reveal Lydia's fundamental heartlessness.

III

THE MOST MEMORABLE black person in *The Virginians,* of course, is Gumbo, and the role of this individual is worth exploring at length. Initially, Gumbo appears to have been conceived simply as a minor character, so minor that Thackeray seems at first to have occasionally confused him with Sady, the other black valet assigned to the twins. Thus chapter 3 of *The Virginians* refers to George's young black servant as Gumbo, while chapter 7 specifically distinguishes between "Sady, George's servant" and "Gumbo, Harry's boy" (15:73). In addition, chapter 3 alludes to "old Gumbo, the child's father" (15:31)—depicted in the chapter's illustrated capital—and implies that George's black servant has been named after his parent. In contrast, chapter 9 of the novel offers the different explanation that little Gumbo was so called because of his fondness for the kind of soup known by that name. A possible reason for such inconsistencies is that Thackeray apparently wrote much of what we now have in chapter 3 about the Virginia Esmonds at a very early stage of his composition of the book. He then decided to open his action in England and present this background information about Virginia as a flashback.[13] Evidently, in the course of rearranging and expanding his material, Thackeray overlooked the fact that he had given conflicting explanations regarding Gumbo's name and the twin to whom he was assigned. However, as the novel develops, the significance of Gumbo grows. In the latter part of the book, Sady, who eventually comes to England with the resurrected George, has to be sent back to Virginia because of illness, leaving George with Gumbo, the servant who originally came to England with Harry, now absent on military service. This somewhat contrived sequence of events may reflect Thackeray's awareness by chapter 72 that Gumbo had become a major character and that Sady was largely irrelevant. The specific assignment of Gumbo to George at this point, when George assumes his position as first-person narrator, may also reflect Thackeray's sense that George and this black servant are creatively linked.

In the course of the novel, the character of Gumbo reveals many of Thackeray's assumptions about blacks. By modern standards, some of these assumptions would be considered racist. Gumbo lies (i.e., he freely exaggerates, on virtually any occasion). He howls (15:211). He blubbers (15:484, 485). He is both idle and greedy (15:673). He is also "trusty" (15:673), "faithful" (15:857), and attached with doglike devotion to his masters, both Harry and George. When Harry is confined for debt, Gumbo "flung himself, roaring with grief, at Harry's feet: and with a thousand vows of fidelity, expressed himself ready to die, to sell himself into slavery over again, to do anything to rescue his beloved Master Harry from this calamitous position" (15:474–75). Gumbo's proposal is slightly confusing, and perhaps means that Gumbo is offering to sell himself to someone else, since there is no previous mention of Gumbo's being freed, and in Harry's subsequent letter to George (15:672) Gumbo is evidently still a slave. (A landmark judicial decision in the case of James Somerset in 1772 established that any slave became free while in England and could not be compelled to leave England involuntarily.[14] However, the novel contains no specific reference to the Somerset case, and Harry's incarceration in 1757 predates this decision by fifteen years.) At any rate, in the context of the novel, Gumbo's shortcomings are outweighed by his fidelity.

In depicting such stereotypical details about Gumbo's behavior, Thackeray was undoubtedly influenced by what he had observed or been told by his Southern hosts about black people in America, as well as by his own notions of the ideal relationship between masters and servants. However, Gumbo is far from being a simple stereotype. Much of the amusement associated with this character in the novel lies in his off-stage amorous successes with white serving women in England, one of whom he eventually marries. As the omniscient narrator emphasizes: "Wherever that dusky youth was, he sought comfort in the society of females. Their fair and tender bosoms knew how to feel pity for the poor African, and the darkness of Gumbo's complexion was no more repulsive to them than Othello's to Desdemona. I believe Europe has never been so squeamish in regard to Africa, as a certain other respected Quarter" (15:673). That quarter is presumably the United States, embodied later by Lydia, who reacts to Gumbo's wooing of his female fellow-servant with disgust: "Fogh! guess they ain't particular, these English people!" (15:858). In reality, there were a number of black serving men in England in the eighteenth century, and many of these married white serving women.[15] What Thackeray seems to be trying to do here is to create a black servant who is as historically accurate as possible and also an individual in his own right. The fact that Gumbo eventually earns his freedom and remains in England on the Warrington estate reflects both Thackeray's personal conviction of the wrongness of slavery and his artistic sense of the underlying relationship that has evolved in the novel between Gumbo and George.

To a striking extent, by the end of the book, Gumbo serves as a foil to George, with whom Gumbo also has a kind of symbiotic relationship. The mutuality of these two individuals is suggested by three whipping episodes in the novel. While such episodes may reflect Thackeray's peculiar preoccupation with flagellation, they are primarily worth noting as indicative of the link between Gumbo and George.[16] In the first, as discussed earlier, young Gumbo is whipped in chapter 3 for falling asleep on George's bed, a punishment that results in George's first "passionate rebellion" in opposition to his mother's wishes. In chapter 5, George himself, who is described as a "little rebel" (15:50), almost receives a whipping when his mother, encouraged by their neighbor George Washington, directs the Warrington boys' tutor to chastise George for insubordination. George breaks his mother's power over him by breaking her favorite cup. He and Harry thus force their tutor to acknowledge his inability to discipline them. However, George Warrington continues to nourish a grudge toward George Washington for his part in this episode. As the former subsequently says to Washington when challenging him to a duel on the grounds of an insulting remark, "It is not the first time you have chosen to take me for a negro, and talked of the whip for me" (15:107). Finally, in chapter 87, entitled "The Last of 'God Save the King,' " the now emancipated Gumbo returns with George for a visit to Virginia, where Gumbo becomes "a centre of insurrection" among Madam Esmond's servants (15:934). Since he is free while the other blacks are not, jealousies arise.

His white wife, Molly, the servant of George's English wife, is not accepted by the black servants. In turn, Molly becomes jealous of one of these black servants who she fancies is having an affair with Gumbo. When this story reaches Madam Esmond and Gumbo denies it to her "with asperity" (15:935), Madam Esmond forgets that he is now "a free gentleman" and orders that he be whipped. Again, George defends Gumbo, and "there was a rebellion in our house at Castlewood" (15:935). In this case, the disagreement is settled by resolving to send "the Standard of Insurrection" (15:935) back to England, along with his wife, whose wrath at her husband's supposed behavior has been swiftly replaced by wrath at Madam Esmond's proposed punishment. Each of these three episodes suggests the motif of rebellion that runs throughout the novel. They also show the analogy between Gumbo and George as insurrectionists, despite the obvious black and white differences between the two men.

The conclusion of *The Virginians* underscores both the contrast and the inseparable connection between Gumbo and George. At the end of one of the last paragraphs of the book, George jokingly refers to "a family sketch by my ingenious neighbour, Mr. Bunbury, who has drawn me and my lady with Monsieur Gumbo following us, and written under the piece, 'SIR GEORGE, MY LADY, AND THEIR MASTER' " (15:1001). As the next paragraph makes clear, the "master" is Gumbo. In George's words, "Here my master comes; he has poked out all the house-fires, has looked to all the bolts, has ordered the whole male and female crew to their chambers; and begins to blow my candles out, and says, 'Time, Sir George, to go to bed! Twelve o'clock!' " (15:1001). The significance of what might seem simply incidental humor here is indicated by the fact that the illustration to which George alludes (reprinted in *Works* 15:1000) appeared as the frontispiece of volume two of the first edition, in book form, of *The Virginians*.[17] What Thackeray is suggesting is that George is dependent on his servant, who manages the practical details of George's life. Where George is a bookish idealist, Gumbo is a practical man of affairs. In the illustration (fig. 18), Gumbo walks stiffly behind Sir George and Lady Warrington and appears proud of his position, whereas George has earlier described himself as subject to fits of "moodiness" (15:904) and discontent. In George's words, "There came a period of my life, when having reached the summit of felicity I was quite tired of the prospect I had there: I yawned in Eden, and said, 'Is this all? What, no lions to bite? no rain to fall? no thorns to prick you in the rose-bush when you sit down?—only Eve, for ever sweet and tender, and figs for breakfast, dinner, supper, from week's end to week's end!' " (15:905). As the illustration empha-

Fig. 18. "SIR GEORGE, MY LADY, AND THEIR MASTER" (The Virginians).

sizes, both the melancholy employer and the down-to-earth servant are inseparably linked. Indeed, although the relationship of the fraternal twins, George and Harry, grows artistically less significant as the book progresses, by the close of the novel their relationship is at least partly replaced by the psychological duality of George and Gumbo.

The fact that Gumbo appears more content than George with his ultimate lot is perhaps explainable in the sense that George, unlike his servant, suffers from a condition that Florence Nightingale described in *Cassandra* as "nothing to do."[18] George himself asks, "Does a man sleep the better who has four-and-twenty hours to doze in?" (15:907). His doctor observes to George's wife when asked about George's malaise, "My dear lady, his inheritance has been his ruin, and a little poverty and a great deal of occupation would do him all the good in life" (15:907). As Ina Ferris has argued, one of the most disturbing aspects of the world of *The Virginians* is that it ultimately seems nihilistic.[19] Comparing this sequel with the earlier *Henry Esmond*, Jack Rawlins writes that *The Virginians* "is meaningless *where once there was meaning.*"[20] In this late novel in which even the ideal of retirement at the end of *Esmond* is questioned, the only qualified contentment that exists seems to lie in domestic relations, including those between master and servant. As Ferris observes, "The general tone of George's narration reinforces the sense that despite his genuine and lasting love for his wife and family, he has spent a large part of his life in melancholy and boredom for which there is no relief. For self-conscious and skeptical spirits like George, the novel suggests, there is no answer, no possibility of profound fulfillment in life."[21] In his depiction of George and Gumbo at the end of the novel, Thackeray indicates that the relation between master and slave should be replaced by that between master and servant, and that compassion rather than compulsion will best secure whatever kind of permanency can be found in this meaningless world.

CHAPTER EIGHT

Seeming, Being, and Racism
in Philip

But Sarah saw the son of Hagar the Egyptian, whom she had
borne to Abraham, playing with her son Isaac. So she said to Abraham, "Cast out this slave woman with her son; for the son of this
slave woman shall not be heir with my son Isaac."

—GENESIS 21:9-10

Pilate said to him, "What is truth?"
—JOHN 18:38

I

*T*HE *ADVENTURES OF PHILIP* is Thackeray's last completed novel and
his most puzzling. Stylistically, it is peculiar. It features an unlike-
able hero who (contrary to Thackeray's usual treatment of heroes in
his fiction) is conspicuous throughout the novel and an insecure narrator who has little confidence in his tale.[1] For modern readers, its content is even more disturbing. In contrast to Thackeray's earlier full-
length novels from *Barry Lyndon* to *The Virginians, Philip* for the most
part sidesteps the image of slavery and instead includes an important,
racially mixed character of West Indian origin and presumably slave
descent. However, this character—a wealthy mulatto called Mr. Woolcomb, who owns a vast estate in the West Indies as well as property in
England—is even less likeable than the protagonist Philip. Throughout
the book, Woolcomb is repeatedly described in racist terms.[2] Worse
yet, in an ethnocentric action as flagrant as Sarah's banishment of Ish-
mael and Hagar in the biblical tale from Genesis, the conclusion of
Thackeray's novel turns on an episode in which Philip publicly ridi-
cules Woolcomb's candidacy for a Parliament seat by unpleasantly

mocking his racial background and parodying an antislavery slogan. Serialized in the *Cornhill Magazine* from January 1861 to August 1862, *The Adventures of Philip* is not one of Thackeray's better books. While its structure is more tightly controlled than that of the poorly organized *Virginians,* evidence of Thackeray's weariness in *Philip* can be seen in the way in which the book reworks material (derived from its author's own early life) which had already been used more effectively in *Pendennis* and *The Newcomes.* Even the origin of *Philip* suggests some paucity of inspiration. Thackeray returned for the idea behind this novel to "A Shabby Genteel Story" published in *Fraser's Magazine* in 1840 and left in a form in which it might or might not be continued, although he was careful to compose *Philip* in such a way that it was independent of the early tale.[3] Nonetheless, despite the book's problematic material and signs of authorial fatigue, portions of *The Adventures of Philip* remain powerful. Although the novel as a whole artistically falls short, as the final finished work of a major author and a work with many dazzlingly well-written parts, it should not be lightly dismissed.

Unfortunately, most modern readers do dismiss this book, or just do not open it at all. What little modern scholarship there is of *Philip* has generally taken one of two approaches. By concentrating on the technique of this work and saying little about its racist dimensions, a few recent critics have offered highly perceptive comments about such stylistic features as *Philip's* distinctive narrative method or the book's recurrent imagery of death.[4] In contrast, two earlier critics, Gordon N. Ray and Joseph E. Baker, said little or nothing about Thackeray's stylistic virtuosity in *Philip* but called attention to what they felt were the historical or humanitarian implications of Thackeray's intolerant depiction of Woolcomb.[5] A complete discussion of the book must combine both of these scholarly approaches and take both elements of *Philip*—racist and stylistic—into account. The existence of Woolcomb in *Philip* is definitely relevant to Thackeray's fascination throughout his career with blacks and with slavery. In addition, as John Sutherland has accurately pointed out, the episode mocking Woolcomb at the end of *The Adventures of Philip* is clear evidence of Thackeray's Victorian racism, as well as the "hardening" of "his views on race . . . as he grew older."[6] Sutherland does not explore the reasons behind this heightened racism in *Philip,* and the reasons offered by Ray and Baker to explain it, along with the troubling ending, appear misguided. At the core of *The Adventures of Philip* lies the question of truth, a question probed so deeply in this novel that even the racism that mars the Woolcomb sections is undercut. However, before turning to an analysis of *Philip* and Woolcomb's role in it, a more detailed examination of the ideas proposed by Ray and Baker regarding Woolcomb is in order.

II

(a)

RAY'S CONJECTURE ABOUT Woolcomb links the unpleasant attributes of this character with the war that erupted in the United States a few months after Thackeray began publishing *Philip*. In a speculative foot-note in his otherwise admirable biography of Thackeray, Ray suggests that "the effrontery and generally objectionable behaviour" of Wool-comb—especially in the last chapter of the novel—show Thackeray's proslavery attitude at the time of the American Civil War and seem "almost to be implying that this is the sort of thing Americans must expect from Negroes who have been given their freedom."[7] The prob-lem with Ray's speculation is that it is not consistent with either the main current of contemporary British public opinion about freed blacks and the American Civil War or with Thackeray's thinking on the sub-ject of slavery at this time. Woolcomb's affluence, energy, and finan-cial acumen in no way correspond to reports that had begun appearing in the British press in the 1840s and 1850s about the laziness of the blacks who had been freed in the 1830s in the British West Indies.[8] Even more significant is the fact that at the time of *Philip*, abolition of slavery was not generally seen in England as one of the goals of the American war between northern and southern states. The date on which Thackeray finished his writing of *Philip* (3 July 1862) was well in advance of Lincoln's Emancipation Proclamation of 1 January 1863 and even the preliminary emancipation proclamation of 22 September 1862. In addition, strange as this circumstance now seems, especially to mod-ern Americans, most British men and women in the early 1860s did not perceive the conflict that began in America with the fall of Fort Sum-ter to the Confederates on 13 April 1861 as a war to liberate the slaves. As Douglas A. Lorimer points out in *Colour, Class and the Victorians:*

> From the disinterested distance of a century or more, the Ameri-can Civil War takes on the appearance of a great morality play. Lincoln, the knight in shining armour, and his Federal Forces of Good fight for abolition, while a Satanic South vainly struggles for slavery, and justly falls because of its hellish institution. As in-terested spectators in this great moral drama, many mid-Victorians became confused, and ended up cheering for the South in flagrant violation of England's honoured anti-slavery tradition.[9]

Part of the confusion in British thinking stemmed from Lincoln's cautious approach to emancipation. Since freedom for slaves was not announced as a goal of the war until September 1862, many British anti-slavery observers became disillusioned with the North at the outset of the struggle and concluded that the slaves would fare better in a victorious South where "inexorable laws of political economy and moral progress" would eventually lead to their freedom.[10] Distrust of the North for many reasons—including this failure to declare an immediate war of abolition—led to the widespread sympathy with the South that Henry Adams was shocked to encounter on his arrival in England in May of 1861.[11] According to the British point of view, Lorimer notes, "If the war was not fought to end slavery, the Confederacy had every right to self-determination."[12] As Davis observes, this sympathetic attitude toward the Confederacy, along with the belief that the issue of slavery was not a major factor in the conflict between North and South, dominated British public opinion in the first two years of the war: "By the second year of the war there could be no doubt that from the *Times* to the *Edinburgh Review,* the most respected British newspapers and journals vehemently opposed the Lincoln administration's attempt to conquer the South. This view was shared not only by the aristocracy but also by much of the middle class, Lancashire workers, and even abolitionists who were appalled by the carnage of a modern war that bore no apparent relation to slave emancipation or any idealistic cause."[13] Thackeray's decision in *Philip* to avoid as much as possible the motif of slavery that had surfaced in his six previous books and instead in this novel to substitute an important character of black descent may reflect a personal feeling, based on his visits to America, that the topic of slavery had become too hot to handle. However, in the context of the widespread perception among British readers in 1861 and much of 1862 that the question of slavery was not a significant element in the war, it seems doubtful that the unappealing qualities of Woolcomb represent Thackeray's attempt to make a statement about abolition in connection with the current American conflict.

To be sure, Thackeray had his own reasons for sympathizing with the South at the outset of the Civil War. He had particularly enjoyed his visits to the South on his American tours in the 1850s and had formed warm friendships with some of his Southern hosts, such as Andrew Low, in whose home he had stayed on both of his visits to Savannah. More important, Sally Baxter—the New York girl of whom he had become platonically enamoured on his first visit to the United States—had married a Southerner, Frank Hampton of South Carolina, in 1855. Sally died of consumption in South Carolina on 10 September

1862 without being able to see her father and sister, who had travelled to visit her but had not been permitted by Federal authorities to continue their journey.[14] When Thackeray learned of her death and its attendant circumstances, his reaction was one of rage at Abraham Lincoln, as Henry Adams records in his *Education:*

> The last time Henry Adams saw Thackeray, before his sudden death at Christmas in 1863, was in entering the house of Sir Henry Holland for an evening reception. Thackeray was pulling on his coat downstairs, laughing because, in his usual blind way, he had stumbled into the wrong house and not found it out till he shook hands with old Sir Henry, whom he knew very well, but who was not the host he expected. Then his tone changed as he spoke of his—and Adams's friend, Mrs. Frank Hampton, of South Carolina, whom he had loved as Sally Baxter and painted as Ethel Newcome. Though he had never quite forgiven her marriage, his warmth of feeling revived when he heard that she had died of consumption at Columbia while her parents and sister were refused permission to pass through the lines to see her. In speaking of it, Thackeray's voice trembled and his eyes filled with tears. The coarse cruelty of Lincoln and his hirelings was notorious. He never doubted that the Federals made a business of harrowing the tenderest feelings of women—particularly of women—in order to punish their opponents. On quite insufficient evidence he burst into violent reproach.[15]

Nevertheless, although Thackeray had private motives (or believed he did) for despising Lincoln in late 1862, his contemporaries in London commonly shared his negative opinion of the Lincoln administration. Indeed, Adams's reason for citing the encounter with Thackeray is to demonstrate the point that in 1862 in London "the belief in poor Mr. Lincoln's brutality and Seward's ferocity became a dogma of popular faith."[16] In other words, in the early years of the American Civil War, Thackeray's own positive feelings toward the South were only corroborated by British public opinion.

In any case, despite his sympathy with the South during as much as he lived to know of the American conflict, Thackeray did not abandon the conviction he expressed in 1853 that "Slavery is a wrong."[17] Although he continued to say little about slavery in public, one of his private letters as editor of the *Cornhill Magazine* shortly before the outbreak of the war makes clear that Thackeray was not at all the supporter of slavery that—in the subsequent upheaval in the United States—at least one of his American friends believed him to be.[18] In 1860, Thackeray wrote to the *Cornhill's* publisher, George Smith, explaining that a proposed contributor was unsuitable because, among other reasons, "he is committed to Slave-advocacy which is not our side at all."[19] As explained in chapter 6, Thackeray was certainly not an abolitionist; nonetheless, he was also certainly not a believer in the proslavery position.

After the outbreak of the war, one of Thackeray's own Roundabout papers for the *Cornhill* offers an illuminating glimpse at his thinking on the topic of slavery at this point. This piece, published in December 1861 and entitled "A Mississippi Bubble," suggests that the idea of slavery continued to fascinate him, that he felt he ought to pay tribute to his Southern friends without condoning what was sometimes called their "peculiar institution," and that he definitely did not wish to become embroiled in any debate on an issue that he saw as complex and potentially inflammatory. The essay begins with an illustrated capital (fig. 19) showing a black nursemaid with a white infant and several black children, a drawing, Thackeray explains, "made in a country where there was such hospitality, friendship, kindness shown to the humble designer, that his eyes do not care to look out for faults, or his pen to note them" (17:537). In the first paragraph of the essay, which contains a brief recollection of some of his experiences in the antebellum South, Thackeray stresses the hospitality of his hosts, the material

Fig. 19. Capital for "A Mississippi Bubble" (Roundabout Papers).

comfort of their slaves, and the fact that his observations were limited by his inability to see much of plantation life:

> How they sang; how they laughed and grinned; how they scraped, bowed, and complimented you and each other, those negroes of the cities of the southern parts of the then United States! My business kept me in the towns; I was but in one negro plantation-village, and there were only women and little children, the men being out afield. But there was plenty of cheerfulness in the huts, under the great trees—I speak of what I saw—and amidst the dusky bondsmen of the cities. I witnessed a curious gaiety; heard amongst the black folk endless singing, shouting, and laughter; and saw on holidays black gentlemen and ladies arrayed in such splendour and comfort as freeborn workmen in our towns seldom exhibit. (17:537)

In this fleeting reminiscence, Thackeray indicates that the slaves whom he saw during his prewar visits to the American South did not seem discontented with their lot.

Simultaneously, in this revealing paragraph at the outset of "A Mississippi Bubble," Thackeray also makes clear that—contrary to the erroneous assumption of a hypothetical, indignant reader—he is by no means a supporter of slavery: "I am not going into the slavery question, I am not an advocate for 'the institution', as I know, madam, by that angry toss of your head, you are about to declare me to be" (17:537). As in his earlier letters from America, Thackeray contends in this essay that a major argument against slave labor is its economic inefficiency—illustrated in these introductory remarks to "A Mississippi Bubble" by the contrast between the "immense crew" of slaves maintained by a Southern slaveholder in order to achieve the domestic work that can be accomplished in London by "half a dozen willing hands" (17:538). Finally, he calls attention to the paradox inherent in the recent defense of American slavery by the journalist John Mitchel, who had been transported from Ireland for his advocacy of violent resistance against England and who had subsequently fled from Van Diemen's Land to the United States: "Let Mitchel, the exile from poor dear enslaved Ireland, wish for a gang of 'fat niggers'; I would as soon you should make me a present of a score of Bengal elephants, when I need but a single stout horse to pull my brougham" (17:538). For Thackeray, at this point, the subject of slavery is quite clearly a ground which interests him but on which he does not wish to tread.[20] The remainder of the essay deals with his journey by Mississippi steamer in the company of "the Vermont Giant and the famous Bearded Lady of Kentucky and her son" (17:540). The topic of slavery has been broached only to be dropped. As in his letters from the United States in the 1850s, Thackeray demonstrably perceives slavery as both a complex subject about which his readers have strong opinions and a subject fraught with paradox.

Since Thackeray died in December 1863, almost a year and a half before the end of the Civil War, it is dangerous to guess whether his thoughts about events in America and American slavery would have changed as the war progressed. Certainly, in late 1862, at the time of Sally Baxter's death, he was irrationally hostile to the Lincoln administration, but his attitude was supported by the widespread opinion of his contemporaries in England. The Trent affair had occurred earlier in 1862; two diplomats representing the Confederacy were forcibly removed from a British ship in international waters by members of the Union navy, and Thackeray, like his British contemporaries, was particularly incensed with the United States. Feelings between the two countries ran high over this incident, although the diplomats were soon released. Some American journalists recommended that the United States government use the threat of confiscating property held in America by British citizens to keep Great Britain from declaring war on the United States. Thackeray's response to this threat was to instruct his bankers in New York to sell his investments in America and send the proceeds to him in London, as he explained in the intemperate Roundabout paper "On Half a Loaf" (February 1862). However, according to his American friend Bayard Taylor, a few months later Thackeray indicated that he regretted the article and attributed his splenetic behavior on this occasion to one of his periodic attacks of illness.[21] In a similar fashion, had he lived long enough, Thackeray's congenital tendency to try to see all sides of any issue might have led him to moderate the hostility he had expressed to Henry Adams, at the time of Sally's death, concerning the government in Washington. Gradually, a shift in opinion in favor of the Union side occurred among British intellectuals.[22] Had Thackeray lived to see the end of the war, it is possible that he might have modified his sympathy for the South, since his opinions on the war generally mirrored those of the majority of his intellectual peers in England. Alternatively, his loyalty to his Southern friends might have caused him to remain steadfast in his positive feelings toward the Confederacy. Ultimately, what Thackeray might have done cannot be known. What is known is that his sympathetic attitude toward the Southern side in the American Civil War at the time of writing *Philip* was in keeping with current public opinion in England, but that attitude did not alter his earlier belief that slavery was wrong.

(b)

WHAT DID ALTER IN Thackeray's thinking and that of most of his contemporaries was an attitude toward race. In a sweeping indictment not just of the depiction of Woolcomb in *Philip* but of Thackeray's entire outlook at the end of his career, Baker contends that *The Adventures of Philip* represents "Thackeray's Recantation" of his earlier humanitarian sensitivity.[23] The trouble with this indictment is that it is based on insufficient evidence regarding Victorian racial attitudes in 1861–62. In the 1840s (following the abolition of British West Indian slavery in the 1830s), black American travellers (such as Frederick Douglass) frequently commented on what seemed to them to be an astonishing lack of racial prejudice in England.[24] Despite the eloquent testimony of black visitors like Douglass, racial prejudice was certainly not unknown in England in the 1840s and earlier. Nevertheless, in the next two decades this kind of prejudice on the part of British men and women became far more widespread and pronounced. In Lorimer's words, "The 1850s and 1860s saw the birth of scientific racism and a change in English racial attitudes from the humanitarian response of the early nineteenth century to the racialism of the imperialist era at the close of the Victorian age."[25]

The reasons for the heightened racism in mid-nineteenth-century England remain unclear. Certainly, one factor that troubled observers in mid-century England (including many abolitionists) was the reluctance of the recently freed blacks to continue working on plantations in the British West Indies. The result of this reluctance was a sharp decline in exports, a decline that in turn led to a disastrous weakening of the sugar-based British West Indian economy.[26] It was in this context of growing British disillusionment over the effects of emancipation that Carlyle published his strident "Occasional Discourse on the Negro Question" (1849), reprinted in 1853 with the word "Negro" in the title changed to the more racist term "Nigger." Another factor contributing to British racism in the 1850s and 1860s may have been the fear of what Kipling later described as "lesser breeds without the Law," a fear that was heightened by the insurrections in India in 1857–58, especially the killing of a large number of British women as well as children in an uprising at Cawnpore in 1857.[27] Dickens's racist reaction to the Cawnpore massacre can be seen in his 1857 Christmas number, *The Perils of Certain English Prisoners,* set in the West Indies and featuring a treacherous "Sambo."[28] A third factor may have been the efforts in the 1850s and 1860s by men like the anatomist Robert Knox and the physician James Hunt to promote what they considered "scientific" theories of anthropology, stressing what they believed were the separate origins of the different races of man, in contrast to the biblical version of human genesis. Such anthropological speculations seemed to offer proof of the notion that blacks were intrinsically inferior to Europeans.[29] Nevertheless, the racism that became so pronounced in Victorian thinking in the middle of the nineteenth century cannot simply be explained as a response to the widely perceived failure of the West Indian experiment (when judged by the standards of the Victorian work ethic), as a reaction to mutiny in India, or as the result of anthropological theories. As Davis explains:

> There were no direct ties . . . between the politics of emancipation and the racial theories that began to preoccupy the international scientific community by the mid-nineteenth century. Britain, which could justly pride itself on an absence of discrimination against individual blacks, was swept with degrading stereotypes of colored peoples which ranged from the mania for comic blackfaced minstrelsy to sober scientific treatises. Disillusion over the consequences of West Indian emancipation mixed with a broader reaction against sentimental reformers and "Nigger Philanthropy." This heightened racial consciousness appealed to workingmen who felt they suffered far worse hardships than the supposedly coddled blacks of the New World, and also to the upper classes who feared that sympathy for downtrodden slaves had already been extended dangerously close to their own proletariat. For reasons that have not yet been fully explained, most of the Western world began accepting racist theories that had earlier lacked the sanction of science and that had generally been limited to the United States.[30]

The blatant racism that seems so disturbing to modern readers of Thackeray's *Philip* must be viewed in the context of this widespread shift in contemporary British attitudes.

One aspect of this intensified racism in England was an increased concern with the questions of who was a gentleman and who was not. According to Lorimer, in the first half of the nineteenth century through the 1850s, "Englishmen responded to the social rather than to the physical attributes of black residents and visitors."[31] Thus, if an educated black visitor like Frederick Douglass behaved like a gentleman, he was generally perceived as one. However, by the 1860s,

> the quest for gentle status within English society intensified, and the aspirants for gentility became more concerned about excluding those of questionable status. Blacks were identified by their race and history with servitude and savagery. For those mid-

Victorians who placed increased emphasis upon the visible signs
of gentility, and who perceived race relations as a particular form
of class relationship, blacks could no longer qualify as gentlemen.
As a consequence all Negroes were classed in a common category
of the brutish and perpetually inferior lower orders. . . . gentlemen were now seen to share a common nobility of character
which was learned at the public schools, but which they liked to
think they inherited. Lacking the common inheritance of aristocratic birth, the seekers of gentility founded a new racial aristocracy. Henceforth, only Anglo-Saxons could be gentlemen.[32]

As Hannah Arendt has observed, "race-thinking" in Victorian England
was part of an effort by the middle class to give itself a common, national identity that encompassed colonists of English descent throughout the world.[33] Since mid-Victorians typically saw race relationships
in terms of the hierarchical class distinctions that they took for granted
in Victorian England, they readily viewed blacks as belonging to the
laboring rather than the "gentle" class.[34] By the time of *Philip's* publication in 1861–62, in Lorimer's words, "A white skin . . . [had be-
come] one essential quality of a gentleman."[35]

In the context of these pervasive racial assumptions in England in
the 1860s, some of Thackeray's remarks in *Philip* become more com-
prehensible. In particular, the emphasis throughout the novel on the
ungentlemanly nature of "the tawny Woolcomb" (16:173) can be seen
as a reflection not just of Thackeray's personal thinking but of the
widespread view among his contemporaries during this period that
blacks could not be gentlemen. Catherine Peters is certainly correct
when she says that "something seems to have gone badly wrong with
the ideal of the gentleman in *Philip*."[36] However, this wrongness was
not confined to Thackeray but was rather endemic in Victorian thinking in the 1860s. John Sutherland is also correct in calling attention to
the contrast between Thackeray's relatively congenial depiction of the
kindhearted Miss Swartz in *Vanity Fair* and his later, much more blatantly racist treatment of Woolcomb.[37] Nevertheless, this regrettable
calcification of Thackeray's racial attitudes should be seen primarily
not as his individual humanitarian failure but rather as a manifestation
of a general hardening of attitudes on the subject of race in British
thinking in the 1850s and 1860s.[38] An example of this trend is Thackeray's changing use of the abolitionist slogan "Am I Not a Man and a
Brother?"—employed good-humoredly by the narrator at the end of
Pendennis and parodied vindictively by Philip at the end of *The Adventures of Philip* in order to mock the pretensions of Woolcomb. As the
Morning Herald observed in 1865, illustrating what it saw as a significant

shift in British public opinion, "The world-renowned question, once thought so convincing, of 'Am I not a man and brother?' would nowadays be answered with some hesitation by many—with a flat negative to its latter half by those who regard the blacks as an inferior race."[39] A demonstration of this common 1860s British repudiation of the idea of interracial brotherhood occurs in *Philip* when the narrator remarks snidely that Woolcomb's hair is "so *very* black and curly, that I really almost think in some of the Southern States of America he would be likely to meet with rudeness in a railway car" and then observes ironically that "in England we know better. In England Grenville Woolcomb is a man and a brother. Half of Arrowroot Island . . . belongs to him; besides [other properties] . . . and that fine house in Berkeley Square" (16:105). The point of this transatlantic contrast is that in the narrator's eyes the American South is candid in denying a mulatto like Woolcomb status as a gentleman, whereas contemporary English society is hypocritical when it pretends to overlook Woolcomb's racial background for the sake of his wealth.

Undoubtedly, much of the reason for Woolcomb's prominence in this novel is Thackeray's well-known concern with the concept of the gentleman, a concern that seems to have become acute in his later years. What Ray describes as Thackeray's "intensified crusade for the gentlemanly standard" in his late writings can be seen at least in part as a reflection of the heightened "quest for gentle status" which Lorimer perceives as a general characteristic of British society in the 1860s.[40] As Ray points out, throughout his life, Thackeray's sense of class distinctions was strong. Even early in his career, "he makes sure in his fiction . . . that lower-middle-class men who assume gentlemanly airs get an emphatic come-uppance."[41] The conspicuousness of Woolcomb's "come-uppance" at the end of *The Adventures of Philip* can be seen as a reflection of the intensity with which Thackeray pursues the idea of the gentleman in this late book. For better or worse, the idea behind Thackeray's presentation of Woolcomb in this novel seems to be a conviction that blacks inherently cannot be gentlemen. In contrast, the relatively favorable picture of Gumbo in *The Virginians* shows a black who is content with his role as servant and makes no effort to aspire to a higher class. In Thackeray's outlook, as in that of his contemporaries, racial differences in both of these books are perceived in terms of familiar class distinctions.

In light of the consistent similarity between Thackeray's views on race and class and the views of his contemporaries, it seems an error to see, as Baker does, the social attitudes expressed in *Philip* as a calculating betrayal of humanitarianism on Thackeray's part.[42] Despite the significance of Baker's essay as one of the few critical efforts prior to the 1970s to deal with this difficult novel, there are several flaws in his argument. Lionel Stevenson has called attention to the way in which Baker's article misreads *Philip* by ignoring its ironic dimensions, and Jack P. Rawlins has suggested that Thackeray's ultimate espousal of the principle of friendship in this book—rather than being a submission to "The Establishment" as Baker claims—is a reflection of Thackeray's skepticism concerning any other basis for certitude than friendship in an uncertain world.[43] Indeed, Baker's contention that *The Adventures of Philip* shows Thackeray's late-in-life contempt for those belonging to a lower social class is undercut by Thackeray's next novel, the uncompleted *Denis Duval*, which was apparently intended to show how the grandson of a French emigré barber and smuggler became a gentleman. However, the most serious weakness in Baker's argument concerning *Philip* is his failure to consider the cultural context of the book. Despite the incisiveness with which he anatomized snobbism from *The Book of Snobs* to *Philip* itself, Thackeray was never a democrat. He wrote in "Charity and Humour" (1853) that one mark of a gentleman is kindness to "those below us in degree; for people above us and below us we must find, in whatever hemisphere we dwell, whether kings or presidents govern us" (10:619). The opinions concerning the hierarchy of social classes expressed in *Philip* are opinions that Thackeray had held throughout his career and that he and most of his Victorian readers accepted as part of the inevitable order of life. The ideas of racial superiority in the book are ones that merged in the 1850s and 1860s with this underlying class consciousness and that also came to seem part of the natural order of things to the average Victorian. In expressing such attitudes, Thackeray is simply showing that he is a man of his own time, not of ours. The important issue with which we should be concerned as critics is how Thackeray deals with this material in expressing the fundamental theme of *Philip*—the question of what is truth.

III

LIONEL STEVENSON SUGGESTS that the idea of "the relativity of truth" is a pervasive characteristic of Victorian thought.[44] Thackeray is certainly concerned with the issue of truth in all his fiction and, as Stevenson points out, shows his sense of the subjectivity of individual points of view as early as the *Yellowplush Papers* and *Barry Lyndon*.[45] In *The Adventures of Philip*, however, Thackeray focuses directly and emphatically on what the narrator describes as "the question of seeming and being in the world" (16:30). Previous criticism has touched on the problematic nature of truth in this late novel but has not really examined the matter in detail.[46] Nonetheless, in this book the question of what constitutes truth is an overriding theme, linking its racial assumptions to its handling of setting, characterization, and narration. The connection between these three elements and that theme creates an artistic context within which Thackeray's depiction of Woolcomb can ultimately be understood.

(a)

THE SETTING OF *Philip* is that of a society where truth is elusive. The inquiry with which the book's narrator, Arthur Pendennis, begins chapter 4 concentrates explicitly on the difference between appearance and reality: "Have you made up your mind on the question of seeming and being in the world? I mean, suppose you *are* poor, is it right for you to *seem* to be well off? Have people an honest right to keep up appearances?" (16:30). While the question may seem simple (most readers would probably say, "Yes"), Pendennis's next queries complicate the issue: "Are you justified in starving your dinner-table in order to keep a carriage; to have such an expensive house that you can't by any possibility help a poor relation; to array your daughters in costly milliners' wares because they live with girls whose parents are twice as rich?" (16:33). Pendennis then generalizes regarding the confusion he has intentionally evoked:

> Sometimes it is hard to say where honest pride ends and hypocrisy begins. To obtrude your poverty is mean and slavish; as it is odious for a begger to ask compassion by showing his sores. But to simulate prosperity—to be wealthy and lavish thrice a year when you ask your friends, and for the rest of the time to munch a crust and sit by one candle—are the folks who practise this deceit worthy of applause or a whipping? Sometimes it is noble pride, sometimes shabby swindling. When I see Eugenia with her dear children exquisitely neat and cheerful; not showing the slightest semblance of poverty, or uttering the smallest complaint; persisting that Squanderfield, her husband, treats her well, and is good at heart; and denying that he leaves her and her young ones in want; I admire and reverence that noble falsehood—that beautiful constancy and endurance which disdains to ask compassion. When I sit at poor Jezebella's table, and am treated to her sham bounties and shabby splendour, I only feel anger for the hospitality, and that dinner, and guest, and host, are humbugs together. (16:33)

The answer to the narrator's questions seems to be that "honest pride" is justified while hypocrisy is not. However, the boundary between the two is difficult to discern.

Later, in chapter 21, Pendennis returns explicitly to the problem of seeming versus being with an ironic allusion to a recent play by Bulwer-Lytton: "A distinguished writer has composed, in not very late days, a comedy of which the cheerful moral is, that we are 'not so bad as we seem' " (16:307). In its context in the novel, this reference to Bulwer-Lytton's *Not So Bad as We Seem; or, Many Sides to a Character* (1851) corroborates a person's comment on Pendennis himself, whose "manner is cold, not to say 'aughty," and who "seems to be laughing at people sometimes," but "when you know him, his heart is good" (16:307). Nevertheless, the tone of Pendennis's remark after alluding to Bulwer-Lytton's play suggests that the cliché "not so bad as we seem" should not be taken as the entire truth: "Give us thy hearty hand, Iago! Tartuffe, how the world has been mistaken in you! Macbeth! put that little affair of the murder out of your mind. It was a momentary weakness; and who is not weak at times? Blifil, a more maligned man than you does not exist! O humanity! how we have been mistaken in you! Let us expunge the vulgar expression 'miserable sinners' out of all prayer-books; open the portholes of all hulks; break the chains of all convicts; and unlock the boxes of all spoons" (16:307).[47] In other words, "the question of seeming and being in the world" is deliberately raised here as at the beginning of chapter 4 only to suggest that the question has no clear-cut answer. Shakespeare's Iago and Macbeth, Molière's Tartuffe, and Fielding's Blifil initially give the impression of being upright yet are eventually found to be just the opposite. Pendennis's remarks suggest that some people, like these notorious wrongdoers, *are* as bad as we may ultimately discover them to be, while others, like Pendennis himself, may not be so bad as they first appear. This idea of the impossibility of finding some simple principle by which to distinguish between truth and falsehood pervades the milieu in which the action of *Philip* occurs.

The environment of *Philip* is one in which sham proliferates. The most visible examples are the dinner parties given by Philip's uncle (husband of his mother's sister), Talbot Twysden. After introducing the subject of "seeming and being" in chapter 4, Pendennis illustrates the topic by explaining that the Twysden dinners superficially appear splendid but are actually hollow feasts for both body and spirit:

> Talbot Twysden's dinner-table is large, and the guests most respectable. There is always a bigwig or two present, and a dining

dowager who fréquents the greatest houses. There is a butler who
offers you wine; there's a *menu du dîner* before Mrs. Twysden; and
to read it you would fancy you were at a good dinner. It tastes of
chopped straw. Oh, the dreary sparkle of that feeble champagne;
the audacity of that public-house sherry; the swindle of that acrid
claret; the fiery twang of that clammy port! I have tried them all,
I tell you! It is sham wine, a sham dinner, a sham welcome, a sham
cheerfulness, among the guests assembled. (16:33)[48]

Pendennis's voice predominates in *The Adventures of Philip*. Hence, the
Twysdens are presented as Pendennis perceives them—grasping, self-
advancing, stingy, and hypocritical—yet Pendennis is also aware of the
potential bias inherent in his words. He remarks after his exposé of the
Twysden dinners: "What is this? Am I angry because Twysden has left
off asking me to his vinegar and chopped hay? No. I think not. Am I
hurt because Mrs. Twysden sometimes patronizes my wife, and sometimes cuts her? Perhaps" (16:34). Moreover, Pendennis is acutely conscious that the Twysdens themselves could tell a different tale: "By the
way, whilst I am giving this candid opinion of the Twysdens, do I
sometimes pause to consider what they think of *me?*" (16:35). However, while Pendennis is by no means infallible, his assessments of the
other characters appear to be ones that Thackeray intends the reader
to accept. As Pendennis describes it in this book, the society in which
the Twysdens wriggle themselves forward and other individuals must
live as best they can is a world in which concealment and prevarication
are routine.

Further evidence of the chronic confusion in this book between
seeming and being lies in the unresolved question of legitimacy which
hangs over Philip, as well as in the discovery of the apparently destroyed
will—enriching Philip—around which the plot revolves. The shifting
names of some of the characters likewise contribute to this sense of
ambiguity. George Brand Firmin called himself George Brandon at the
time of his early deception (described in "A Shabby Genteel Story") of
Caroline Gann. Now, years later (in *Philip*), Caroline calls herself Mrs.
Brandon. Others frequently refer to her as "the Little Sister," and in
the penultimate paragraph of the novel, she wildly presents herself in
public as Mrs. Firmin. Even Philip's fiancée, Charlotte Baynes, for a
time is designated by the alias, "Miss Grigsby," as emphasized by the
title of chapter 31, which "Narrates That Famous Joke about Miss
Grigsby." However, while seeming and being are repeatedly confused
in *The Adventures of Philip,* the novel also repeatedly conveys the sense
that, if the truth could only be found, a great gulf would be obvious between what things are and what they often appear to be. Juliet

McMaster has perceptively called attention to the preoccupation with death in this book and its recurrent sense of contrast between "the tidy surface, the horror beneath."[49] In addition, a chronic disjunction between appearance and actuality exists in this novel even in contexts that do not explicitly remind us of the skull beneath the flesh. Pendennis observes about the youthful Philip's mistaking of appearance for reality at the ballet: "The simple young fellow . . . mistook carmine for blushes, pearl powder for native snows, and cotton-wool for natural symmetry; and I dare say when he went into the world, he was not more clear-sighted about its rouged innocence, its padded pretension, and its painted candour" (16:38–41). The events of *Philip* occur in a slippery milieu—an intensified version of the world of *Vanity Fair*—where even good-hearted characters resort to stratagems as a matter of course. When the kindly Madame de Smolensk dresses for dinner with the lodgers at her Paris boarding house, she takes a "smile out of some cunning box on her scanty toilet-table—that smile which she wore all the evening along with the rest of her toilette, and took out of her mouth when she went to bed" (16:277). Her removable smile is merely a symptom of a world where masks prevail.

(b)

LIKE THE SETTING, the other characters are part of the artistic context for Woolcomb, and four of the major characters in *Philip*—including the narrator—offer different approaches to this setting where pretense is so common. The first, Philip's father, Dr. Firmin, epitomizes the cleavage between seeming and being in this book. In the past, he has secretly seduced and abandoned a lower-class girl, marrying her in a false ceremony and under a false name. ("A Shabby Genteel Story" concludes shortly after the false marriage.) After her abandonment, this wronged woman appears in *Philip* as the nurse, Caroline Brandon. Once Firmin has jettisoned Caroline, he marries a niece of the Earl of Ringwood and, after her death, appropriates and speculates away the sizable inheritance that has been left in trust for his son, Philip. Fleeing from England as his financial affairs crumble around him, Firmin evades his creditors and then repeatedly drains more money from the impoverished Philip. Moreover, the hypocritical Dr. Firmin never fully pays the penalty for his misdeeds. In America, where he settles and eventually marries yet again, he is believed to have been ruined and forced to emigrate by the extravagance of his son. Just as Becky Sharp embodies the aggressive self-seeking at the core of *Vanity Fair*, so Dr. Firmin personifies the separation between seeming and being that lies at the heart of *Philip*.

Deceit is the essence of Dr. Firmin's approach to life. As the narrating Pendennis observes, Dr. Firmin "told lies, and told lies habitually and easily" (16:131). Even his profession, as Firmin practices it, involves deception. When his secret concerning Caroline threatens to surface and it appears that the false marriage may have been valid after all, Dr. Firmin conceals his private misery and continues to see his patients: "He has to wear the inspiriting smile, to breathe the gentle joke, to console, to whisper hope, to administer remedy; and all day, perhaps, he sees no one so utterly sick, so sad, so despairing, as himself" (16:152). Unlike Becky Sharp, who does not love her son, Dr. Firmin holds at least some degree of affection for Philip and, according to Pendennis, feels "real grief" (16:58) at Philip's estrangement from him early in the novel. However, Dr. Firmin has so confounded illusion and truth that he has come to believe his own pretenses. From America, as a preface to demanding more money from his son, he regularly writes to Philip concerning speculations and inventions with which the doctor "was always about to make his fortune" (16:547). Occasionally, he sends Philip samples and proposals concerning which "the sanguine doctor got to believe that he really was endowing his son with large sums of money" (16:548–49). Appropriately, the one useful discovery for which he (characteristically falsely) takes credit is chloroform, a drug that induces a false sleep, i.e., unconsciousness. As the novel progresses, Dr. Firmin emits an atmosphere that Robert A. Colby describes as "moral miasma."[50] Firmin's fundamental inability to separate truth and falsehood is especially evident late in the novel in some of his letters to Philip, such as the one in which the doctor claims that "I was the dupe of villains" (16:502). Dr. Firmin's social success first in England and then in the United States is a sign of the extent to which mendacity prevails in the world of Philip.

While Dr. Firmin's *modus operandi* is prevarication, Caroline Brandon's approach to life in *Philip* is a pragmatic awareness that the world is full of lies. Deceived in the trust that she placed at the age of sixteen in Firmin, impregnated by him, and cast off by both him and her family, Caroline survives with the help of a friend who discovers her in poverty in London and brings the benevolent Dr. Goodenough to tend her through illness, childbirth, and the death of her infant son. With Goodenough's help, Caroline eventually becomes a nurse—known affectionately as "the Little Sister"—who supplements her income by keeping a lodging-house. Mrs. Brandon, as she terms herself, is a clear-eyed realist. Forgiving her father for his earlier rejection of her, she shares her home with him in his old age, yet, unlike her former self, she no longer has any illusion that this elderly braggart and toper is "a man of remarkably good manners." As the narrator explains, "This illusion about pa, I suppose, had vanished along with some other fancies of her poor little maiden youth" (16:67). Caroline's wariness about illusions extends to her attitude toward fiction. Like Plato viewing poets as liars, she sees novelists as simply purveyors of make-believe: " 'When I was a girl I used to be always reading novels,' she said; 'but, la, they're mostly nonsense" (16:71). However, in the world of *Philip,* where deceptions are paramount, even the skeptical Little Sister cannot wholly escape unscathed, as is evidenced by the "strange delusion under which the little woman laboured, that . . . [Philip] was her dead child come back to her" (16:581) when she nurses Philip through a childhood illness. Because of this delusion and her resulting love for Philip, despite evidence that her marriage to his father may in fact have been valid, Caroline refuses to challenge the doctor's subsequent marriage to Philip's mother, since invalidation of the later marriage would result in the loss of Philip's inheritance. Quietly but steadfastly convinced that Philip is the reincarnation of her dead infant, she mothers Philip throughout the novel, using every opportunity to put her worldly wisdom to use on his behalf.

This combination of pragmatism and protectiveness toward Philip is the motivation behind the Little Sister's most important scene. In chapter 38 she chloroforms the disreputable Tufton Hunt, the clergyman who had performed the long-ago ceremony uniting her to Firmin, and robs Hunt of a bill to which Dr. Firmin has forged Philip's signature. When Philip learns of this bill, which commits him to pay its owner almost four hundred pounds, he decides that his only recourse is to honor it, although he cannot afford to do so and is aware that payment will only encourage his father to draw on him again. Philip remarks bitterly to Pendennis in an ironic allusion to Abraham's near sacrifice of Isaac, "My patriarch has tied me up, and had the knife in me repeatedly. He does not sacrifice me at one operation; but there will be a final one some day, and I shall bleed no more. It's gay and amusing, isn't it? Especially when one has a wife and children" (16:555).

However, while Philip is prepared to pay the bill, the Little Sister is prepared to fight. Her method of combatting Hunt and by extension Dr. Firmin is to use their own technique—deception. To win Hunt's confidence when he first visits her after returning to England with the bill, she feigns hostility toward Philip. She continues this pretense on Hunt's second visit, when she first tries to buy the bill at a discount. After he refuses to sell the bill and drunkenly makes advances toward her, she chloroforms him, robs him of the document in question, and burns it. Her conduct on both occasions is applauded by Dr. Goodenough, a minor character who functions as a foil to Dr. Firmin and an exemplar of generosity and decency. After Hunt's first visit, when lending Caroline money with which to attempt to buy the bill, Goodenough advises her to "tell him plenty of lies, my dear" (16:568). When he learns of her success over Hunt, Goodenough declares "that his little nurse Brandon was *splendide mendax,* and that her robbery was a sublime and courageous act of war" (16:586). He also terms her action a "glorious crime, and most righteous robbery" (16:580). At least one reader of this book finds the latter description puzzling and morally disturbing.[51] Nonetheless, Thackeray's point in using this rhetorically striking pair of antitheses is evidently to stress just how far removed the world of *Philip* is from an ideal one in which traditional standards of morality prevail. Goodenough's phrases "glorious crime" and "righteous robbery" suggest the gulf between appearance and reality in *Philip.* For the sake of her beloved Philip, Caroline Brandon is temporarily scoring a major success in the world of this novel by going counter to her better nature and using Dr. Firmin's own mode of deceit. Her achievement is emotionally so taxing for her that as soon as Hunt recovers she rushes to Goodenough's house and collapses in hysterics.

The aftermath of this episode comically emphasizes the difficulty of distinguishing between falsehood and truth in many of the characters' assertions in *Philip.* Hunt returns to Mrs. Brandon's house, publicly claiming that she has tricked and robbed him. However, because of Caroline's good reputation and evidence of Hunt's intoxication on the night in question as well as on an earlier occasion, his true story is not believed, and he is arrested for being "Drunk and disorderly" (16:583). When Hunt—"professing to be a clergyman, but wearing an appearance of extreme squalor"—subsequently repeats in court his accusation "that he had been stupefied and hocussed . . . by means of some drug, and that whilst in this state he had been robbed," the charge against Mrs. Brandon is dismissed and Hunt is "called upon to pay a fine for drunkenness" (16:585). Caroline is fundamentally honest, yet she knows how easily truth can be confused with falsehood, and she is not above taking advantage of this confusion to help the young man whom she loves.[52]

In contrast to his father's hypocrisy and Caroline's disillusioned consciousness of the presence of deceit, Philip's attitude is one of utter frankness. Unfortunately for the novel, this frankness often strikes a reader as equivalent to rudeness. Ferris describes Philip as "Thackeray's most obnoxious hero," and Saintsbury remarks, "One does not want Philip, at least so much of him, so constantly."[53] Since there are a number of undeniable parallels between Philip's life and Thackeray's own early struggles, readers have frequently viewed this unappealing young man as simply a biographical projection of Thackeray's younger self.[54] Nevertheless, in this late novel as in his earlier writings, Thackeray is certainly capable of distancing himself from a created character, and he does so, at least to some extent, in *The Adventures of Philip.* One of the reasons that Philip's personal shortcomings are so obvious to the reader is that the narrator makes a point of underlining these flaws, as in the passage where Pendennis remarks, "Philip is so rude and overbearing that I really have a mind to depose him from his place of hero" (16:144). In addition, Philip is far more consistent in his attitudes than the ambivalent Thackeray in real life was ever likely to have been.[55] In the context of this novel's obsession with seeming and being, Philip is best viewed as a character whose personality, like that of a figure in a "humours" comedy by Ben Jonson or later writers in this tradition, has been deliberately narrowed to one dimension.[56] Like Manly in Wycherley's *The Plain-Dealer* (1677), Philip's "humour" is always to speak the truth or what he believes is truth. As Pendennis explains when describing his first, youthful encounter with Philip: "He was a simple little man; an artless child. . . . He was quite unabashed in talking to me and other persons, and has remained so ever since" (16:9). Throughout the book, like the youthful observer who pointed out the nonexistence of the Emperor's clothes in Andersen's tale, Philip retains a childlike penchant for saying exactly what he sees and thinks.

In the mendacious world of *The Adventures of Philip,* Philip is thus an *enfant terrible.* In polite society, he crashes through conventions, "treading upon everybody's dress skirts, smashing the little Dresden ornaments and the pretty little decorous gimcracks of society, life, conversation" (16:104). Such behavior is epitomized by the episode at the Embassy ball in chapter 24, in which Philip expresses his outrage over his treatment at the hands of Ringwood Twysden by kicking him into a fountain. Even before he loses his fortune, Philip shuns the upper-class, silver-fork world, claiming that "the atmosphere of those polite drawing-rooms stifles me" (16:79). He freely characterizes his friend Pendennis as a "worldling," and according to Pendennis, Philip "would tear at his cravat, as though the mere thought of the world's conventionality well nigh strangled him" (16:79, 80). Later, when his refusal to toady to his wealthy granduncle, Lord Ringwood, apparently results in Philip's disinheritance, Pendennis describes this young man who steadfastly resists civilized dissembling even when his future prosperity depends on it as a "Huron" (16:310). Pendennis depicts Philip's penchant throughout the book for bluntly expressing what he feels is truth as a response to his father's habit of prevarication, a compulsive openness that seems to be a reaction to Dr. Firmin's chronic deceitfulness: "The elder's comedy-smiles, and solemn hypocritical politeness, caused scorn and revolt on the part of the younger man. Philip despised the humbug, and the world to which such humbug could be welcome" (16:354; see also 62). Not surprisingly, while Dr. Firmin flourishes in the society of this novel where his hypocrisy is so well suited, "poor downright Phil" is a social misfit (16:76). Once he loses the wealth that to some extent insulates him from the consequences of his plain speaking, Philip struggles to make his way.

However, fortunately for his own sake and that of his eventual wife and family, Philip is assisted by others who are more worldly than himself. While his own natural candor gets him into trouble, he is helped by a safety net of friends who pervert truth on his behalf. These friends are the Good Samaritans indicated in the book's full title: *The Adventures of Philip on His Way through the World, Shewing Who Robbed Him, Who Helped Him and Who Passed Him By.* For example, not only does the Little Sister commit her "glorious crime" in chapter 38 for Philip's sake, she exerts herself in chapter 30 to obtain a position for him as sub-editor of the *Pall Mall Gazette,* without being especially scrupulous regarding Philip's background for the post: "She was as intrepid a little jobber as ever lived, and never scrupled to go any length to serve a friend. To be Archbishop of Canterbury, to be professor of Hebrew, to be teacher of a dancing-school, to be organist for a church: for any conceivable place or function this little person would have asserted Philip's capability" (16:452). Both Rawlins and Baker have criticized what they see as the absence of morality in this novel, contending, in Rawlins's words, that "Philip lies his way through a number of jobs for which he has no qualifications."[57] Nevertheless, in *The Adventures of Philip,* Thackeray is far from oblivious to conventional morality to which the narrator repeatedly alludes even while he repeatedly shows that characters are forced to accept the omnipresence of deceit in order to survive. By demonstrating that even the forthright Philip necessarily becomes involved in deception in his efforts to make a living, Thackeray emphasizes the extent to which prevarication prevails in the society depicted in this book.

In addition, close examination of the three jobs held by Philip for which he seems especially unqualified reveals that his helpers are responsible for much of the trickery involved. In one instance, as a result of "wheedling and blandishments" (16:541) by Pendennis's wife, Philip is hired to appear in a case of law; having been called to the bar, he is technically qualified to practice that profession but has never adequately studied it. When Philip hesitates because of his lack of legal knowledge, Pendennis and Caroline Brandon encourage him to act as the knowledgeable barrister that he is believed to be. A college friend, also involved in a legal capacity in the case, privately coaches him, and Philip's successful appearance in court is followed by his being hired for a few other legal cases. In another instance, Philip is employed as an English correspondent to supply gossip for an American newspaper, a job arranged by that master of deceit, his father. Philip's friends, who "made a vow to help him" (16:498), fabricate stories that Philip then presents in letters to this paper—letters ironically signed "Philalethes," i.e., Lover of Truth. Nonetheless, Philip's reluctance to distort truth as much as he might leads to a poor evaluation of his job performance. From America Dr. Firmin writes that Philip's employer finds these letters "not *quite spicy* enough . . . and I recommend P. F. to put a little more pepper in his dishes" (16:503). In the third situation, again at the insistence of Pendennis's wife, Laura, Philip is hired as sub-editor to produce the *European Review,* a journal founded by a well-to-do member of Parliament to promote his own political views. For a time, to support his growing family, Philip engages in hack writing for this periodical, composing articles on subjects such as "Persian politics, and the intrigues at the Court of Teheran" (16:515) about which he knows nothing. Once more, despite what necessity brings him to write, Philip's natural bent toward plain speaking leads to trouble. His wealthy employer eventually terminates the journal and discharges Philip as a result of the latter's failure to curry favor with this employer as well as Philip's "candid" declaration "that the *Review* was not getting on" (16:613). In all cases, Philip shows little enthusiasm for the ruses that his well-meaning allies push upon him in their efforts to help him make his way through a murky world.

This conception of Philip as essentially a plain-speaking individual results in two artistic problems that significantly affect the novel as a whole. One is the fact that, by envisioning Philip as fundamentally a one-dimensional character, Thackeray has lost the opportunity to give Philip the sort of complexity demonstrated by figures like Becky Sharp, Major Pendennis, or Rachel Esmond—mixed characters of the type at which, as David Masson pointed out long ago, Thackeray excelled.[58] In dealing with Philip, the only way Thackeray can approach his usual practice of showing, in Masson's words, "that mixture of good and evil and of strength and foible" in a character is to stress Philip's rudeness as well as his impulse toward honesty and to point out that not all of what Philip believes to be truth is actually correct: "He said everything that came into his mind about things and people; and, of course, was often wrong and often prejudiced, and often occasioned howls of indignation or malignant whispers of hatred by his free speaking" (16:80). Nevertheless, emphasis on Philip's faults does not really make Philip an interesting character. From an artistic point of view, this "simple little man" as he is termed at the beginning of the book is too simplistic.

The second problem is that Philip does not change. To be sure, most of Thackeray's characters do not really change. As Geoffrey Tillotson has remarked about characters in Thackeray's fiction, "Although a personage in a novel exists through time, and often through a considerable stretch of time, the whole boxful of him was available from the start, and . . . as we learn more we are merely having more of him taken out of the box."[59] The trouble with Philip is that there is so little of him to unfold. Once Thackeray has established Philip as a simple character whose ruling passion is speaking the truth as he sees it, there is nothing left to do with Philip in the book except show him growing older and having occasional confrontations with others as he expresses his opinions. The fact that one of Philip's rare efforts at deceit warrants a chapter title (ch. 34, "In which I Own that Philip Tells an Untruth") highlights the extent to which, throughout the book, frankness is intended to be seen as his dominant trait. Unfortunately, this character trait alone is not enough to carry the weight of the novel, and the depiction of Philip soon appears repetitive.

While Dr. Firmin's deceitfulness, Caroline's wariness, and Philip's openness offer three variations on the theme of seeming versus being, a fourth approach is presented by the chronic uncertainty of the narrator, Pendennis. For Pendennis, as his query at the start of chapter 4 makes clear, "the question of seeming and being in the world" is a matter of constant anxiety. Near the beginning of his story, he cautiously asserts that "the reader need only give such an amount of credence to it as he may judge that its verisimilitude warrants" (16:26). Near the end of his narration, alluding to Philip's callous treatment by his Twysden relatives, Pendennis speculates that a different narrator might have told an entirely different tale:

> People there are in our history who do not seem to me to have kindly hearts at all; and yet, perhaps, if a biography could be written from their point of view, some other novelist might show how Philip and *his* biographer were a pair of selfish worldlings unworthy of credit: how Uncle and Aunt Twysden were most ex-

emplary people, and so forth. . . . I protest as I look back at the
past portions of this history, I begin to have qualms, and ask myself whether the folks of whom we have been prattling have had
justice done to them; whether Agnes Twysden is not a suffering
martyr justly offended by Philip's turbulent behaviour, and whether
Philip deserves any particular attention or kindness at all." (16:618)

Ferris has perceptively analyzed the effect on the novel of this "nervous,
self-mocking, and equivocal" narrator and has correctly observed that
"Pen's attitude to his narrative reflects Thackeray's heightened awareness of the difficulty of penetrating to the truth of things." However,
it is also worth noting that Pendennis is not so thoroughly reliable a
narrator as Ferris and other readers of this novel have frequently taken
him to be.[60]

To be sure, Pendennis is the best guide that we have to the slippery
world depicted in *Philip*. Yet, as the conclusion makes clear, Pendennis
himself has deliberately deceived us by concealing one crucial secret
throughout the book. At several points, like the narrator in a famous
passage in chapter 15 of Trollope's *Barchester Towers*, Pendennis insists
that "I do not seek to create even surprises in this modest history"
(16:103; see also 332 and 372). He demonstrates his candor by giving the
reader advance information regarding the eventual outcome of Philip's
love affairs. Despite this Trollopian disclaimer, however, Thackeray
allows Pendennis for twenty chapters to keep from the reader the truth
regarding the Earl of Ringwood's will. For half the novel, from chapter 22 to the end of chapter 42, this will, which leaves Philip a large legacy, is believed to have been destroyed. The fact that Pendennis begins
chapter 42 (which will eventually result in the climactic discovery of
the will) with the teasing question "Have I had any secrets from you
all through the piece?" (16:624) underscores the book's preoccupation
with the theme of truth. His question at this juncture—implying that
he has kept nothing from the reader—also suggests that Pendennis
himself is not entirely above deceit. Such deception by a narrator who
professes candor and shows such anxiety about the accuracy of his tale
only corroborates this novel's underlying concern with the elusiveness
of truth.

(c)

IN A WORLD where truth is impossible to find, where does Woolcomb fit?
On the level of structure, he is clearly conceived as a foil to Philip, just
as in a less prominent way in this novel Dr. Goodenough serves as the
opposite of Dr. Firmin. Barbara Hardy has suggested that Thackeray's

use of "the grand comparative method" of antithetical characters is confined to his depiction of Becky and Amelia in *Vanity Fair*.[61] However, he also seems to have been intrigued by this type of duality in his late fiction—for example, in the contrast between the twin brothers Harry and George Warrington in *The Virginians*. The literal black-and-white polarity between Woolcomb and Philip in Thackeray's next full-length novel is merely a more extreme version of this kind of contrast. Lorimer writes that the standard Victorian view of blacks during this period was as opposites of whites: "The Victorians looked upon the Negro as the photographic negative of the Anglo-Saxon, and they seemed to get a clearer perception of their own supposed racial uniqueness from the inverted image of the black man."[62] In this fashion, Woolcomb functions in *The Adventures of Philip* as the "photographic negative" of the hero Philip, revealing by contrast the distinctive features of Philip himself.

More specifically, in terms of the structure of the novel, Woolcomb seems designed to demonstrate the idea of the false gentleman just as Philip, despite his faults, seems intended to show the idea of the true one. At the end of his lecture on George the Fourth, which was published in the *Cornhill* in 1860, Thackeray asked: "What is it to be a gentleman? Is it to have lofty aims, to lead a pure life, to keep your honour virgin; to have the esteem of your fellow citizens, and the love of your fireside; to bear good fortune meekly; to suffer evil with constancy; and through evil or good to maintain truth always?" (13:811). The answer, in Thackeray's words, is clear: "Show me the happy man whose life exhibits these qualities, and him we will salute as gentleman, whatever his rank may be" (13:811). The most important ingredients in this concept of the gentleman in Thackeray's view were maintaining truth and adhering to fireside virtues.[63] As Caroline remarks simply to Dr. Firmin in *The Adventures of Philip*, "Gentlemen tell the truth! Gentlemen don't deceive poor innocent girls, and desert 'em without a penny!" (16:133). Despite Philip's crudeness and rudeness, the hallmark of his character is his underlying honesty. He is also a loving husband and father whose worst vice seems to be a fondness for an occasional cigar. Although not personally ambitious, he dedicates himself to providing for the welfare of his wife and growing family. He bears ill fortune with few complaints (little information is given about his reaction to his unexpected good fortune at the end of the novel). Moreover, at least some of his fellow citizens—the friends who help him and know his private acts of charity—esteem him. In the words of the coarse but good-hearted publisher Mugford, who eventually hires, fires, and then rehires Philip: "Young one [Philip] is a gentleman—passionate fellow, hawhaw fellow, but kind to the poor. Father never was a gentleman,

with all his fine airs and fine waistcoats. I don't set up in that line myself . . . but I tell you I know 'em when I see 'em" (16:219). Unlike
his father and the despicable Tufton Hunt, another false gentleman,
who ironically prides himself on what he erroneously perceives as his
gentle status, Philip is presented in this book as an example of an authentic gentleman. The glaring differences between Philip and Woolcomb—a young man of roughly Philip's age who marries the girl
whom Philip once loved—underscore the novel's concern with the distinction between truth and pretense.

In contrast to Philip, the mulatto Woolcomb is visibly not a gentleman, an idea that modern readers can only find repugnant but that, as
we we have seen, readers at the time of the book's first publication
would have generally accepted as routine. Contrary to Philip's honesty
and openness, Woolcomb joins with the Twysdens in spreading falsehoods and distortions regarding Philip behind the latter's back. As the
narrator explains, after Agnes Twysden has jilted Philip to marry
Woolcomb and Philip has kicked the offensive Ringwood Twysden
into the fountain, "Of course all the Twysdens, male and female, and
Woolcomb, the dusky husband of Philip's former love, hated and feared
and maligned him; and were in the habit of speaking of him as a trucu-
lent and reckless savage and monster, coarse and brutal in his language
and behaviour, ragged, dirty and reckless in his personal appearance;
reeking with smoke, perpetually reeling in drink, indulging in oaths,
actions, laughter, which rendered him intolerable in civilized society"
(16:537–38). Worse yet, contrary to Philip's devotion to his family,
Woolcomb allows one of his children to die because he is too stingy to
send for a doctor, and he abuses his wife, who ultimately leaves him.
While Philip is generous, Woolcomb is avaricious. While Philip, despite
his poverty, is loved by many, Woolcomb is eventually scorned by virtually everyone in the novel and is tolerated by society only for the sake
of his wealth. Although Philip is well educated as a result of his Grey
Friars and university background and can earn his living by his pen
when necessity warrants, Woolcomb cannot "spell or speak two sentences of decent English" (16:638) and is unable to memorize a speech
that he is supposed to deliver as a political candidate at the end of the
novel. Even the eyes of the two men reflect the difference in their
characters. Where Philip's "honest blue eyes" (16:337) are clearly defined, Woolcomb's eyes are "opal" and thus evidently changeable,
suggesting among other things, as Geoffrey Tillotson has observed,
Woolcomb's "moral instability."[64] Like that of Spenser's monster Er-
rour in *The Faerie Queene*, Woolcomb's outward appearance is presented in this novel as a sign of his inner nature.

However, a basic artistic defect in *The Adventures of Philip* is that this black-and-white contrast between the false and the true gentleman around which the novel is constructed is at odds with the book's theme concerning the impossibility of determining what is truth. To be sure, Thackeray seems to have taken more pains than are often recognized to tie together the threads of the book's plot. Philip's brutal ridicule of Woolcomb's parliamentary aspirations at the end of the novel (just before Woolcomb wins the election) is anticipated by the emphasis on the animosity between these two men throughout the book. According to Pendennis's description of the unpleasant scene orchestrated by Philip in the final chapter: "The gates of our inn courtyard, which had been closed, were suddenly flung open, and, amidst the roar of the multitude, there issued out a cart drawn by two donkeys, and driven by a negro, beasts and man all wearing Woolcomb's colours. In the cart was fixed a placard, on which a most undeniable likeness of Mr. Woolcomb was designed: who was made to say, 'VOTE FOR ME! AM I NOT A MAN AND A BRUDDER?' " (16:642). Philip's method of using a lower-class black man, elsewhere described as a "mulatto" and "an itinerant tradesman" (16:643), as the willing instrument of this ridicule only underscores the racist idea evident earlier in the novel that blacks and mulattoes do not belong in the class of gentlemen.

In addition, Philip's intense hostility toward Woolcomb in this episode can be explained by the fact that the latter has not only supplanted Philip in his courtship of Agnes but has also now become the candidate designated by the Ringwood family for the Parliament seat that—had Philip been wealthy, less radical, and in favor with his family—he might have been expected to fill (see 16:57, 154, and 633). Philip has hitherto shown little interest in this seat and is campaigning at this point not on his own behalf but on that of an old friend from Grey Friars school, yet like Hamlet, Philip could still justly complain that Woolcomb has "Popped in between the election and my hopes." In a similar manner, despite complaints that some readers have raised about the perfunctoriness and apparent irrelevance of the discovery to the book as a whole, the sensational finding of the will enriching Philip is actually foreshadowed earlier in the work.[65] Philip's angry confrontation with the Earl of Ringwood at the midway point in the novel in chapter 21 covertly prepares for what proves to be a fortunate accident—involving a different kind of run-in with a representation of the late earl—at the end of the parliamentary episode in chapter 42. During the uproar evoked by the donkey cart, the late Lord Ringwood's carriage in which Woolcomb is riding collides with a railing around a statue of the lord himself. The carriage is overturned only to reveal the supposedly destroyed will benefitting Philip hidden in the sword-case of the ancient chariot. Nevertheless, despite these connections of plot between the earlier portions of the novel and the finale, the book does not hold together.[66] The underlying message of the ugly, climactic confrontation between Philip and Woolcomb—the message that the forthright Philip can legitimately show up Woolcomb as a false gentleman—is seriously undercut by the theme throughout the book that truth and falsehood cannot ultimately be distinguished. When Pendennis self-consciously wonders late in the novel "whether the folks of whom we have been prattling have had justice done to them . . . and whether Philip deserves any particular attention or kindness at all," this narrative uncertainty throws into question the issue not only of Philip's character but also that of Woolcomb. In a world where all truths are relative—as is suggested by the theme of *Philip*—racist "truths" may not be so accurate as they seem.

Furthermore, while the structure of the novel stresses the contrast between Philip and Woolcomb, indications of an underlying mutuality between these two individuals can be found. Not only do they both love Agnes Twysden, although Philip's love is eventually dismissed as "only a little brief delusion of the senses" (16:107); they are also both hot-blooded young men who vigorously pursue what they desire. Regarding Woolcomb's marriage to the mercenary and unfeeling Agnes, Pendennis observes: "Though you may have thought Woolcomb an odious, ignorant, and underbred little wretch, you must own that at least he had red blood in his veins. Did he not spend a great part of his fortune for the possession of this cold wife?" (16:598). In his subsequent triumphs over adversity in his wooing of Charlotte—after having been jilted by Agnes—Philip shows that he too has "red blood in his veins." For example, his ardor is visibly manifested in the comic episode in which he stands outside the lodging-house where Charlotte and her family are staying in Paris while a furious argument concerning him rages within among Charlotte's relatives, only to "burst like a bombshell" (16:403) into the midst of the fray because he has heard Charlotte shriek.

Even more important, like Henry Esmond, both Woolcomb and Philip are repeatedly compared to Shakespeare's Othello. Woolcomb is disparagingly nicknamed "Othello" by various characters in the book in an obvious reference to his racial background (16:339, 600), just as he is implicitly compared to Othello in Thackeray's illustrated capital for chapter 9 (fig. 20). Also like Othello, Woolcomb is "diabolically jealous of his wife" (16:339). In a similar vein, Philip's jealousy concerning Charlotte at one point in their courtship prompts Pendennis to comment: "I could fancy Philip hectoring through the part of Othello,

Fig. 20. Capital for chapter 9 of Philip, showing Othello wooing Desdemona as her father naps. Thackeray's drawing implicitly compares Woolcomb to Othello.

and his poor young Desdemona not a little frightened at his black humours" (16:288). Indeed, Philip himself is conscious of the Othello-strain in his personality. Late in the book, he congratulates himself on his escape from marriage to Agnes and remarks, "If she had married me, I might have turned Othello, and have been hung for smothering her" (16:597). In this context, the abusive Woolcomb is seen by Philip as remarkably forbearing in his treatment of Agnes, who is now evidently leading a scandalous life. Philip observes concerning the couple: "I wonder he has not Othello'd her. . . . I should, if she had been mine, and gone on as they say she is going on" (16:597). By suggesting these underlying affinities between the "true" gentleman and his apparent polar opposite in this book, Thackeray once again suggests that what is truth is difficult to discern. The fundamental flaw at the heart of The Adventures of Philip is that its plot and structure are not consistent with this underlying theme.

IV

HENCE, IN THE END, The Adventures of Philip must be seen as an artistic failure. It has many individually brilliant sections, and it wrestles provocatively with the timeless question "What is truth?," yet its parts do not add up to a unified whole. The presence of Woolcomb in this late novel shows Thackeray's continued fascination with black characters. Nevertheless, the idea of slavery is not really a potent image in *Philip*, perhaps because Thackeray was consciously trying to avoid what "A Mississippi Bubble" indicates he rightly perceived as an exceedingly touchy contemporary issue. Thackeray's decision to eschew the topic of slavery in this book, despite his continued interest in the subject as evidenced by "A Mississippi Bubble," may be one reason underlying his artistic difficulties with *Philip*.

In any case, the racist aspects of *The Adventures of Philip* which modern readers find so troubling are not really compatible with the novel's primary theme of "the question of seeming and being," introduced in chapter 4 and reiterated throughout the book as the principal question of the novel. Even after the book's conclusion, Thackeray continued to ponder this issue. In the Roundabout paper "De Finibus" (August 1862), written just after the conclusion of *Philip,* he reveals that he had originally planned to drown Dr. Firmin but decided not to do so in order to give the latter an opportunity to repent. Thackeray then suggests that Firmin probably would not have repented but would instead have groundlessly forgiven his son. That idea, in turn, prompts Thackeray to wonder if anyone sees his or her own actions as they really are: "Do you imagine there is a great deal of genuine right-down remorse in the world? Don't people rather find excuses which make their minds easy; endeavour to prove to themselves that they have been lamentably belied and misunderstood; and try and forgive the persecutors who *will* present that bill when it is due; and not bear malice against the cruel ruffian who takes them to the police-office for stealing the spoons?" (17:595). For Thackeray, such radical skepticism concerning the nature of what we see as truth constitutes the heart of *The Adventures of Philip.* Furthermore, this epistemological skepticism at the heart of the book ultimately contradicts the racism that mars its surface. *Philip* is not an artistically good book, but it is not so narrow-minded a book as it may at first appear.

CHAPTER NINE

Slavery as Creative Image

Was not poor Cervantes also a captive amongst the Moors? Did
not Fielding, and Goldsmith, and Smollett, too, die at the chain as
well as poor Hood?
                    —THACKERAY, "ON A JOKE I ONCE HEARD
                    FROM THE LATE THOMAS HOOD"

THROUGHOUT THACKERAY'S CAREER, the idea of slavery persistently
attracted his attention. Edmund Burke described slavery as "a weed
that grows in every soil."[1] In Thackeray's case, slavery became a potent
image that took root in many contexts in his writings. It was an image
he often applied to his own experience. In 1832, as a student of law, he
wrote to his mother, "This lawyers [sic] preparatory education is certainly one of the most cold blooded prejudiced pieces of invention that
ever a man was slave to."[2] In 1854, describing his daughters' illness
with scarlet fever during his visit to Naples with them while writing
The Newcomes, he began a letter to Percival Leigh, "We are the slaves
of Fate."[3] In 1859, according to William Bradford Reed, Thackeray
remarked that "he had sold himself to slavery for two years" to the
Cornhill Magazine.[4] The most significant manifestations of this image,
however, appear not in Thackeray's comments about himself but in his
literary works.

Preceding chapters of this study have traced the presence of the image of slavery in Thackeray's major fiction, and while slavery is not
always a dominant image in any given novel, the recurrence of this image clearly indicates its creative hold on Thackeray's imagination.
That recurrence is evident elsewhere in his canon. His transformation
of The Wolves and the Lamb into Lovel the Widower demonstrates in passing the tenacity of the idea of slavery as a metaphor in Thackeray's
mind. In The Wolves and the Lamb, a play written by Thackeray around

1854 but not published until after his death, the competent, well-read, and largely self-educated butler John Howell complains to his fellow servant Mary, who lacks his intellectual abilities and is content with her social condition: "Have *you* ever felt the pangs of imprisoned genius? have you ever felt what 'tis to be a slave?" (17:6). In *Lovel the Widower,* a short novel published in the *Cornhill* in 1860 based on the earlier drama, John Howell becomes Dick Bedford. Once again, Thackeray emphasizes this serving man's competence, intelligence, and voracious appetite for reading. In addition, Thackeray again invokes the idea of slavery to indicate the disparity between Dick Bedford's abilities and his lowly social role. According to *Lovel*'s narrator, Mr. Batchelor, "I have thought of this little Dick as of Swift at Sheen hard by, with Sir William Temple: or Spartacus when he was as yet the servant of the fortunate Roman gentleman who owned him" (17:108). As discussed in chapter 5, Thackeray's remarks in *The English Humourists* indicate that he envisioned the youthful Swift as holding a slave-like role in the household of his patron Temple, a view of Swift reinforced here by the analogy with Spartacus, the leader of a slave uprising in the first century B.C. While Thackeray does not elaborate on the notion of Howell/Bedford as a slave whose role restricts fulfillment of his native abilities, the mere fact that Thackeray deepens and carries over the metaphor of slavery from the play to the novel demonstrates the importance to him of this figure of speech.

Even *Denis Duval,* which was left unfinished at the time of Thackeray's death in 1863, briefly invokes the image of slavery. According to Denis, who narrates the novel, the unhappily married Countess de Saverne can be compared to a slave when she feigns contentment in front of her husband: "If, while trembling before him, she yet had dissimulation enough to smile and be merry, I suppose no preacher or husband would be very angry with her for *that* hypocrisy. I have seen a slave in the West Indies soundly cuffed for looking sulky; we expect our negroes to be obedient and to be happy too" (17:214–15). Likewise, in a passing allusion to the notion of the marriage market (developed earlier in more detail in *The Newcomes*), Madame de Saverne is depicted as a slave who has been purchased by her husband: "She was sold, and went to her slavery. . . . She bore no especial malice, and was as gentle, subordinate a slave as ever you shall see in Jamaica or Barbadoes" (17:218–19). *Denis Duval* breaks off with Denis, on board the *Serapis,* about to participate in the famous naval battle that culminated in the surrender of that ship to John Paul Jones during the American Revolutionary War. One of Thackeray's notes, copied from the *Gentleman's Magazine,* raises the intriguing possibility that Thackeray may have envisioned Denis himself, after the surrender of the *Serapis*, as having narrowly escaped some kind of "perpetual slavery."[5] It is clear, then, that from "Timbuctoo" near the beginning of Thackeray's literary life to *Denis Duval* at its end, the notion of slavery recurs. Whether it is literal enslavement of blacks as in "Timbuctoo" or figurative enslavement in marriage in *Denis Duval* or any of the other variations on the motif of bondage that abound in Thackeray's fiction, the idea of slavery is deeply embedded in his creative imagination. The question one may well ask is, Why does the topic of slavery play such a conspicuous role in Thackeray's writing?

That question can never be completely answered. As discussed in earlier chapters, some of the possible reasons for Thackeray's preoccupation with the subject can be found partly in his environment and partly in Thackeray himself. Among his Victorian literary contemporaries, Dickens, Trollope, Carlyle, and Mill expressed themselves forcefully on the matter of literal slavery and occasionally made figurative use of the idea of slavery in their writings. Figurative allusions to slavery can also be found in the work of other Victorian authors as diverse as Tennyson, Arnold, and Charlotte Brontë. Geoffrey Tillotson has discerned in Thackeray a fundamental "fear of being dragged as a person into practical affairs,"[6] but even so impractical and nonpartisan a writer as Thackeray could not help being affected by concepts that were in the atmosphere. M. H. Abrams has observed that ideas of "mastery, servitude, and freedom"—derived from social contexts—became potent "metaphors of mind" which permeated much Romantic literature at the end of the eighteenth and early part of the nineteenth centuries.[7] In the case of Thackeray, a Victorian successor of these Romantic writers, at least one such "metaphor of mind" became a rich creative image in much of his literary work.

Since everyone in Victorian England was exposed to a similar climate of current events, why did slavery become such an especially significant image for Thackeray? As has already been seen, Thackeray may well have felt an unarticulated but powerful nostalgia for his early childhood in India, cared for by dark-skinned native servants. While such dimly recalled childhood memories may have provided the groundwork for a positive feeling in his mind toward slavery, his mother's evangelicalism served as the basis for his firm conviction that slavery was immoral, a belief that he held throughout his life. As a result of his childhood experiences, Thackeray was conditioned to see slavery from two different points of view. Not surprisingly, when he encountered the subject of slavery in adult life, it held his interest. The rich connotations of this subject in his fiction may partly stem from the wide-ranging reverberations of the topic in his psyche.

In addition, Thackeray seems to have been fascinated by figurative slavery in the way one can be intrigued by something that is a polar opposite. According to his friend Bayard Taylor, Thackeray described his own personal "dragons to fight" as "Indolence and Luxury."[8] When, as Thackeray often did, he referred to himself as a slave to his work—or when he depicted a character like Pendennis with autobiographical ingredients as such a slave—Thackeray was describing a situation just the opposite of what he evidently perceived as his own natural tendency toward idleness. For example, in *The Adventures of Philip,* both the protagonist Philip and the narrator Pendennis are briefly described as slaves to their jobs just as, to a much greater extent, Pendennis was depicted as a slave to his work as a writer in the earlier novel that bears his name. In chapter 19 of *The Adventures of Philip,* containing an illustrated capital showing a man chained to a pen (fig. 21), the unmarried, youthful bohemian Philip says to his married, older friend, "You are a slave: not a man" (16:271) because Pendennis must constantly struggle to make enough money to support his middle-class life-style. However, the tables are turned in chapter 34, when the married and financially struggling Philip chafes against his "slavery" (16:509, 510) as sub-editor of the *Pall Mall Gazette,* only to have Pen-

Fig. 21. Capital for chapter 19 of Philip, *suggesting the idea of writing as slavery.*

dennis's wife tell him: "Who has not his work to do, and his burden to bear? . . . Perhaps your slavery, as you call it, may be good for you" (16:510).

Undoubtedly the reason these particular references to work as slavery creep into *Philip* despite their irrelevance to the novel's primary concerns is that for Thackeray, by the end of his career, this figure of speech had become automatic. In the Roundabout paper called "On a Joke I Once Heard from the Late Thomas Hood," published in December 1860, a month before the appearance of the first installment of *Philip,* Thackeray decorated his beginning capital with a design of a galley slave, copied from an antique Dutch silver spoon (fig. 22). He also mused, as the epigraph of this chapter shows, about the applicability of the image of the galley slave to Cervantes's captivity for several years in Algiers, as well as to the literary careers of Fielding, Goldsmith, Smollett, and Hood. Thackeray then broadened this image to encompass mankind in general:

Fig. 22. Capital for "On a Joke I Once Heard from the Late Thomas Hood" (Roundabout Papers). *Thackeray explains: "I copied the little galley-slave who is made to figure in the initial letter of this paper, from a quaint old silver spoon which we purchased in a curiosity-shop at the Hague. . . . Along the stem of the spoon are written the words: 'Anno 1609, Bin ick aldus ghekledt gheghaen'—'In the year 1609 I went thus clad.' The good Dutchman was released from his Algerine captivity (I imagine his figure looks like that of a slave amongst the Moors), and, in his thank-offering to some godchild at home, he thus piously records his escape"* (17:470).

Galley-slaves, indeed! What man has not his oar to pull? . . .
Take the Lawyer's galley, and that dauntless octogenarian in command; when has *he* ever complained or repined about his slavery?
There is the Priest's galley—black and lawn sails—do any mari-
ners out of Thames work harder? When lawyer, and statesman,
and divine, and writer are snug in bed, there is a ring at the poor
Doctor's bell. Forth he must go, in rheumatism or snow; a galley-
slave bearing his galley-pots to quench the flames of fever, to suc-
cour mothers and young children in their hour of peril, and, as
gently and soothingly as may be, to carry the hopeless patient
over to the silent shore. (17:471–72)

In this analogy, Thackeray has ignored the crucial point that the labor
of the doctor, lawyer, statesman, clergyman, and writer is voluntary
while that of the galley slave is involuntary. Nevertheless, Thackeray's
emphasis at the end of this Roundabout paper on the concept that each
individual's occupation is a form of slavery makes clear that the notion
of an inherent tension between the urge to shirk and the need to work
was very much a part of his outlook on life in 1860.

In an extension of this attraction toward something opposite, Thackeray's use of the image of slavery, with its connotations of bondage,
exploitation, domination, and dehumanization, was a deliberate evocation of a state of being that was contrary to all that he most deeply
believed. As the 1843 General Anti-Slavery Convention proclaimed, a
slave is someone who has been reduced to the status of a thing: "His
right to himself is abrogated. If he says *my* hands, *my* body, *my* mind,
Myself, they are figures of speech. To use *himself* for his own good, is a
crime. To keep what he earns is *stealing.* To take his body into his own
keeping, is *insurrection.*"[9] Such a definition suggests that the essence of
enslavement is self-gratification, that is, using a person as a thing to
gratify someone else's ends. In contrast, Thackeray's underlying philosophy was simply that human beings ought, ideally, to behave less
selfishly toward one another. Ray observes that "his servants were uni-
formly devoted to Thackeray, who unlike many Victorian masters
treated them as human beings and made friends of them."[10] Ray also
argues that—after Thackeray's agonizing but fruitless efforts in 1840–41
to seek a cure for Isabella's mental breakdown—affection and charity
came to stand in Thackeray's mind as the supreme values in life.[11]
Hence, the image of slavery was a powerful one that he could employ
to express his disapproval of such exploitive relationships as George's
with Amelia or Amelia's with Dobbin in *Vanity Fair.*

However, slavery was also an image that could sometimes be com-
plicated by Thackeray's tendency to perceive it (like all subjects about
which he thought at any length) from different angles. In any case,

despite his usual reluctance to bring political subjects into his fiction, Thackeray's personal reasons for finding the topic of slavery compelling undoubtedly made him especially susceptible to the metaphors of bondage and freedom that were part of the cultural climate of his day. When he became sensitive to this element in his writing after his visits to America, he was determined not to treat it in any consistently political way. The fact that the concept of slavery is unusually recurrent in Thackeray's fiction in contrast to that of contemporaries like Dickens is an indication not of any proslavery conviction on Thackeray's part but rather of his inability to keep the image of slavery out of his artistic vision.

British thinking on the subject of slavery was neither static nor entirely consistent in the nineteenth century, and Thackeray's treatment of this topic throughout his literary career can generally be seen as reflective of contemporary British public opinion. When the emancipation bill was passed by Parliament in 1833 and when the subsequent apprenticeship system was terminated in 1838, the prevailing attitude in England toward these events was positive. At the time of his lavish praise for Biard's painting about the slave trade in 1840, Thackeray—like most of his contemporaries—clearly took enthusiastic pride in England's accomplishment of "the good end of freeing this hapless people." His negative use of the image of slavery in 1844 to show the bullying mentality of Barry Lyndon demonstrates his participation in this wholehearted, early Victorian disapproval of slavery. Vanity Fair (1847–48) also manifests Thackeray's reflexive antislavery attitude, although (partly under the influence of his recent Mediterranean journey) the most important image of slavery in this novel is "Oriental." During the 1840s, reports of labor problems in the British West Indies reached England, and it became clear that the West Indian economy was in trouble. By the end of the decade, Carlyle was bluntly criticizing the results of abolition, while as Davis writes, "the abolitionists, for all their rhetoric about the debilitating effects of bondage, could not conceal their disappointment or hide their fear that blacks were somehow predisposed to the cardinal sin of idleness."[12] In the context of this growing uncertainty about the benefits of West Indian emancipation, Thackeray's double-edged treatment of the image of slavery in Pendennis (1848–50) and Henry Esmond (1852) does not seem surprising. In the 1850s, disillusionment about the results of the West Indian experiment became even more widespread, although the average Victorian continued to believe—as did Thackeray—that England had taken the moral high road in abolishing slavery. Many writers in the early 1850s, like Dickens in Bleak House with his satiric jabs at Mrs. Jellyby's philanthropic preoccupation with Africa, took the attitude that, while slavery was certainly wrong, it was a mistake to worry about the far-off conditions of blacks when there were so many urgent domestic problems in England.[13] Thackeray's satiric analogy in *The Newcomes* (1853–55) between the British marriage market and the American slave market is indicative of this contemporary feeling that efforts to reform society ought to begin at home.

In the late 1850s, blatant racism emerged as an unpleasant factor in Victorian thinking on the subject of blacks and slavery, and racist attitudes toward blacks grew even more pronounced in the 1860s. Hitherto, such virulent racism had appeared to be primarily an American phenomenon.[14] In this context, Thackeray's visits to the United States in 1852–53 and 1855–56 did him no good, since he seems to have been infected slightly earlier than his Victorian contemporaries with racist attitudes (demonstrated in his letters from America) that the increasingly racist climate of opinion in England, combined with his own Anglo-Indian experiences, only confirmed. Thackeray's trips to America also had a negative result in another respect. Prior to his firsthand encounters with black American servitude, the idea of slavery had a powerful effect on Thackeray's imagination. In novels from *Barry Lyndon* to *Henry Esmond,* he creatively used the image of slavery to express in figurative terms the conditions, desires, and value systems of his central characters. However, after his exposure to slavery in real life in the American South, the image of slavery no longer worked so well in Thackeray's fiction. In *The Newcomes,* after his first visit, he still managed to make compelling artistic use of the notion of slavery. Nevertheless, he did so largely through implication—by presenting a figurative comparison between the "selling of virgins" in England and America and then focussing on the British side of this metaphor and alluding to the American side only in passing. With *The Virginians* (1857–59), after his second visit, he attempted to deal directly with the idea of slavery only to have the book as a whole fall flat. Much of its material is uncontrolled, and Thackeray's efforts to give a realistic picture of slavery as it existed in eighteenth-century Virginia are less effective than his earlier figurative use of a fantasized "Oriental" slavery in *Vanity Fair.* By the time he wrote the also unsuccessful *Adventures of Philip* (1861–62), Thackeray was for the most part sidestepping the matter of slavery, which some of his Roundabout remarks indicate he correctly saw as an inflammatory current issue. Instead, in *Philip,* he created a mulatto character who unpleasantly reflects the racist views that Thackeray shared with his contemporaries in the 1860s. From Thackeray's first significant novel to his last completed one, his shifting approach to the topic of slavery (and the related matter of characters of slave descent) shows the influence both of his own travels and experiences and of the climate of ideas around him.

If, as G. M. Young fancifully suggests, Thackeray is to be seen as a passenger worrying about whether he has a first-class ticket for the railway journey of Victorian life, he should also be seen as a passenger with a newspaper in his hand. According to Ray's picture of Thackeray in his later years, "The *Times* was a daily necessity to him."[15] Early in his career, in *The Irish Sketch Book,* Thackeray gives a vivid picture of himself at breakfast, avidly devouring every detail of the local Dublin newspapers, and it can be safely assumed that this habit of newspaper reading was a chronic one for Thackeray. What he might have read in the London *Times* throughout his career until his death in 1863 would have reinforced his interest in the topic of slavery, as well as his feeling that the topic had more than one side, his eventual belief that it was hypocritical for Englishmen to criticize the institution of slavery before correcting the equally serious evils present in their own society, and regrettably, toward the end of his life, his heightened racism.[16] However, his reading about the subject, along with his encounters with slavery on his lecture tours in the antebellum American South, did not alter his basic conviction that slavery was wrong.

In the end, what matters is how Thackeray used his thinking about slavery in his most successful fiction. With *Vanity Fair, Pendennis, Henry Esmond,* and *The Newcomes,* the idea of slavery becomes an important metaphor that creatively enlarges and deepens the overall meaning of his work. The metaphor functions both negatively and positively. Negatively, in *Vanity Fair, Esmond,* and *The Newcomes,* self-pleasing individuals seek to gratify themselves by binding others, often in the guise of love or marriage. Yet in *Pendennis,* while efforts to bind others are repudiated, the bondage of oneself to marriage, work, and convention appears to be an inevitable and positive part of the maturation process. Even *The Luck of Barry Lyndon*—written near the beginning of Thackeray's flowering as a novelist and still showing signs of relative inexperience—gains artistic power through its figurative (and in this case negative) use of the idea of enslavement. It seems ironic that, after Thackeray's American visits had given him a greater acquaintance with actual slavery than most of his contemporaries in Victorian England, he no longer employed the image of slavery so easily or so effectively in his novels. Nonetheless, at a point when the concept of slavery was primarily only a matter of speculation for him, he used it brilliantly in his fiction to explore the ties that bind and often confine.

Thackeray's eventual efforts to understand the actual phenomenon of slavery were limited by his time and place. In his best novels, however, his imaginative treatment of the idea of slavery transcends historical and geographical limitations.

Notes

UNLESS OTHERWISE INDICATED, citations from Thackeray's works in my text are to *The Oxford Thackeray*, ed. George Saintsbury, 17 vols. (London: Oxford University Press, [1908]). References to this edition are usually given simply by volume and page number; however, where necessary to prevent confusion, I have also included the abbreviation *Works*. Major exceptions are references to modern editions of *Vanity Fair, The History of Pendennis, The History of Henry Esmond,* and *The Luck of Barry Lyndon*. These exceptions are fully cited in notes to chapters 2, 3, 4, and 5.

Among the notes, I have referred in shortened form to the sources specified below:

The Letters and Private Papers of William Makepeace Thackeray.
　　Ed. Gordon N. Ray. 4 vols. Cambridge: Harvard University Press, 1945–46.　　　　　　　　　　　　*Letters*
Ray, Gordon N. *Thackeray: The Uses of Adversity 1811–1846.*
　　New York: McGraw-Hill, 1955.　　　　　　*Uses of Adversity*
　　_____. *Thackeray: The Age of Wisdom 1847–1863.* New York:
　　McGraw-Hill, 1958.　　　　　　　　　　　　*Age of Wisdom*

INTRODUCTION

1. John W. Dodds, *Thackeray: A Critical Portrait* (New York: Oxford University Press, 1941), p. 72.

2. *Letters,* 1:433, to Mrs. Carmichael-Smyth, March 1840.

3. Michel Foucault, *Discipline and Punish: The Birth of the Prison,* trans. Alan Sheridan (New York: Vintage-Random House, 1979), p. 30 (trans. of *Surveiller et Punir: Naissance de la prison* [Paris: Editions Gallimard, 1975]). According to Foucault, "The disappearance of public executions [such as the horrific 1757 execution of Damiens described at the outset of *Discipline and Punish* or the grisly 1726 execution of Catherine by burning presented at the end of Thackeray's novel] marks a slackening of the hold on the body" (p. 10). Foucault also suggests that slavery represents another manifestation of bodily control (pp. 137, 314 n. 1).

CHAPTER 1

1. *Works* 10:623; originally delivered as a lecture in New York, 31 January 1853.

2. *Letters* 3:198–99, to Mrs. Carmichael-Smyth, 13 February 1853.

3. See William Makepeace Thackeray, *Contributions to the "Morning Chronicle,"* ed. Gordon N. Ray (Urbana: Univesity of Illinois Press, 1955), reviews of 3 April, 13 May, and 31 December 1845, pp. 70–86, 101–6, and Ray, *Uses of Adversity,* pp. 326–27. See also Charles Mauskopf, "Thackeray's Concept of the Novel: A Study of Conflict," *Philological Quarterly* 50 (1971): 243. I discuss Thackeray's view of fiction further in chapter 6, in connection with his objection to Harriet Beecher Stowe's *Uncle Tom's Cabin.*

4. See Keats's remark, "We hate poetry that has a palpable design upon us," in "To John Hamilton Reynolds," [3 February 1818], *Selected Poems and Letters,* ed. Douglas Bush [Boston: Riverside-Houghton Mifflin, 1959], p. 263.

5. [G. H. Lewes], *Morning Chronicle,* 6 March 1848, reprinted in *Thackeray: The Critical Heritage,* ed. Geoffrey Tillotson and Donald Hawes (London: Routledge & Kegan Paul; New York: Barnes & Noble, 1968), p. 45.

6. G. M. Young, "Thackeray," *Victorian Essays* (London: Oxford University Press, 1962), pp. 81, 82.

7. Dodds, p. 213. Geoffrey Tillotson has called attention to the contrast between the relative absence "in Thackeray's novels of ideas about matters much under discussion at the time" and the presence of such "ideas of contemporary interest" in Thackeray's writings other than his novels (*Thackeray the Novelist* [Cambridge: Cambridge University Press, 1954], pp. 181 and 181 n. 1).

8. David Brion Davis, *The Problem of Slavery in Western Culture* (Ithaca: Cornell University Press, 1966), p. 10.

9. Wylie Sypher, *Guinea's Captive Kings: British Anti-Slavery Literature of the XVIIIth Century* (1942; rpt., New York: Octagon, 1969), p. 25.

10. Edward W. Said, *Orientalism* (1978; rpt., New York: Vintage-Random, 1979), p. 5. Said has perceptively argued that the term "Orientalism" carries a weight of imperialist connotations and that the word itself is a form of "cultural domination" (p. 28). For a further discussion of "Orientalism" in Said's sense and its relevance to Thackeray's concept of "Oriental" slavery, see my chapter 3, " 'Oriental' Slavery in *Vanity Fair.*"

11. Foucault, pp. 257–64. See also Gordon Wright, *Between the Guillotine and Liberty: Two Centuries of the Crime Problem in France* (New York: Oxford University Press, 1983), pp. 6, 70.

12. For example, see Thackeray's illustrated capital for the Roundabout Paper "On a Joke I Once Heard from the Late Thomas Hood" (December 1860), as well as his Roundabout remarks concerning this illustration (17:460, 470–72). See also his joking allusion to himself as "Enchainé (pauvre forçat de

la Presse!) a son banc de travail," *Letters* 2:86, to Charles Lever, 26 October 1842.

13. William Law Mathieson, *Great Britain and the Slave Trade, 1839–1865* (1929; rpt., New York: Octagon Books, 1967), p. 1.

14. James Walvin, introd., *Slavery and British Society, 1776–1846,* ed. James Walvin (Baton Rouge: Louisiana State University Press, 1982), p. 16. See also Seymour Drescher, "Public Opinion and the Destruction of British Colonial Slavery" and James Walvin, "The Propaganda of Anti-Slavery," in *Slavery and British Society, 1776–1846,* ed. Walvin, pp. 22–68, as well as James Walvin, "The Rise of British Popular Sentiment for Abolition, 1787–1832," in *Anti-Slavery, Religion, and Reform: Essays in Memory of Roger Anstey,* ed. Christine Bolt and Seymour Drescher (Folkestone, Eng.: Dawson; Hamden, CT: Archon, 1980), pp. 149–62.

15. Walvin, "The Rise of British Popular Sentiment for Abolition," p. 159.

16. See William Law Mathieson, *British Slave Emancipation, 1838–1849* (1932; rpt., New York: Octagon, 1967), p. 2, and Walvin, introd., *Slavery and British Society, 1776–1846,* pp. 16–17.

17. Mathieson, *British Slave Emancipation,* pp. 12, 15. See also William Law Mathieson, *British Slavery and Its Abolition, 1823–1838* (1926; rpt., New York: Octagon, 1967), pp. 283–86.

18. Mathieson, *British Slavery and Its Abolition,* pp. 256, 276–81.

19. For a useful survey of West Indian apprenticeship, see Mathieson, *British Slavery and Its Abolition,* pp. 256–305 and *British Slave Emancipation,* pp. 11–19. According to Seymour Drescher, a major tool used by British antislavery activists to exert influence on Parliament was the petition: "During the 1830s no other cause could begin to approach the number of petitions submitted to Parliament against slavery and black apprenticeship. Foreigners noted with awe that a British MP could cover the floor of the Commons with these petitions, boasting with the assurance of an Inca ruler that he would fill the whole chamber the next time around if Parliament did not act on those before it" ("Public Opinion and the Destruction of British Colonial Slavery," in *Slavery and British Society,* ed. Walvin, p. 47).

20. Anne Thackeray Ritchie, introd., *The Memoirs of Mr. Charles J. Yellowplush, Men's Wives, Character Sketches, and Flore et Zephyr,* reprinted in *The Two Thackerays: Anne Thackeray Ritchie's Centenary Biographical Introductions to the Works of William Makepeace Thackeray,* critical introd. Carol Hanbery MacKay, bibliographical introd. Peter L. Shillingsburg and Julia Maxey (New York: AMS Press, 1988) 1:111. However, Ritchie also observed about her father's political views, "Only he sympathised warmly with his friends and companions, and never hesitated to utter his sympathies" (1:111).

21. *Letters,* 1:246, to Edward FitzGerald, 5–7 July 1832. See also Ray, *Uses of Adversity,* p. 158.

22. For a discussion of Isabella Thackeray's breakdown, see Ray, *Uses of*

Adversity, pp. 250–73, 278, 304–5. Eventually, Thackeray arranged private care for his wife, and he and Isabella Thackeray lived apart.

23. I am grateful to the Houghton Library, Harvard University, which holds a complete run of the *National Standard*, for allowing me to examine this journal.

24. *The National Standard of Literature, Science, Music, Theatricals, and the Fine Arts* 2, no. 31 (3 August 1833): 70.

25. Ibid., 68–71; no. 33 (16 August 1833): 98–100; no. 34 (24 August 1833): 116–18.

26. Ibid., no. 33 (16 August 1833): 95.

27. Ibid., no. 34 (24 August 1833): 118.

28. Ray, *Uses of Adversity*, pp. 160–61.

29. Mathieson, *British Slavery and Its Abolition*, pp. 271–73.

30. *The Constitutional and Public Ledger*, 21 November 1836, p. 2, col. 5; 22 April 1837, p. 3, cols. 2–3; 10 May 1837, p. 2, col. 7.

31. Ibid., 7 December 1836, p. 3, col. 5; 28 December 1836, p. 4, col. 2; 22 April 1837, p. 3, col. 3. See also Mathieson, *British Slavery and Its Abolition*, p. 273 and *British Slave Emancipation*, p. 12.

32. See George Saintsbury, *East India Slavery* (1829; rpt., Shannon, Ireland: Irish University Press, 1972). See also *Minutes of the Proceedings of the General Anti-Slavery Convention, Called by the Committee of the British and Foreign Anti-Slavery Society, Held in London on the 12th of June, 1840, and Continued by Adjournments to the 23rd of the Same Month* (London: Johnston & Barrett, 1840). According to David Brion Davis, the 1843 abolition of slavery in British India was more a matter of law than of actual practice: "The government . . . annulled all legal sanctions for slavery without taking direct steps to destroy the institution" (*Slavery and Human Progress* [New York: Oxford University Press, 1984], p. 308).

33. As an adult, Thackeray possessed an obsessive aversion to leave-taking, and scholars have attributed this aversion to the pain of his youthful departure from India and separation from his mother; see J. Y. T. Greig, *Thackeray: A Reconsideration* (1950; rpt., [Hamden, CT]: Archon, 1967), pp. 10–11 and Ina Ferris, *William Makepeace Thackeray* (Boston: Twayne, 1983), p. 3. Catherine Peters observes that "Thackeray's early separation from his mother, and his unhappiness at school, were not extreme or unknown experiences for a boy of his background, but they left a mark as profound as Dickens's more obviously traumatic background, repeatedly referred to in his writing" (*Thackeray's Universe: Shifting Worlds of Imagination and Reality* [New York: Oxford University Press, 1987], p. 79). Thackeray himself remarked to his mother in 1845, when he was nearly 34, "I never could bear to think of children parted from their parents somehow without a tendency to blubbering: and am as weak to this day upon the point, as I used to be at school" (*Letters* 2:197, to Mrs. Carmichael-Smyth, June 1845).

34. Ray, *Uses of Adversity*, pp. 48–49.

35. Ibid., p. 61.

36. *Letters* 1:4, to Mrs. Richmond Thackeray, 3 July 1817.

37. Ibid. 2:34, to Mrs. Ritchie, 19 August 1841. See also Ray, *Uses of Adversity*, pp. 49–50, 64, 273.

38. *Letters* 1:245, to Mrs. Carmichael-Smyth, 25 June 1832. See also Thackeray's diary entry for 10 June 1832, *Letters* 1:208.

39. Diary entry for 6 August 1841, *Letters* 2:32.

40. Thackeray wrote to Edward FitzGerald about this visit: "I have got a black niece staying with me: daughter of a natural sister of mine. She was never in Europe before & wrote to my mother the other day as her 'dear Grandmamma' Fancy the astonishment of that dear majestic old woman!" (*Letters* 2:367, March–May 1848). After his niece's departure, Thackeray wrote to his mother describing a successful dinner party he had just hosted and explaining that his young daughters and their governess "had fled the premises previously—What a mercy it is too to have got rid of my niece!" (*Letters* 2:381, to Mrs. Carmichael-Smyth, 15–16 May 1848).

41. Phillips George Davies, "The Miscegenation Theme in the Works of Thackeray," *MLN* 76 (1961): 326–31.

42. See Gordon N. Ray, *The Buried Life: A Study of the Relation between Thackeray's Fiction and His Personal History* (Cambridge: Harvard University Press, 1952).

43. Ray, *Uses of Adversity*, p. 54.

44. Patrick Brantlinger, *Rule of Darkness: British Literature and Imperialism, 1830–1914* (Ithaca: Cornell University Press, 1988), pp. 104, 106–7. See also John Sutherland, "Thackeray as Victorian Racialist," *Essays in Criticism* 20 (1970): 441–45.

45. Hannah Arendt, *The Origins of Totalitarianism*, 2d ed. (Cleveland: World, 1958), pp. 180–82.

46. Davis, *Slavery and Human Progress*, p. 139. See also Raymond G. Cowherd, *The Politics of English Dissent: The Religious Aspects of Liberal and Humanitarian Reform Movements from 1815 to 1848* (New York: New York University Press, 1956), pp. 46–63.

47. Roger Anstey, "The Pattern of British Abolitionism in the Eighteenth and Nineteenth Centuries," in *Anti-Slavery, Religion, and Reform*, p. 21.

48. Ray, *Uses of Adversity*, p. 110.

49. Anne Thackeray Ritchie, introd., *The Newcomes*, reprinted in *The Two Thackerays* 1:386.

50. *Letters* 3:93–94, to Anne Thackeray, October 1852.

51. Anthony Trollope, *Thackeray* (1887; rpt., New York: AMS Press,

1968), p. 4. (Trollope's study of Thackeray originally appeared in 1879.) See also Greig, pp. 17–18, and Ray, *Uses of Adversity,* p. 110.

52. Greig, p. 28.

53. *Letters* 2:205, to Mrs. Carmichael-Smyth, 2 August 1845. See also *Letters* 2:204, to Mrs. Carmichael-Smyth, 26 July 1845, and 2:209, to Charlotte Ritchie, August 1845.

54. Ibid. 2:206–7, to Mrs. Carmichael-Smyth, 2 August 1845.

55. Greig, p. 18.

56. [G. H. Lewes], rev. of *Pendennis,* in *Leader,* 21 December 1850, reprinted in *Critical Heritage,* ed. Tillotson and Hawes, p. 108.

CHAPTER 2

1. Chapter references to this novel, as well as citations in my text, are to the critical edition of *The Luck of Barry Lyndon,* ed. Martin J. Anisman (New York: New York University Press, 1970). Anisman generally restores the original 1844 text, including the original chapter numbers, and indicates what sections were omitted or modified in the 1856 edition.

2. C. Duncan Rice, "Literary Sources and the Revolution in British Attitudes to Slavery," in *Anti-Slavery, Religion, and Reform,* ed. Bolt and Drescher, Drescher, p. 329.

3. Ibid., p. 330.

4. Hallman B. Bryant, "The African Genesis of Tennyson's 'Timbuctoo,' " *Tennyson Research Bulletin* 3, no. 5 (1981): 198–200.

5. Ibid., pp. 200–201. See also Aidan Day, "The Spirit of Fable: Arthur Hallam and Romantic Values in Tennyson's 'Timbuctoo,' " *Tennyson Research Bulletin* 4, no. 2 (1983): 59–71.

6. See Day, p. 70 n. 1, on the deadline for the contest, as well as the date of the announcement that Tennyson had won the competition.

7. Ray, *Uses of Adversity,* p. 119.

8. Arthur Henry Hallam, *The Poems of Arthur Henry Hallam together with His Essay on the Lyrical Poems of Alfred Tennyson,* ed. Richard Le Gallienne (1893; rpt., New York: AMS Press, 1973), pp. 17–27.

9. Patrick Brantlinger has recently remarked that Thackeray's poem was "written for the same contest that Tennyson's poem won" and that Thackeray's poem "parodied abolitionist propaganda" (*Rule of Darkness,* p. 188). However, as discussed in my text, Thackeray's own prefatory comments, as well as the poem's date of appearance in the *Snob,* make clear that the piece could not have been an actual submission into the competition. Moreover, these preliminary comments, along with the verse form of the poem and its apparatus of mock footnotes, suggest that the principal object of Thack-

eray's parody in "Timbuctoo" was the prize-poem genre (as Ray indiates; see my n. 7 in this chapter, as well as Ray, *Uses of Adversity*, p. 457 n. 26).

10. *Letters* 2:172; to Mrs. Carmichael-Smyth and Anne Thackeray, 11 June 1844.

11. Ray, *Uses of Adversity*, p. 323; see also *Letters* 2:229, to Mrs. Carmichael-Smyth, 16 February 1846.

12. Ray, *Uses of Adversity*, p. 323; *Letters* 2:225, to Major Carmichael-Smyth, January[?] 1846.

13. Ray, *Uses of Adversity*, pp. 330–32.

14. *Letters* 2:190–91, to Thomas Longman, 6 April 1845.

15. Rice, p. 322. In the *Zong* case, publicized by the antislavery activist Granville Sharp in 1783, more than one hundred and thirty slaves from the ship *Zong* were thrown overboard, allegedly because of insufficient rations. Sharp's efforts to have those responsible for this atrocity prosecuted for murder were unsuccessful, and the case was tried as an insurance dispute. See Frank J. Klingberg, *The Anti-Slavery Movement in England: A Study in English Humanitarianism* (1926; rpt., [Hamden, CT]: Archon Books, 1968, pp. 59–60; and David Brion Davis, *The Problem of Slavery in the Age of Revolution 1770–1823* (Ithaca: Cornell University Press, 1975), pp. 25, 220n, and 405–6.

16. Helene E. Roberts, " 'The Sentiment of Reality': Thackeray's Art Criticism," *Studies in the Novel* 13 (1981): 27.

17. Ibid., p. 25. Roberts notes that, in addition to the criteria mentioned in my text, Thackeray's third criterion for judging a work of art was "the technical excellence of the painting" (p. 25).

18. Ibid., pp. 32–33.

19. Ray, *Age of Wisdom*, p. 48.

20. William A. Green, *British Slave Emancipation: The Sugar Colonies and the Great Experiment 1830–1865* (Oxford: Clarendon Press, 1976), p. 268.

21. William Allen and T. R. H. Thomson, *A Narrative of the Expedition Sent by Her Majesty's Government to the River Niger, in 1841* (London: Richard Bentley, 1848) 2:335–77; Mathieson, *Great Britain and the Slave Trade*, pp. 53–57.

22. Mathieson, *Great Britain and the Slave Trade*, p. 56.

23. *Letters* 2:43, to Edward FitzGerald, 9 March 1842.

24. For example, see Bird Allen's discussion of some of his feelings about the Niger Expedition in a letter to Mrs. John Allen (10 September 1840), quoted in R. M. Grier, *John Allen* (London: Rivingtons, 1889), p. 71.

25. George Saintsbury and Gordon Ray, among others, attribute authorship to Thackeray. Saintsbury says that the attribution of this piece to Thackeray is "exceedingly probably" (*Words* 5:xiv). Ray says that for "French Romancers on England" and another piece in the same category in the *Foreign Quarterly Review*, "The stylistic evidence is so strong that I am inclined to join

Garnett, Melville, and Gulliver (supported by Saintsbury . . .) in assigning them to Thackeray," *Uses of Adversity*, p. 485 n. 11. See also the attributions of "French Romancers on England" to Thackeray by Robert S. Garnett, *The New Sketch Book: Being Essays Now First Collected from "The Foreign Quarterly Review"* (London: Alston Rivers, 1906); Lewis Melville [Lewis S. Benjamin], *Some Aspects of Thackeray* (Longdon: Stephen Swift & Co. [1911]), pp. 261–63; Melville [Benjamin] *William Makepeace Thackeray: A Biography Including Hitherto Uncollected Letters & Speeches & a Bibliography of 1300 Items* (London: John Lane, Bodley Head, 1910), 2:188; and Harold Strong Gulliver, *Thackeray's Literary Apprenticeship* (Valdosta, Georgia: Southern Stationery and Printing Company, 1934), pp. 133–36. *The Wellesley Index to Victorian Periodicals 1824–1900* also attributes this review essay to "W. M. Thackeray, prob." (vol. 2, ed. Walter E. Houghton et al. [Toronto: University of Toronto Press, 1972], p. 166).

26. For example, see Ray, *Uses of Adversity*, pp. 326–27, and Charles Mauskopf, "Thackeray's Concept of the Novel: A Study of Conflict, *Philological Quarterly* 50 (1971): 242–43.

27. See Rice's remark about American audiences, referenced in note 2, this chapter.

28. See Thackeray's reviews in the *Morning Chronicle* for 3 April 1845, 13 May 1845, and 31 December 1845, reprinted in Gordon N. Ray, ed., *William Makepeace Thackeray: Contributions to the "Morning Chronicle,"* pp. 70–86, and pp. 101–6. *Punch's Prize Novelists* was subsequently retitled *Novels by Eminent Hands*.

29. For example, see Trollope, *Thackeray*, p. 75; Ferris, *William Makepeace Thackeray*, pp. 18, 20; and Ray, *Uses of Adversity*, p. 345.

30. For examples of discussions of this novel in terms of the idea of luck, see Ray, *The Buried Life*, pp. 27, 28; Ray, *Uses of Adversity*, p. 345; and Anisman, ed., *The Luck of Barry Lyndon*, pp. 2, 17. This concern with luck is evident in the title under which the novel was originally serialized in *Fraser's Magazine* (*The Luck of Barry Lyndon; A Romance of the Last Century. By Fitz-Boodle*) rather than the later title (*The Memoirs of Barry Lyndon, Esq.*) under which a much revised version of the novel appeared in book form in 1856. The alteration of the title was not authorized by Thackeray (Ray, *The Buried Life*, p. 131 n. 60).

31. For a contemporary (early 1840s) English view of Frederick the Great's army, see [John Mitchell], "Tableaux of the Most Eminent Soldiers of the Eighteenth Century: Frederick II," *Fraser's Magazine* 23 (May 1841): 559–74. Anisman suggests (pp. 31–32) that this article may have served as a source for Thackeray's account of the religious candidate who is entrapped into the Prussian service in *The Luck of Barry Lyndon*.

32. Foucault, *Discipline and Punish*, p. 136.

33. For example, see George Saintsbury, introd., *Works* 6:xi; and Robert Alter, *Rogue's Progress: Studies in the Picaresque Novel* (Cambridge: Harvard University Press, 1964), pp. 116, 117.

34. See Ray's remarks in *The Buried Life* (pp. 112–14) about Colonel Newcome's vindictiveness toward his nephew Barnes and the Colonel's

eventual purification from all hostile feelings. Unlike Colonel Newcome, Barry Lyndon is never purged of his negative attitudes toward others. For useful discussions of Thackeray's concept of character, see Kathleen Tillotson, *Novels of the Eighteen-Forties* (Oxford: Clarendon Press, 1954), p. 239, and Geoffrey Tillotson, *Thackeray the Novelist*, p. 153.

35. Juliet McMaster, *Thackeray: The Major Novels* (1971; rpt., Toronto: University of Toronto Press, 1976), pp. 189–90.

36. Viscountess [Margaret Jean Trevelyan Holland] Knutsford, *Life and Letters of Zachary Macaulay* (London: Edward Arnold, 1900) [Ann Arbor, MI: Published on demand by University Microfilms, 1973], p. 394.

37. Anne Thackeray Ritchie, introd., *The Memoirs of Barry Lyndon, Esq., Written by Himself, and The Fatal Boots*, reprinted in *The Two Thackerays* 1:202.

38. Ibid.

39. Trollope, p. 70.

40. See Ray, *Uses of Adversity*, pp. 339–43; and Anisman, ed., *The Luck of Barry Lyndon*, pp. 23–27.

41. Jesse Foot, *The Lives of Andrew Robinson Bowes, Esq., and the Countess of Strathmore, Written from Thirty-Three Years Professional Attendance, from Letters, and Other Well Authenticated Documents* (London: Becket and Porter; and Sherwood, Neely, and Jones, [1810?]). Foot deliberately gives little information about Bowes's background. In Foot's words (explaining why he does not wish to reveal Bowes's original name):

> as his original name is not seen in his signature, I have no right to disturb it; for if I did, I must expose his place of nativity, his family, and relatives, who I know are in possession of wealth, respectability, and honourable connexion. . . . Nor shall I bring names into this relation which I can by any means keep out, as I know it was always not only possible, but desirable in Bowes to introduce himself to others upon false pretences. What he wanted of them, was never that he first spoke to them about. The first introduction was merely to get a hearing from them, and by that to have the power, by the most artful and insidious means, to bend them and make them instrumental to his purposes. (Pp. 2–3)

CHAPTER 3

1. *Letters* 2:309, to Mrs. Carmichael-Smyth, 2 July 1847.

2. Citations from this novel in my text are to *Vanity Fair: A Novel without a Hero*, ed. Peter L. Shillingsburg (New York: Garland, 1989). As an aid to readers who may be familiar with other editions of *Vanity Fair*, chapter numbers as well as page numbers are included in my text. For discussions of the role of the illustrations—"the Author's own candles"—in *Vanity Fair*, see Joan Stevens, "Thackeray's 'Vanity Fair,'" *Review of English Literature* 6 (January 1965): 19–38; J. R. Harvey, " 'A Voice Concurrent or Prophetical': The

Illustrated Novels of W. M. Thackeray," in *Victorian Novelists and Their Illustrators* (London: Sidgwick & Jackson, 1970), pp. 76–102; and Teona Tone Gneiting, "The Pencil's Role in *Vanity Fair*," *Huntington Library Quarterly* 39 (1976): 171–202; as well as Nicholas Pickwoad, "Commentary on Illustrations," in *Vanity Fair*, ed. Shillingsburg, pp. 641–47.

3. For remarks about the aggressive nature of the world depicted in *Vanity Fair*, see Edgar F. Harden, "The Fields of Mars in *Vanity Fair*," *Tennessee Studies in Literature* 10 (1965): 123–32, as well as Robert E. Lougy, "Vision and Satire: The Warped Looking Glass in *Vanity Fair*," *PMLA* 90 (1975): 260; and Bernard J. Paris, "The Psychic Structure of *Vanity Fair*," in *A Psychological Approach to Fiction: Studies in Thackeray, Stendhal, George Eliot, Dostoevsky, and Conrad* (Bloomington: Indiana University Press, 1974), pp. 86–95, 106, et passim. For discussions of the implications of slavery in certain aspects of this novel, see Maria DiBattista, "The Triumph of Clytemnestra: The Charades in *Vanity Fair*," *PMLA* 95 (1980): 829–30, and Paris, pp. 78 and 93.

4. Wylie Sypher, *Guinea's Captive Kings*, pp. 25–27.

5. Edward W. Said, *Orientalism*, pp. 1–2. See also Said, pp. 1–7, for a further discussion of the Eastern-Western antithesis.

6. See Said, pp. 4 and 17, as well as his discussion (pp. 25–28) of why he has focussed in *Orientalism* on the Near East. See Thackeray, *Works* 9:135, 150–51, 185, and 246–47 for examples of his use of the term "Oriental" (with and without the initial capital letter).

7. See *Works* 9:149 and 249 for examples of Thackeray's generalizing use of the term "Turkish."

8. Said, p. 188. The pornographic novel *The Lustful Turk* (1828), analyzed by Steven Marcus in *The Other Victorians*, offers an early nineteenth-century illustration of this stereotype (see *The Other Victorians: A Study of Sexuality and Pornography in Mid-Nineteenth-Century England* [1966; rpt. with new introd. by author, New York: Meridian-NAL, 1974], pp. 197–216). See also Rana Kabbani's discussion (pp. 67–85) of "The Salon Seraglio" in *Europe's Myths of Orient* (Bloomington: Indiana University Press, 1986). Kabbani observes that such nineteenth-century European "myths of Orient" included a distinction "between the barbarity of the Eastern male and the civilised behaviour of the Western male. One tied women up and sold them at slave auctions; the other revered them and placed them on pedestals" (p. 78).

9. *The Selected Letters of Lady Mary Wortley Montagu*, ed. Robert Halsband (London: Longman, 1970), pp. 96–97, to Lady Mar, 1 April 1717.

10. See *Letters* 2:190, to Mrs. Carmichael-Smyth, 28 March 1845, and Ray, *Uses of Adversity*, p. 384, for evidence that Thackeray was thinking about *Vanity Fair* while preparing *Notes of a Journey from Cornhill to Grand Cairo* for publication. For a good discussion of Thackeray's familiarity with other writings about the East, see Rida Hawari, "Thackeray's Oriental Reading," *Revue de Littérature Comparée* 48 (1974): 114–27.

11. See *Letters* 2:150 (diary entries for 19 to 22 August 1844) and Ray, *Uses of Adversity*, p. 297. According to his diary, Thackeray attended the fateful

dinner on 19 August and sailed in the *Lady Mary Wood* from Southampton in the early morning of 22 August. In his preface to *Notes of a Journey from Cornhill to Grand Cairo,* Thackeray observes that "Mr. Titmarsh . . . had but six-and-thirty hours to get ready for so portentous a journey" (9:81).

12. See *Letters* 1:283, diary entry for 20 April 1835 (actually 19 April 1835 according to Ray 1:282 n. 15); and 1:281–82, to John Payne Collier, 22 April 1835.

13. Lionel Stevenson, *The Showman of Vanity Fair* (New York: Charles Scribner's Sons, 1947), p. 125. Thackeray left India at the age of five—in December 1816—to return to England, while his widowed mother remained behind in India to marry Captain Henry Carmichael-Smyth. Thackeray did not see his mother again until three and a half years later—in July 1820—when the Carmichael-Smyths also returned to England.

14. *The Luck of Barry Lyndon,* ed. Anisman. This passage appears near the end of the September 1844 installment (part 2, chapter 1, "Barry Appears at the Summit of His Fortune") in *Fraser's Magazine.* Thackeray describes himself in his diary as writing *Barry Lyndon* "all day" on 19 August, the date of the eventful dinner, and then working on the novel again on 20 and 21 August along with making necessary arrangements for his trip. His frantic efforts to complete as much writing as possible before departure can be seen in his diary entry for 22 August, evidently describing his boarding of the *Lady Mary Wood* on the previous evening: "came on to Southampton writing for Punch the whole way, & finished my article just as we got in" (*Letters* 2:150).

15. David Brion Davis observes that "in the 1820s the owners of most West Indian estates lived in Britain and included some of the richest and most influential members of the landed and mercantile ruling class" (*Slavery and Human Progress,* p. 192). See also Klingberg, *The Anti-Slavery Movement in England,* pp. 7–8.

16. The narrator also observes ironically about Lady Emily that "It is to her, I believe, we owe that beautiful poem,—

'Lead us to some sunny isle,
Yonder in the western deep;
Where the skies for ever smile,
And the blacks for ever weep,' &c." (293; ch. 33)

As Geoffrey and Kathleen Tillotson note about Lady Emily's supposed poem, "This is the third verse of No. xci in *A selection of hymns used in Trinity Church, Lower Gardiner-Street, Dublin* (1841), beginning 'Go! ye messengers of God' . . . . Thackeray had already quoted the verse (beginning 'Hasten to some distant isle'), saying he had heard the hymn in a Dublin church, in *Irish Sketch Book" (Vanity Fair: A Novel Without a Hero,* ed. Geoffrey and Kathleen Tillotson [Boston: Houghton Mifflin, 1963], p. 320 n. 2).

Thackeray's ironic treatment of this hymn (and Lady Emily) shows his distaste for evangelicalism, a distaste even more pronounced in his comments in *The Irish Sketch Book* about the hour-and-twenty-minute sermon of the preacher who used this hymn in his service. In the hymn itself, one line in particular evoked Thackeray's criticism—"And the blacks for ever weep"—

which he italicized in *The Irish Sketch Book,* remarking, "Is it not a shame that such nonsensical false twaddle should be sung in a house of the Church of England, and by people assembled for grave and decent worship?" (5:263–64n). The problem with this line is that it invites misreading as a neutral description of perpetually weeping blacks. If the line is misread in this way, the stanza as a whole sounds like a desire to escape to a faraway land of black oppression, an idea which is indeed, as Thackeray points out, "nonsensical false twaddle" and inappropriate in a house of worship.

Moreover, the subtle change that Thackeray makes in this hymn in transferring it from *The Irish Sketch Book* to *Vanity Fair* heightens the sense of an apparent escapist urge on the part of its speaker. In *The Irish Sketch Book,* the first line of the quoted stanza is "Hasten to some distant isle," while in *Vanity Fair* the first line is "Lead us to some sunny isle." (In the original, as given in the Tillotsons' edition, p. 320 n. 2, the line is "Go to many a tropic isle.") This change in the opening line as it appears in *Vanity Fair* causes the stanza as a whole to seem more directly applicable to Lady Emily—ironically suggesting both the desire to evade ordinary reality inherent in her yearning to leave England for "some sunny isle" and the muddled nature of her professed concern for blacks. (In Lady Emily's vision of the future, as suggested by her poem, the blacks appear to be "for ever" weeping even after her arrival in the "sunny isle.")

Readers should be cautious about viewing Thackeray's ironic treatment of Lady Emily and her "beautiful poem" as indicative of his own views concerning black slavery. As discussed in the preceding chapter of this study, at the time at which he first ridiculed the language of this hymn in *The Irish Sketch Book* (1843), Thackeray was evidently very much in favor of the recent emancipation of blacks in the British West Indies.

17. John Carey, *Thackeray: Prodigal Genius* (London: Faber & Faber, 1977), p. 107; see also p. 106.

18. In his notes on *Vanity Fair,* Edgar F. Harden explains that "The *Forty Thieves* was a musical drama first performed at Drury Lane Theatre in 1806 with Miss De Camp dancing in the part of Morgiana. Maria Theresa Kemble (1774–1838) danced and acted under her maiden name of De Camp until her marriage in 1806 to Charles Kemble (1775–1854)" (*Annotations for the Selected Works of William Makepeace Thackeray,* ed. Edgar F. Harden [New York: Garland, 1990] 1:426).

19. Ibid., p. 500.

20. See Jack P. Rawlins, *Thackeray's Novels: A Fiction that Is True* (Berkeley and Los Angeles: University of California Press, 1974), pp. 21, 22.

21. Walter Besant, *The Queen's Reign* (London: Werner, 1897), pp. 48–53.

22. See Richard D. Altick, *The Shows of London* (Cambridge: Belknap-Harvard University Press, 1978), pp. 268–72, and Sander L. Gilman, *Sexuality: An Illustrated History, Representing the Sexual in Medicine and Culture from the Middle Ages to the Age of AIDS* (New York: Wiley, 1989), pp. 292–94. My remarks about the Hottentot Venus derive from these discussions, although Altick and Gilman do not mention Thackeray's reference to the Hottentot Venus in *Vanity Fair.* See also the contemporary documents, primarily relating to the un-

successful attempt by British abolitionists to rescue this black woman from her deplorable situation, reprinted in Paul Edwards and James Walvin, *Black Personalities in the Era of the Slave Trade* (Baton Rouge: Louisiana State University Press, 1983), pp. 171–81. The spelling of the given name of the Hottentot Venus varies. Altick spells it "Sartje," Gilman "Saartje" or "Saat-Jee," and Edwards and Walvin "Saartjie." Altick observes (p. 271) that she is believed to have been christened in England as Sarah Bartmann.

23. DiBattista, p. 830. For the incorrect placement of the scene between George and Amelia, see p. 829. There are several other small slips in this paragraph by DiBattista. One of the passages that she cites from the episode on page 187 of the Tillotsons' edition of *Vanity Fair* is misquoted. The phrase "the knowledge of his complete power" (enclosed in quotation marks by DiBattista) should be simply "the knowledge of his power." The phrase "Sultan's thrill" (also placed in quotation marks by DiBattista in connection with this scene) does not appear on page 187. Thackeray's text says about George Osborne: "He would be generous-minded, Sultan as he was, and raise up this kneeling Esther and make a queen of her" (p. 187). In the first charade, the Nubian slave salaams not "to the Kislar Aga" as DiBattista indicates but to the Aga, i.e., the Turkish potentate being portrayed in the tableau.

24. *Letters* 2:23, to Mrs. Procter, 28 May–5 June 1841.

25. DiBattista, p. 830.

26. *The History of Pendennis,* ed. Peter L. Shillingsburg (New York: Garland, 1991); the abbreviation *P2* refers to the second volume of *Pendennis* in this edition.

27. Ray, *Age of Wisdom,* p. 96.

28. For example, see Ray, *Uses of Adversity,* p. 422; and Kathleen Tillotson, *Novels of the Eighteen-Forties,* pp. 234, 240, 241.

29. For a psychological discussion of the contrast between Becky's and Amelia's attitudes toward the world, see Paris, pp. 89–91.

30. DiBattista, pp. 827, 829–30, 832–34.

31. Ibid., p. 832.

32. The illustrated capital also contains an allusion to the tale of "The Barber's Fifth Brother" in the *Arabian Nights' Entertainments,* covertly implying that Steyne's expectations regarding Becky will eventually be dashed. In "The Barber's Fifth Brother," a man buys a stock of glassware and fantasizes about the wealth and resulting sexual power he will derive from its sale. However, at the height of his fantasy, he destroys the glassware by kicking over the tray on which he has placed it—as the figure is kicking over a tray in Thackeray's illustrated capital for chapter 52. (I am indebted to a note by Edgar F. Harden for this reference. See *Annotations for the Selected Works of William Makepeace Thackeray,* ed. Harden 1:494.)

33. DiBattista, p. 832.

34. See John A. Lester, Jr., "Thackeray's Narrative Technique," *PMLA*

(1954), reprinted in *Victorian Literature: Selected Essays,* ed. Robert O. Preyer (1966; rpt., New York: Harper & Row, 1967) for a discussion of what Lester calls the "characteristic redoublings" (p. 162) in Thackeray's fiction.

35. According to James Hannay, Thackeray remarked about this sentence describing Becky's admiration of her husband after his chastisement of Lord Steyne: "When I wrote the sentence, I slapped my fist on the table, and said '*that* is a touch of genius!' " (from *A Brief Memoir of the late Mr. Thackeray* [1864], reprinted in *Critical Heritage,* ed. Tillotson and Hawes, p. 317).

36. Paris, pp. 93, 110.

37. See my *Dickens and the Short Story* (Philadelphia: University of Pennsylvania Press, 1982), p. 58.

38. *Letters* 1:423, to Mrs. Procter, 16 February 1840. According to Ray's headnote (p. 422), the text of this letter comes "from a transcript given to Lady Ritchie by George Murray Smith." The letter is followed by a description, in brackets, of a sketch by which it was originally accompanied— "representing 'Orson going to Court, after having been conquered, enslaved and finally polished and presented to the world by Valentine.' " It is not clear who wrote this description of the sketch, including the word "enslaved."

39. U. C. Knoepflmacher, *Laughter and Despair: Readings in Ten Novels of the Victorian Era* (Berkeley and Los Angeles: University of California Press, 1971), p. 80.

40. The similarity between Amelia with infant George in the "Major Sugarplums" illustration and traditional representations of "Madonna and Child" has been pointed out by Gneiting, p. 197.

41. Paris, p. 112.

42. *An Epitome of Anti-Slavery Information: Or a Condensed View of Slavery and the Slave-Trade* (London: T. Ward, 1842), p. 4

43. Davis, *The Problem of Slavery in Western Culture,* p. 35. See also Davis's similar but slightly longer formulation (*The Problem of Slavery in Western Culture,* p. 10) cited in my first chapter, n. 8.

44. See *Middlemarch,* ed. W. J. Harvey (Harmondsworth, Eng.: Penguin, 1965), p. 243 (ch. 21). George Eliot's Dorothea eventually outgrows the element of self-centeredness that initially—despite her ardent desire to do good in the world—leads her to see Casaubon as something other than the person he really is. In contrast, Thackeray's George Osborne remains consistently selfish.

45. See Barbara Hardy, *The Exposure of Luxury: Radical Themes in Thackeray* ([Pittsburgh]: University of Pittsburgh Press, 1972), ch. 4 ("The Expressive Things"), especially pp. 102–4, 106–8, and 110. See also Juliet McMaster's discussion of "Thackeray's Things: Time's Local Habitation," in *The Victorian Experience: The Novelists,* ed. Richard A. Levine (Athens: Ohio University Press, 1976), pp. 49–86.

Chapter 4

1. Citations from this novel in my text are to *The History of Pendennis,* ed. Peter L. Shillingsburg (New York: Garland, 1991), which preserves the division into two volumes of the first edition in book form. To avoid confusion with the multivolume *Works,* cited elsewhere in this study, references to the two volumes of *Pendennis* are preceded by a capital *P.*

2. Ray observes that *Pendennis* was "a book for which . . . [Thackeray's] contemporaries felt particular affection as the epitome of his genial wisdom" (*Age of Wisdom,* p. 108). Samuel C. Chew and Richard D. Altick remark that "*Pendennis* . . . has had its enthusiastic admirers but is little read today" (*A Literary History of England,* ed. Albert C. Baugh, 2d ed. [New York: Appleton-Century-Crofts, 1967], p. 1358).

3. Introduction, *Works* 12: xviii-xix, xvii. Ensuing Saintsbury quotations are all from *Works.*

4. Anthony Burton, *Josiah Wedgwood: A Biography* (New York: Stein and Day, 1976), caption for illustration facing p. 176. For additional discussions of the Wedgwood emblem, see Burton, pp. 199–203; Eliza Meteyard, *The Life of Josiah Wedgwood* (London: Hurst and Blackett, 1866) 2:565–67; Howard Temperly, *British Antislavery, 1833–1870* (Columbia: University of South Carolina Press, 1972), p. 3; and Jean Fagan Yellin, *Women & Sisters: The Antislavery Feminists in American Culture* (New Haven: Yale University Press, 1989), pp. 5–7.

5. Michael Steig, *Dickens and Phiz* (Bloomington: Indiana University Press, 1978), p. 14. See Steig's illustration 22.

6. Charles Dickens, *Bleak House,* ed. George Ford and Sylvère Monod (New York: Norton, 1977), pp. 166–67.

7. William Makepeace Thackeray, *The Book of Snobs,* ed. John Sutherland (New York: St. Martin's, 1978), p. 72. See also *Works* 9:337.

8. *The Book of Snobs,* ed. Sutherland, p. 221 n. 1.

9. John Sutherland, "Thackeray as Victorian Racialist," p. 443. As I shall discuss in chapters 6 and 8, Sutherland points out in this article that many of Thackeray's comments about blacks reflect racist attitudes.

10. Barbara Hardy also discusses the episode involving Morgan and the Major which is analyzed in my text, although Hardy stresses the element of reversal in this series of events (*The Exposure of Luxury,* pp. 37–44).

11. John Bunyan, *The Pilgrim's Progress,* ed. Roger Sharrock (Harmondsworth, Eng.: Penguin, 1965), p. 125.

12. For examples of articles about the blockade, see the *Times,* 13 January 1849, p. 4, cols. 4–5; 27 April 1849, p. 4, cols. 5–6; 24 May 1849, p. 4, cols. 5–6; 21 June 1849, p. 4, col. 6–p. 5, col. 1; 16 November 1849, p. 4, cols. 3–4; 22 July 1850, p. 4, cols. 3–4; 17 August 1850, p. 4, cols. 5–6. For examples of articles about slavery in the United States, see the *Times,* 11 January 1849, p. 4, col. 6–p. 5, col. 1; 24 January 1850, p. 4, cols. 2–3; 23 March 1850, p. 5, cols.

3–5; 30 August 1850, p. 4, cols. 3–4; 12 September 1850, p. 4, col. 6–p. 5, col. 1; 20 September 1850, p. 4, cols. 3–4; 25 October 1850, p. 4, cols. 2–3; 8 November 1850, p. 4, cols. 4–5; 19 November 1850, p. 4, cols. 1–3.

13. For examples of the *Times*'s effort at evenhandedness in its treatment of the topic of slavery, see the articles of 8 May 1849, p. 5, cols. 5–6 (in which the *Times* objects to accusations that the British press is cold or hostile to the antislavery cause) and 13 December 1850, p. 4, cols. 3–4 (in which the *Times* declares that "Except under the just provocation caused by the exuberant impudence of brother JONATHAN in his remarks on the country of his ancestors, no prudent Englishman would deny that there are two sides to the question of American Slavery"—p. 4, col. 3).

14. [Thomas Carlyle], "Occasional Discourse on the Negro Question" *Fraser's Magazine* 40 (1849): 675; [John Stuart Mill], "The Negro Question," *Fraser's Magazine* 41 (1850): 25–31. Carlyle subsequently reprinted his essay as *Occasional Discourse on the Nigger Question* (1853). In 1865–67, Carlyle and Mill were again emphatically at odds in the racially related Governor Eyre case— a controversy involving a British governor of Jamaica who had harshly suppressed a Negro insurrection. For a discussion of this case, as well as the different positions taken by Carlyle, Mill, and their followers, see George H. Ford, "The Governor Eyre Case in England," *University of Toronto Quarterly* 17 (1948): 219–33. See also Gillian Workman, "Thomas Carlyle and the Governor Eyre Controversy: An Account with Some New Material," *Victorian Studies* 18 (1974): 77–102.

15. *The Odes of Horace,* trans. James Michie (New York: Orion Press, 1963), p. 157. A literal translation of "Nec tenui penna" is "and not upon a thin wing." Donald Hawes gives the translation of this motto as "[Mine are] no weak wings" (*The History of Pendennis*, ed. Donald Hawes, introd. J. I. M. Stewart [Harmondsworth, Eng.: Penguin, 1972], p. 789 n. 8. Edgar F. Harden translates it as "Nor on feeble wing" (*Annotations for the Selected Works of William Makepeace Thackeray*, ed. Harden 1:580).

16. *The Odes of Horace,* pp. 157, 159.

17. As Thackeray remarked later in a letter to his daughters, "You see what you do when you marry.—what slaves you become—well? and what immense happiness you enjoy I daresay with the right man" (*Letters* 4:28, to Anne and Harriet Thackeray, 8 March 1857).

18. Robert Bledsoe, "*Pendennis* and the Power of Sentimentality: A Study of Motherly Love," *PMLA* 91 (1976): 871, 882. George Levine aptly observes about Laura and Pen, "she is . . . his mother's childhood gift to him, as Elizabeth is a gift to Victor Frankenstein" (*The Realistic Imagination: English Fiction from Frankenstein to Lady Chatterley* [Chicago: University of Chicago Press, 1981], p. 170).

19. For example, see Walter E. Houghton, *The Victorian Frame of Mind, 1830–1870* (New Haven: Yale University Press, 1957), pp. 94–99, 218–62, 341–48, as well as Alexander Welsh's discussions of "The Hearth" and "The Spirit of Love and Truth" in *The City of Dickens* (Oxford: Clarendon, 1971), pp. 141–79.

20. Bledsoe, p. 876.

21. Juliet McMaster, *Thackeray: The Major Novels,* p. 202.

22. Robert A. Colby, *Thackeray's Canvass of Humanity: An Author and His Public* (Columbus: Ohio State University Press, 1979), pp. 301–3.

23. Robert A. Colby, *Fiction with a Purpose: Major and Minor Nineteenth-Century Novels* (Bloomington: Indiana University Press, 1967), p. 144.

CHAPTER 5

1. For example, John Sutherland observes that "the thoroughness of the imposture is remarkable" and "the consistency of the anachronism amounted to benevolent forgery" (introd. to *The History of Henry Esmond,* ed. John Sutherland and Michael Greenfield [Harmondsworth, Eng.: Penguin, 1970], p. 14). However, while awarding this novel high praise, Gordon N. Ray notes that in it "Thackeray is not so consistently successful in historical as in stylistic reconstruction" (*Age of Wisdom,* p. 178). Contemporary reviewers frequently commented on the skill with which Thackeray caught the flavor of a bygone age in this book. John Forster remarked in the *Examiner* (13 November 1852) that in *Esmond* "Mr Thackeray has caught the true tone of the writers of Queen Anne's time" (reprinted in *Thackeray: The Critical Heritage,* ed. Tillotson and Hawes, p. 145. Nevertheless, not all early reviewers agreed that the imposture was worthwhile. Samuel Phillips queried rhetorically in the *Times* (22 December 1852), "Why, Mr. Thackeray, in the name of all that is rational, why write in fetters?" (reprinted in *Critical Heritage,* p. 155).

2. Trollope, *Thackeray,* p. 122; Ray, *Age of Wisdom,* p. 176. However, Sutherland challenges the widespread view that Thackeray's accomplishment in *Esmond* resulted from careful revision (see *Thackeray at Work* [London: Athlone Press, 1974], pp. 58, 66).

3. Hardy, *The Exposure of Luxury,* p. 131.

4. See Ferris, *William Makepeace Thackeray,* p. 61; James H. Wheatley, *Patterns in Thackeray's Fiction* (Cambridge, MA: M.I.T. Press, 1969), pp. 96, 105.

5. Ray, *Buried Life,* p. 96; *Age of Wisdom,* p. 189.

6. For a discussion of the Brookfield affair and its bearing on *Esmond,* see *Buried Life,* pp. 78–96, as well as *Age of Wisdom,* pp. 58–91, 157–67, and 180–88. See also Ray's remarks about the Brookfields in *Letters* 1:xcv–c.

7. Citations from this novel in my text are to *The History of Henry Esmond,* ed. Edgar F. Harden (New York: Garland, 1989). As an aid to readers who may be familiar with other editions of *Henry Esmond,* book and chapter numbers as well as page numbers have been included.

8. Andrew Sanders, *The Victorian Historical Novel 1840–1880* (New York: St. Martin's Press, 1979), p. 102.

9. Orlando Patterson, *Slavery and Social Death: A Comparative Study* (Cam-

bridge: Harvard University Press, 1982), p. 5. Other characteristic features of slavery, according to Patterson, are "the extremity of power involved . . . and . . . the qualities of coercion that brought the relation into being and sustained it" (p. 2) and "the fact that slaves were always persons who had been dishonored in a generalized way" (p. 10).

10. Patterson, p. 5.

11. Patterson, p. 6. For a detailed analysis of the importance of memory—and the related issue of identity—in this novel, see Henri-A. Talon, "Time and Memory in Thackeray's *Henry Esmond,*" *Review of English Studies,* n.s. 13 (1962): 147–56. For other discussions of Henry Esmond's preoccupation with the question of identity, see Ferris, p. 64, and John Loofbourow, *Thackeray and the Form of Fiction* (Princeton: Princeton University Press, 1964), p. 125.

12. Loofbourow, p. 123.

13. Patterson, pp. 8–9.

14. Ibid., p. 63. The phrase "of the lineage" which Patterson quotes comes from Joseph C. Miller, "Imbangala Lineage Slavery," in Suzanne Miers and Igor Kopytoff, eds., *Slavery in Africa: Historical and Anthropological Perspectives* [Madison: University of Wisconsin Press, 1977], p. 213.

15. John E. Tilford, Jr., "The Love Theme of *Henry Esmond.*" *PMLA* 67 (1952): 684–701, reprinted in *Thackeray: A Collection of Critical Essays,* ed. Alexander Welsh (Englewood Cliffs, NJ: Prentice-Hall, 1968), p. 145. For a good discussion of the way in which the motif of incest "drives the story" (p. 194) in this novel, see Sylvia Manning, "Incest and the Structure of *Henry Esmond,*" *Nineteenth-Century Fiction* 34 (September 1979): 194–213.

16. See *Pendennis,* vol. 2, ch. 16. Major Pendennis alludes to the story of Joseph in a conversation with Helen concerning Pen's relationship with Fanny Bolton: "Young men will be young men; and, begad, my good ma'am, if you think our boy is a Jo___." However, Helen interrupts the Major: "Pray, spare me this" (P2:152). In addition, as mentioned in the following chapter of this study, a reference to the biblical account of Joseph's being sold into bondage appears in *The Newcomes* (*Works* 14:62).

17. See *Esmond,* p. 130 (bk. 1, ch. 14), for an allusion to "Jacob in hairy gloves cheating Isaac of Esau's birthright," depicted on the tiles of the chimney where Henry burns the confession that would have established his legitimacy and inheritance; the biblical story about how Jacob fraudulently obtains his father's blessing appears in Genesis, ch. 27. See p. 298 (bk. 3, ch. 3) for an allusion to the fourteen years that Jacob served the father of Rachel in order to marry her (Genesis, ch. 29).

18. Davis, *Slavery and Human Progress,* p. 17.

19. See my discussion of this tale and its relationship to Dickens's *The Haunted Man* in *Dickens and the Short Story* (Philadelphia: University of Pennsylvania Press, 1982), pp. 56–58.

20. Loofbourow, p. 148.

21. See Douglas A. Lorimer, *Colour, Class and the Victorians: English Attitudes to the Negro in the Mid-Nineteenth Century* ([Leicester, Eng.]: Leicester University Press, 1978), pp. 25, 28.

22. For a useful summary of Johnson's opposition to slavery, see the appendix on "Johnson's Sentiments towards his Fellow-subjects in America," *Boswell's Life of Johnson,* ed. George Birkbeck Hill, rev. and enlarged by L. F. Powell (Oxford: Clarendon, 1934) 2:476–77. For a discussion of Washington's posthumous emancipation of his slaves, see James Thomas Flexner, *George Washington: Anguish and Farewell (1793–1799)* (Boston: Little, Brown [1972]), pp. 445–47. On Washington's thinking about emancipation, see also Flexner, pp. 112–25 and 432–45.

23. John Sutherland, introd. *The History of Henry Esmond,* ed. Sutherland and Greenfield, p. 18; J. Hillis Miller, *The Form of Victorian Fiction* (Notre Dame, IN: University of Notre Dame Press, 1968), p. 102. See also J. Hillis Miller's more recent discussion of *Henry Esmond* in *Fiction and Repetition: Seven English Novels* (Cambridge: Harvard University Press, 1982) where Miller presents a similar "alternative portrait of Henry Esmond" (p. 103) but argues that the ironic nature of this novel undercuts even this "alternative" reading. In Miller's words, "Where there is irony there is no authority, not even the authority to know for sure that there is no authority" (p. 108).

24. Juliet McMaster, *Thackeray: The Major Novels,* pp. 110, 124; Lionel Stevenson, "Thackeray's Dramatic Monologues," in *From Smollett to James: Studies in the Novel and Other Essays Presented to Edgar Johnson,* ed. Samuel I. Mintz, Alice Chandler, and Christopher Mulvey (Charlottesville: University Press of Virginia, 1981), p. 155 (see also p. 153); and Ferris, *William Makepeace Thackeray,* pp. 73–74.

25. Sixteen years after *Esmond,* another sophisticated nineteenth-century fictional work reflecting this type of ambiguity is Dickens's "George Silverman's Explanation" (1868). See my discussion of the latter in *Dickens and the Short Story,* pp. 121–31.

26. See *The History of Henry Esmond,* ed. Sutherland and Greenfield, p. 528 n. 6; this note also calls attention to the "affinity" between Esmond and Othello.

27. *Letters* 3:15, to Mrs. Carmichael-Smyth, 26 February 1852.

CHAPTER 6

1. Ray, *Age of Wisdom,* p. 239. For a famous view of *The Newcomes* as a work lacking in artistic unity, see Henry James's description of *The Newcomes,* Dumas's *Les Trois Mousquetaires,* and Tolstoy's *War and Peace* as "large loose baggy monsters" (preface to *The Tragic Muse,* in *The Art of the Novel: Critical Prefaces by Henry James,* introd. Richard P. Blackmur (New York: Charles Scribner's Sons, 1934), p. 84. For a refutation of this assessment of *The Newcomes,* see Juliet McMaster, *Thackeray: The Major Novels,* p. 176. (See also Juliet McMaster's remark about the difference between the setting of *Vanity Fair* and *The Newcomes,* p. 155.) Michael Lund has suggested that James's famous

remark reveals a "spatial" framework rather than "the kind of temporal framework" that is more appropriate for considering a lengthy, serialized novel such as *The Newcomes* (*Reading Thackeray* [Detroit: Wayne State University Press, 1988], p. 106).

2. [Whitwell Elwin], from a review, *Quarterly Review* (September 1855), reprinted in *Critical Heritage,* ed. Tillotson and Hawes, pp. 230–31.

3. For examples of discussions dealing with the theme of respectability and the idea of mercenary marriage in *The Newcomes,* see Ray, *Age of Wisdom,* pp. 238–43; Juliet McMaster, *Thackeray: The Major Novels,* pp. 133–34, 155–58; Colby, *Thackeray's Canvass of Humanity,* pp. 362, 371–72; and Ferris, *William Makepeace Thackeray,* pp. 85–89. See also *Letters* 3:297n, as well as Jean Sudrann, " 'The Philosopher's Property': Thackeray and the Use of Time," *Victorian Studies* 10 (1967) on "the selling of hearts" (p. 386) in *The Newcomes.* On Colonel Newcome "as the perfect embodiment, for all his eccentricities, of the gentlemanly ideal," see Ray, *Age of Wisdom,* p. 245.

4. R. D. McMaster has recently mentioned that "the analogy between the position of women and slavery was much in the air in the early fifties and forms a background against which one should examine the women of Thackeray's novel" (*Thackeray's Cultural Frame of Reference: Allusion in "The Newcomes"* [Montreal & Kingston: McGill-Queen's University Press, 1991], p. 6), but he does not pursue this analogy in much detail. He correctly identifies the allusion in chapter 28 of *The Newcomes* to "the address to Mrs. Stowe" as a reference to the 1852 antislavery document treated in my present chapter (see *Thackeray's Cultural Frame of Reference,* pp. 5–6, 84, and *Annotations for the Selected Works of William Makepeace Thackeray,* ed. Harden 2:195). However, R. D. McMaster does not discuss the conspicuous association of upper-class British women with this particular antislavery document or the specific objections to slavery on which this "address to Mrs. Stowe" focuses.

5. *Age of Wisdom,* p. 216.

6. On Thackeray's arranged visit to a plantation in Georgia, see *Letters* 3:241–42, to Anne and Harriet Thackeray, 14–19 March 1853, as well as 3:241n.

7. *Letters* 3:252, to Mrs. Procter, 4 April 1853.

8. James Grant Wilson, *Thackeray in the United States 1852–3, 1855–6* (1904; rpt., New York: Dodd, Mead, 1909) 1:118. See also *Journals of Ralph Waldo Emerson,* ed. Edward Waldo Emerson and Waldo Emerson Forbes (Boston: Houghton Mifflin, 1912) 8:393; Ray, *Age of Wisdom,* p. 119, as well as *Letters* 3:142n; and Barbara Hardy, *The Exposure of Luxury,* p. 110n.

A contemporary reviewer in the London *Times* complained about Thackeray, "His chief and important defect, . . . is, that he fails on the side of imagination. He is always restricted to the domain of pure facts. He has no dreams, no superstitions, no tentative aspirations to the unseen. What he can see, hear, smell, touch, and taste he can describe, and even idealize, but he can go no further than the range of his five senses" (29 August 1855; reprinted in *Critical Heritage,* p. 227).

9. John Sutherland, "Thackeray as Victorian Racialist," p. 441-45.

10. *Letters* 3:199, to Mrs. Carmichael-Smyth, 13 February 1853.

11. *Letters* 3:235, to Harriet Thackeray, 11 March 1853.

12. For example, see *Letters* 3:223, to Anne Thackeray, 3 March 1853; 3:229, to Albany Fonblanque, 4 March 1853; 3:248, to Mrs. Carmichael-Smyth, 25-28 March 1853; 3:252, to Mrs. Procter, 4 April 1853.

13. On Thackeray's treatment of his servants, see Ray, *Uses of Adversity,* p. 202, quoted in my chapter 9.

14. He wrote to Mrs. Procter, "The Southern gentry are as a body the most generous and kind people" (*Letters* 3:252, 4 April 1853).

15. Geoffrey Tillotson, *Thackeray the Novelist,* p. 246.

16. Davis, *Slavery and Human Progress,* p. 80.

17. Ibid., p. 147.

18. *Letters* 3:245, 25 March 1853.

19. Eugene D. Genovese, *Roll, Jordan, Roll: The World the Slaves Made* (1974; rpt., New York: Vintage-Random, 1976), p. 51. Genovese writes that the motive behind the movement among Southern slaveholders to render slavery more humane without abolishing it was to "make the South safe for slaveholders by confirming the blacks in perpetual slavery and by making it possible for them to accept their fate" (ibid.).

20. Ibid., p. 58; see also pp. 58–63.

21. Ibid., p. 61.

22. This view of American slavery as an economically dying institution has been notably contested by Robert William Fogel and Stanley L. Engerman in their controversial *Time on the Cross: The Economics of American Negro Slavery* (Boston: Little, Brown, 1974). What is of primary concern to the present study, of course, is what Thackeray thought.

23. *Letters* 3:252, to Mrs. Procter, 4 April 1853. See also Thackeray's remark to his daughter Minny, "besides its being wrong: slavery is 6 times as dear as free labour" (*Letters* 3:236, to Harriet Thackeray, 11 March 1853).

24. *Letters* 3:229, to Albany Fonblanque, 4 March 1853.

25. Ibid., p. 254, to Mrs. Bayne, 5 April 1853.

26. Ibid., p. 242, to Anne and Harriet Thackeray, 14-19 March 1853.

27. Ibid., p. 224, to Anne Thackeray, 3 March 1853.

28. Ibid., p. 555, to Anne and Harriet Thackeray, 2–7 February 1856. See Ray, *The Age of Wisdom,* pp. 257 and 263–64, for a discussion of Thackeray's ill health at the time of his second visit and his dissatisfaction with the United States as a result of this second tour.

29. *Letters* 3:567, to Anne and Harriet Thackeray, 15 February 1856.

30. Ray, *Age of Wisdom*, p. 217.

31. *Letters* 3:229, to Albany Fonblanque, March 1853.

32. Ann Douglas, ed., *Uncle Tom's Cabin; or, Life among the Lowly*, by Harriet Beecher Stowe (Harmondsworth, Eng.: Penguin, 1981), p. 9.

33. As Ray has observed, Thackeray's primary reason for going to the United States as a lecturer was to earn enough money "to replace for his children's use the fortune of £20,000 which he had lost as a young man" (*Age of Wisdom*, p. 195; see also *Age of Wisdom*, p. 257). Thackeray himself explained in a letter to his daughter Anne: "I must and will go to America not because I like it, but because it is right I should secure some money against my death for your poor mother and you 2 girls—And I think if I have luck I may secure nearly a third of the sum that I think I ought to leave behind me by a six month's tour in the States" (*Letters* 3:93, October 1852). In view of this determination to accrue enough money through his lectures to provide for his unmarried daughters and insane wife in the event of his death, it is not surprising that Thackeray was anxious to avoid any public statements or activities on his American tours that might jeopardize his popularity.

34. Eyre Crowe, *With Thackeray in America* (New York: Charles Scribner's Sons, 1893), p. 35.

35. *Letters* 3:187, to Mrs. Carmichael-Smyth. One discussion of slavery that Thackeray is known to have read while in the United States and which would certainly have corroborated his feeling that the issue was more complex than indicated by *Uncle Tom's Cabin* was an article entitled "Concerning Free British Negros" [*sic*] (*Fraser's Magazine* 47 [1853]: 114–26). The article presents a negative picture of the recently emancipated blacks—"suspicious, slothful, filthy, and half-clad" (p. 116)—in the British West Indies. While believing that slavery is wrong, the author contends that West Indian emancipation came about too abruptly. The essay sees the former slaves as analogous to children who must be properly trained and guided by laws instituted by the British government. In several footnotes, the British West Indian colony of Demerara is singled out because of its high rate of murder and robbery, as well as the large number of blacks who "subsist without even the pretence of earning an honest living" (p. 117n)—circumstances which the essay implies are attributable to precipitous and unregulated emancipation. In one of his letters, Thackeray specifically urges his mother to read this article (*Letters* 3:247, 25–28 March 1853). The article appears in the same issue of *Fraser's Magazine* as "Mr. Thackeray in the United States," a spoofing account of Thackeray's supposed personal characteristics—parodying contemporary American journalistic style—commonly attributed to Thackeray himself.

36. *Letters* 3:273, to Mrs. Baxter, 3 June 1853.

37. *Catalogue of the Library of Charles Dickens from Gadshill, Catalogue of His Pictures and Objects of Art, Catalogue of the Library of W. M. Thackeray, and Relics from His Library*, ed. J. H. Stonehouse (London: Piccadilly Fountain Press, 1935).

38. Wilson 2:144; Thackeray's sketch is reproduced (without some of the facial details) in *Letters* 3:655, to Mrs. Dunlop, 12 December 1856.

39. *Letters* 3:293, to William Bradford Reed, 21 July 1853.

40. Charles Mauskopf, "Thackeray's Concept of the Novel: A Study of Conflict," *Philological Quarterly* 50 (1971): 242.

41. Review in the *Morning Chronicle*, 3 April 1845, reprinted in *William Makepeace Thackeray: Contributions to the "Morning Chronicle,"* ed. Ray, p. 72; also quoted by Mauskopf, p. 243. See also Ray, *Uses of Adversity*, pp. 326–28.

42. According to Geoffrey Tillotson, "Thackeray contemplates what offers with an openness of mind, an untendentious readiness to see all sides of a thing" (*Thackeray the Novelist*, p. 236).

43. For example, see Ray, *Letters* 1:lxxxviii–xc; Ray, *Age of Wisdom*, pp. 207–11; Juliet McMaster, *Thackeray: The Major Novels*, p. 163; and Ferris, *William Makepeace Thackeray*, p. 85. For a good discussion of the impact of Thackeray's affection for Sally on his subsequent feelings about America at the time of the Civil War, see Arnold Whitridge, "Dickens and Thackeray in America," *The New York Historical Society Quarterly* 62 (1978): 231–36.

44. *Times* (London), 29 November 1852, p. 8, col. 3.

45. In R. D. McMaster's *Thackeray's Cultural Frame of Reference* (p. 6), as well as his notes on *The Newcomes* in *Annotations for the Selected Works of William Makepeace Thackeray*, ed. Harden (2:195), "Strafford" is apparently a slip for "Stafford." The name of the house appears as "Stafford" in many sources including the *Times* (cited above in note 44), the *Illustrated London News* (cited below in note 47), and Rice's *The Scots Abolitionists* (cited below in note 48).

46. See Edwin Hodder, *The Life and Work of the Seventh Earl of Shaftesbury* (London: Cassell & Company, 1886) 2:395.

47. *Illustrated London News*, 26 March 1853, p. 231. The *Times* (London) cited the same statistic and commented: "Nothing can be more intelligible, more gratifying, and more utterly inconclusive than this immense number of signatures" (21 March 1853, p. 4, col. 3).

48. C. Duncan Rice, *The Scots Abolitionists 1833–1861* (Baton Rouge: Louisiana State University Press, 1981), p. 183. See also Margaret Howitt, ed. *Mary Howitt: An Autobiography* (London: William Isbister, 1889), 2:92–93.

49. *Times* (London), 13 December 1852, p. 6, col. 5.

50. *Times* (London), 2 December 1852, p. 6, col. 3.

51. "Mrs. Ex-President John Tyler to the Duchess of Sutherland and Others," *Richmond Enquirer*, 28 January 1853; reprinted in the *Times* (London), 15 February 1853, p. 8, col. 6.

52. *Letters* 3:228, to Albany Fonblanque, 4 March 1853; see also *Letters* 3:251–52, to Mrs. Procter, 4 April 1853.

53. *Letters* 3:181, 21 January 1853.

54. Rice, p. 183; see also *Illustrated London News*, 9 April 1853, p. 276.

55. *Letters* 3:181n.

56. *Letters* 3:296–97, to Sarah Baxter, 26 July–7 August 1853.

57. Colby, p. 390 n. 22; Caroline Norton [*English Laws for Women in the Nineteenth Century*, 1854], *Caroline Norton's Defense: English Laws for Women in the Nineteenth Century*, introd. Joan Huddleston (Chicago: Academy Chicago, 1982), pp. 15–18.

58. *Letters* 3:428, to Mrs. Carmichael-Smyth, 6–7 March 1855.

59. For example, see Juliet McMaster, *Thackeray: The Major Novels*, p. 163, and Ferris, *William Makepeace Thackeray*, pp. 89–92.

60. *Times* (London), 15 February 1853, p. 8, col. 5. Genovese puts this disagreement over the religious instruction of American slaves into context by observing that by the 1830s Southern slaveholders commonly encouraged Christianity among their slaves "as a means of social control" (p. 186). According to Genovese: "Hence the apparent contradictions of the period: a decline of antislavery sentiment in the southern churches; laws against black preachers; laws against teaching slaves to read and write; encouragement of oral instruction of slaves in the Christian faith; and campaigns to encourage more humane treatment of slaves. The religious history of the period formed part of the great thrust to reform slavery as a way of life and to make it bearable for the slaves" (p. 186). Genovese also notes that "In terms recognizable to the white America in which the black development was lodged, the mass of the slaves apparently became Christians during the late eighteenth and early nineteenth centuries. By the last antebellum decade blacks constituted a large proportion of those attending Christian services" (p. 184).

61. As R. D. McMaster points out, Warrington's thought about taking "a savage woman, who should nurse my dusky brood" is an allusion to Tennyson's "Locksley Hall," line 168 (*Annotations for the Selected Works of William Makepeace Thackeray*, ed. Harden 2:224).

62. Thackeray described the episode as "such a piece of imprudence" on Crowe's part (*Letters* 3:222, to Mrs. Elliot and Kate Perry, 3 March 1853).

63. Eyre Crowe, *With Thackeray in America*, pp. 132–33.

CHAPTER 7

1. From Thackeray's day to our own, readers have commonly called attention to the artistic flaws of *The Virginians*. In 1859, Goldwin Smith acidly observed: "Of the plot of *The Virginians* we have only to say what the topographer said of the snakes in Iceland. There is none" (review, *Edinburgh Review*, October 1859; reprinted in *Critical Heritage*, ed. Tillotson and Hawes, p. 292). More recently, Gordon N. Ray has remarked that Thackeray "may be said to have reached an acme of formlessness in *The Virginians*" (*Age of Wisdom*, p. 373). Using a phrase frequently but apocryphally attributed to Douglas Jerrold, John Sutherland entitles his chapter about *The Virginians* in *Thackeray at Work* ([London: Athlone Press, 1974], pp. 86–109) "The Worst Novel Anyone Ever Wrote."

2. In 1864, a year after Thackeray's death, his American friend William Bradford Reed argued that *The Virginians* displayed Thackeray's proslavery views: "More than any Englishman of letters I have ever known, he was free from that sentimental disease of 'Abolitionism'. His American novel, and his pictures of life in ancient days at Castlewood, on the Potomac, show this abundantly" (William Bradford Reed, from *Haud Immemor* [Philadelphia, 1864]; reprinted as "His Simple Naturalness," in *Thackeray: Interviews and Recollections*, ed. Philip Collins [New York: St. Martin's, 1983] 1:191). Described by James Grant Wilson as "a Northern proslavery sympathiser," Reed was essentially claiming that his own position was supported by Thackeray (see Wilson, *Thackeray in the United States*, 2:73).

3. *Letters* 3:226, to Albany Fonblanque, 4 March 1853.

4. Louise H. Johnson, "The Source of the Chapter on Slavery in Dickens's *American Notes*," *American Literature* 14 (January 1943): 427–30. See also Arthur A. Adrian, "Dickens on American Slavery: A Carlylean Slant," *PMLA* 67 (1952): 319n. Adrian observes that Dickens's remarks about American slavery in the years after the publication of *American Notes* show "a lessening concern for the welfare of the colored race" (p. 328) and, especially in the latter part of Dickens's career, a similarity with the views of Carlyle.

5. *Letters* 4:73–74, from Frederick Swartout Cozzens, 21 March 1858.

6. Charles Mauskopf, "Thackeray's Concept of the Novel: A Study of Conflict," *Philological Quarterly* 50 (1971): 242, 244–45, 246, 251–52.

7. Mauskopf, pp. 245, 252.

8. Gerald C. Sorensen, "Beginning and Ending: *The Virginians* as a Sequel," *Studies in the Novel* 13 (1981): 144.

9. Ibid., p. 113. Ironically, in view of Madam Esmond's assessment of her half-brother's limitations, Harry is her favorite son.

10. Juliet McMaster, *Thackeray: The Major Novels*, p. 213.

11. See also Sorensen, p. 116, and Robert A. Colby, *Thackeray's Canvass of Humanity*, pp. 403–4.

12. David Brion Davis, *The Problem of Slavery in the Age of Revolution 1770–1823* (Ithaca: Cornell University Press, 1975), pp. 24, 73, 278.

13. Edgar F. Harden, *The Emergence of Thackeray's Serial Fiction* (Athens: University of Georgia Press, 1979), pp. 139–41.

14. Lorimer, *Colour, Class and the Victorians*, p. 28. See also David M. Turley, " 'Free Air' and Fugitive Slaves: British Abolitionists versus Government over American Fugitives, 1834–61," in *Anti-Slavery, Religion, and Reform*, ed. Bolt and Drescher, p. 179 n. 14, as well as Davis, *The Problem of Slavery in the Age of Revolution*, pp. 23, 471–501.

15. Lorimer, pp. 25–27.

16. For a discussion of what John Carey calls Thackeray's "fixation" (p. 29) with flagellation, see Carey, *Thackeray: Prodigal Genius*, pp. 28–29.

17. See *The Virginians: A Tale of the Last Century*, 2 vols. (London: Bradbury & Evans, 1858–59).

18. Florence Nightingale, *Cassandra* (Old Westbury, NY: Feminist Press, 1979), pp. 32, 34, 36. *Cassandra* was written in 1852 and revised in 1859, when a small number of copies were privately printed, but the work was not published in the true sense of the word until 1928.

19. Ferris, *William Makepeace Thackeray*, pp. 105–7.

20. Rawlins, *Thackeray's Novels: A Fiction that Is True*, p. 201; also quoted by Ferris, *William Makepeace Thackeray*, p. 105.

21. Ferris, *William Makepeace Thackeray*, p. 107.

CHAPTER 8

1. On the difference between Philip's role in this book and the usual place of heroes in Thackeray's novels, see George Saintsbury, introd., *Works* 16:x–xi. The narrative technique of this unconventional novel has been analyzed by Ina Ferris in "Narrative Strategy in Thackeray's *The Adventures of Philip*" (*English Studies in Canada* 5 [1979]: 448–56), as well as in *William Makepeace Thackeray*, pp. 112–16.

2. In his characterization of Woolcomb in *Philip*, Thackeray is guilty of racism in the sense in which Tzvetan Todorov has recently defined it: "a type of behavior which consists in the display of contempt or aggressiveness toward other people on account of physical differences (other than those of sex) between them and oneself" (" 'Race,' Writing, and Culture," trans. Loulou Mack, in *"Race," Writing, and Difference*, ed. Gates, p. 370). However, as Todorov also points out, "Racialist and colonialist authors of the nineteenth century, in promulgating racism, were completely in accordance with popular opinion of their time" (p. 378). Todorov distinguishes between racism and racialism, defining the latter as "theories of race, whose heyday extended from the middle of the eighteenth through the middle of the twentieth centuries" (p. 372). As I shall argue in this chapter, Thackeray's depiction of Woolcomb is in keeping with popular British opinion in the 1860s, but by the end of the novel Thackeray has paradoxically subverted at least some of the racism in this book.

3. For Thackeray's early view of "A Shabby Genteel Story" as a work that might or might not be extended, see *Letters* 1:488, to James Fraser, 3 December 1840.

4. See Ferris, *William Makepeace Thackeray*, and Juliet McMaster, "Funeral Baked Meats: Thackeray's Last Novel," *Studies in the Novel* 13 (1981): 133–55. Another recent critic who has commented on the style of *Philip* is Rawlins, *Thackeray's Novels: A Fiction that Is True*, pp. 86–87, 215–25 et passim. Rawlins also briefly mentions Woolcomb (pp. 86–87, 215).

5. Ray, *Age of Wisdom*, p. 316 and p. 484 n. 11; Joseph E. Baker, "Thackeray's Recantation," *PMLA* 77 (1962): 586–94; reprinted as *"The Adventures of Philip"* in *Thackeray: A Collection of Critical Essays*, ed. Welsh, pp. 174–75.

6. John Sutherland, "Thackeray as Victorian Racialist," pp. 442, 444.

7. Ray, *Age of Wisdom,* p. 484 n. 11.

8. For example, see "Concerning Free British Negros" [*sic*], pp. 114–26, and [Thomas Carlyle], "Occasional Discourse on the Negro Question," pp. 670–79. See also Lorimer, *Colour, Class and the Victorians,* p. 123, and Davis, *Slavery and Human Progress,* pp. 220–21 and 226.

9. Lorimer, pp. 162–63.

10. Lorimer, p. 164. See also Ephraim Douglass Adams, *Great Britain and the American Civil War* (1925; rpt., New York: Russell & Russell, [1958?]), 2:88–90.

11. [Henry Adams], *The Education of Henry Adams,* introd. D. W. Brogan (Boston: Houghton Mifflin, 1961), pp. 114–15. See also Ephraim Douglass Adams, *Great Britain and the American Civil War,* 1:68–69, and Davis, *Slavery and Human Progress,* pp. 246–47.

12. Lorimer, p. 163.

13. Davis, *Slavery and Human Progress,* p. 245.

14. *Age of Wisdom,* p. 319. For Sally's last letter to Thackeray, 5 April 1862, see *Age of Wisdom,* pp. 317–19.

15. *Education of Henry Adams,* p. 131. See also Arnold Whitridge's remarks about the influence of Thackeray's feelings about Sally Baxter on his attitude toward the Confederacy ("Dickens and Thackeray in America," *The New York Historical Society Quarterly* 62 [1978]: 234–36.

16. *Education of Henry Adams,* pp. 130–31.

17. See *Letters* 3:229, to Albany Fonblanque, 4 March 1853 (quoted more extensively in chapter 6 herein), as well as *Letters* 3:235, 236 to Harriet Thackeray, 11 March 1853 (also quoted in chapter 6 and chapter 6, n. 23).

18. Writing in 1864, William Bradford Reed asserted about Thackeray: "More than any Englishman of letters I have ever known, he was free from that sentimental disease of 'Abolitionism'. . . . He had been in the South, and met Southern ladies and gentlemen, the highest types of American civilisation. This I may say now in their hour of suffering and possible disaster" (*Haud Immemor;* reprinted as "His Simple Naturalness" in *Thackeray: Interviews and Recollections,* ed. Collins, 1:191. (See also ch. 7, n. 2 herein, for a further quotation from this passage by Reed, in connection with *The Virginians.*) Collins notes that "Reed's strong views" concerning abolitionism "ruined his career, after the victory of the North" (1:191). In his comments about Thackeray, Reed seems to have misconstrued Thackeray's careful efforts to deal open-mindedly with the subject of slavery as support for Reed's own proslavery stand.

19. *Letters* 4:172, to George Smith, 23 January 1860.

20. A similar approach-avoidance conflict concerning the topic of slavery is evident in Thackeray's "On Two Roundabout Papers which I Intended to

Write" (September 1861), where Thackeray again raises the idea of slavery only to replace it with a less controversial subject—in this case, a fantasy about gorillas (17:532–36). Moreover, on this occasion, Thackeray deals with the subject of slavery in an even more oblique way than in "A Mississippi Bubble." What he presents in this September 1861 essay about a slave-trading expedition resulting in an adventure with gorillas is explicitly described as no more than musing for a nonexistent Roundabout paper (although his musings on this and on another undeveloped subject constitute a Roundabout paper in themselves). While Thackeray plainly does not wish to deal at length with the topic of slavery at this point, it is also plainly one that he is not completely able to leave alone.

21. Wilson 2:45–56.

22. Davis, *Slavery and Human Progress,* p. 250.

23. Baker, pp. 161–77, see especially p. 176.

24. Lorimer, pp. 47–50; Frederick Douglass, *My Bondage and My Freedom* (1855; rpt., New York: Arno, 1968), pp. 370–73. According to Lorimer, "Undoubtedly the violent racism of nineteenth-century America, in both North and South, led these black visitors to interpret the absence of institutionalized discrimination in Britain as a lack of racial antipathy among the British" (p. 47). See also Harriet Jacobs [Linda Brent], *Incidents in the Life of a Slave Girl* (Boston, 1861), reprinted in *The Classic Slave Narratives,* ed. Henry Louis Gates, Jr. (New York: NAL Penguin, 1987), pp. 497–98.

25. Lorimer, p. 13. When the Rev. Samuel Ringgold Ward travelled to Liverpool on the British steamer *Europa* in 1853, he was informed that, as a black passenger, he was expected to eat his meals in his stateroom, rather than at the customary common table, to avoid offending white American passengers. According to Ward, Thackeray was also a passenger on the *Europa* at this time, but unlike the American voyagers who kept aloof from this black antislavery lecturer and in contrast to the rigidity of the British steamship official who ordered Ward's segregation, Thackeray visited Ward daily in his stateroom (*Autobiography of a Fugitive Negro* [1855; rpt. New York: Arno, 1968], pp. 228–36).

26. See Davis, *Slavery and Human Progress,* pp. 219–26, as well as Lorimer, p. 123.

27. Davis, *Slavery and Human Progress,* p. 249.

28. For a discussion of this Christmas number and its connection with the Cawnpore uprising, see William Oddie, "Dickens and the Indian Mutiny," *Dickensian* 68 (1972), 3–15. See also my *Dickens and the Short Story,* pp. 88–89.

29. Lorimer, pp. 137–39. See also Bolt, *Victorian Attitudes to Race,* pp. 1–28. Charles Darwin's *On the Origin of Species by Means of Natural Selection* was published in 1859. (His *Descent of Man* appeared in 1871, eight years after Thackeray's death.) Lorimer observes that "Ultimately Darwin solved the problems of the monogenesis-polygenesis argument simply by making them irrelevant. His theory of evolution greatly extended the time scheme in which the life processes operated, and thereby allowed for the development of the

diverse types of men from a common origin" (p. 142). However, the scientific racists remained committed to the idea of black inferiority. Hence (despite finding his theories "singularly unhelpful" [p. 145]), they adapted Darwin's concept of evolution—along with his idea of natural selection—to support their own belief in Anglo-Saxon superiority (pp. 144–46).

30. Davis, *Slavery and Human Progress*, p. 277.

31. Lorimer, p. 203.

32. Lorimer, pp. 203–4.

33. Arendt, *The Origins of Totalitarianism*, 2d ed., pp. 180–82.

34. Lorimer, pp. 92, 202–3.

35. Lorimer, p. 113.

36. Peters, *Thackeray's Universe: Shifting Worlds of Imagination and Reality*, p. 262.

37. Sutherland, "Thackeray as Victorian Racialist," p. 444.

38. In this context, Sutherland contrasts Thackeray's late-in-life thinking on the subject of race with that of Dickens (p. 442). In fact, however, despite the improvement in his sensitivity toward the feelings of Jewish readers between *Oliver Twist* and *Our Mutual Friend*, Dickens's view of blacks had significantly hardened by the end of his career. See Adrian, "Dickens on American Slavery: A Carlylean Slant," pp. 328–29, as well as Ford, "The Governor Eyre Case in England," pp. 226–28.

39. *The Morning Herald*, 23 November 1865, 4a–b. Sutherland uses Thackeray's changing treatment of this slogan to illustrate the increasing rigidity of Thackeray's racial views. The *Morning Herald*'s observation makes clear that Thackeray's changing attitude toward the well-known slogan was part of a general Victorian trend.

40. Ray, *Age of Wisdom*, p. 375; Lorimer, p. 203.

41. Ray, *Uses of Adversity*, p. 215.

42. Baker, pp. 171, 176.

43. Lionel Stevenson, "William Makepeace Thackeray," in *Victorian Fiction: A Guide to Research*, ed. Lionel Stevenson (1964; rpt., New York: Modern Language Association, 1980), p. 176; Rawlins, pp. 224–25; Baker, p. 171, see also p. 177. Thackeray's emphasis in *Philip* on the principle of friendship in a world where all else seems uncertain can be seen as analogous to Matthew Arnold's famous appeal "Ah, love, let us be true / To one another!" against the background of the "darkling plain" envisioned at the end of "Dover Beach."

44. Lionel Stevenson, "The Relativity of Truth in Victorian Fiction," in *Victorian Essays: A Symposium*, ed. Warren D. Anderson and Thomas D. Clareson ([Kent, OH]: Kent State University Press, 1967), pp. 71–86. See also Stevenson's concluding remark in his 1964 survey of scholarship about a signif-

icant desideratum in Thackeray studies: "Most necessary of all . . . is a perceptive analysis of Thackeray's multiple levels of irony, his double perspective and his elusive changes of tone, with all their implications about the relativity of truth" (*Victorian Fiction: A Guide to Research*, p. 187).

Elsewhere, Stevenson has suggested the relevance to *Philip* of this concept of "the relativity of truth" but has not specifically analyzed the novel in terms of the idea. At the end of an essay on "Thackeray's Dramatic Monologues," after quoting a passage from *Philip* in which Pendennis, the narrator, observes that another narrator might see things entirely differently, Stevenson remarks, "With due allowance for the difference between the condensation of poetry and the expansiveness of the novel, it can be claimed that Browning and Thackeray introduced a new method that rendered their two media responsive to the subtleties and ironies of experience, to the complexities of individual psychology, and to the recognition of the relativity of truth that were coming to dominate the modern mind" (in *From Smollett to James,* ed. Mintz, Chandler, and Mulvey, p. 156). However, Stevenson does not pursue the subject further in terms of *The Adventures of Philip.*

45. For brief remarks about Thackeray's awareness of the subjectivity of individual points of view in the *Yellowplush Papers* and *Barry Lyndon,* see Stevenson, "The Relativity of Truth in Victorian Fiction," p. 80. On Thackeray's fundamental commitment to truth in his writing, for example, see Geoffrey Tillotson, *Thackeray the Novelist,* pp. 206, 209; Ray, *Uses of Adversity,* p. 227; and Ferris, *William Makepeace Thackeray,* p. 121.

46. Ina Ferris approaches this question of what is truth in *Philip* in one of her remarks about the narrative technique of this novel in *William Makepeace Thackeray,* quoted later in my text in this chapter and cited below in note 60. However, Ferris focuses on the way in which Thackeray's "increased skepticism about the adequacy of conventional plot to discover or express what matters . . . generates significant experiments with fictional form" (p. 112). My treatment of the novel is indebted to the insights of Stevenson and Ferris. The purpose of my present discussion is to extend these insights into an analysis of the theme of the relativity of truth in *Philip* as a whole.

47. The installment of *Philip* containing this passage originally appeared in the October 1861 issue of the *Cornhill Magazine.* The reference to hulks and convicts suggests a possible mocking allusion on Thackeray's part to Dickens's *Great Expectations* (serialized in *All the Year Round* from 1 December 1860 to 3 August 1861). Thackeray was undoubtedly aware that Dickens had played the leading role of Lord Wilmot in numerous, well-attended performances of *Not So Bad as We Seem* in 1851–52 to benefit the Guild of Art and Literature—a project designed by Dickens and Bulwer-Lytton to aid impoverished writers and artists. Thackeray strongly opposed the Guild, which he felt was demeaning to the literary profession. See Edgar Johnson, *Charles Dickens: His Tragedy and Triumph* (New York: Simon and Schuster, 1952), 2:723–24, 727–30, 732–39, and Ray, *Age of Wisdom,* pp. 151–53.

48. Barbara Hardy also discusses this description of the Twysden dinners in *The Exposure of Luxury,* pp. 122–23.

49. McMaster, "Funeral Baked Meats," p. 134.

50. Colby, *Thackeray's Canvass of Humanity,* p. 440.

51. Rawlins, pp. 222–23; see also Baker, pp. 161–63.

52. At the conclusion of the novel, Caroline's groundless conviction "that Philip was her own child" (16:647) is emphasized. The end of the book also reveals her perhaps well-grounded and covertly held belief—all along—that her marriage to Philip's father was valid. The conclusion thus suggests the self-sacrifice with which she has previously concealed her opinion regarding her marital status for Philip's sake. Stressing at least one misconception (Caroline's erroneous belief that Philip is her son), the ending only underscores the power of delusion in this novel to infect an otherwise clear-thinking mind.

53. Ferris, *William Makepeace Thackeray,* p. 108; Saintsbury, introd., *Works* 16:xi.

54. See *Letters* 1:clxiv n. 153, as well as—for example—Ray, *Uses of Adversity,* pp. 186, 219; Ray, *Age of Wisdom,* pp. 387–88; and Colby, p. 444. See also McMaster's interesting variation on this idea of the biographical dimensions of *Philip* with the suggestion "that Pen is Thackeray the Older, looking at Philip, who is Thackeray the Younger" ("Funeral Baked Meats," p. 151).

55. On Thackeray's indecisiveness, see J. Y. T. Greig, *Thackeray: A Reconsideration,* pp. 1–6 (ch. 1, "The Indecisive Thackeray"); Geoffrey Tillotson, *Thackeray the Novelist,* p. 240; and Ray, *Age of Wisdom,* p. 123.

56. Geoffrey Tillotson observes that this tendency toward "humours" is implicit in Thackeray's concept of character (*Thackeray the Novelist,* p. 155). In the case of Philip, the tendency seems carried to an extreme.

57. Rawlins, p. 221. See also Baker, pp. 166–67.

58. According to David Masson, "It is Thackeray's aim to represent life as it is actually and historically—men and women, as they are, in those situations in which they are usually placed, with that mixture of good and evil and of strength and foible which is to be found in their characters, and liable only to those incidents which are of ordinary occurrence" (*British Novelists and Their Styles* [Cambridge, 1859]; reprinted as "Dickens and Thackeray," in *The Dickens Critics,* ed. George H. Ford and Lauriat Lane, Jr. [Ithaca: Cornell University Press, 1961], pp. 34–35).

59. Geoffrey Tillotson, *Thackeray the Novelist,* pp. 151–52.

60. On Pendennis as narrator, see Ferris, *William Makepeace Thackeray,* pp. 115, 112. See also Ferris, "Narrative Strategy in Thackeray's *The Adventures of Philip,* pp. 448–56, and Juliet McMaster, "Funeral Baked Meats," pp. 149–53. My reading of the role of Pendennis in *Philip* is indebted to these useful, more detailed analyses of the narrative technique of this book.

Ferris calls attention to Pendennis's "fallibility" (*William Makepeace Thackeray,* p. 115; see also p. 121). However, she indicates that this narrator's chronic tendency to undercut himself is part of Thackeray's narrative strategy in *Philip* and does not mean that Pendennis himself is actually unreliable as a narrator: "This is not to suggest that Pen is unreliable but to stress the extent to which Thackeray works to keep the reader aware of the personal, and therefore limited, perspective disguised by the authoritative narrative voice common to Victorian novels" (*William Makepeace Thackeray*, p. 116). Other critics often view Pendennis in this novel as a spokesman for Thackeray himself. For example, see Baker, p. 165, and Juliet McMaster, "Funeral Baked Meats," pp. 150–51. Certainly, there is a strong autobiographical component to Pendennis in *Philip*, and certainly, many of his remarks in this novel are ones that Thackeray would endorse. Nevertheless—as I argue in my text—by allowing Pendennis to withhold vital information despite his professions of candor, Thackeray suggests that Pendennis is not so completely dependable in his role as narrator as he appears.

61. Hardy, *The Exposure of Luxury*, pp. 18–19.

62. Lorimer, p. 11. Edgar Harden refers to Woolcomb as Philip's "dusky opposite," although Harden does not elaborate on this point (*The Emergence of Thackeray's Serial Fiction*, p. 278).

63. In practice, somewhat inconsistently, Thackeray seems to have assumed that a true gentleman would also be well educated and well spoken. However, while a good education and the ability to speak what educated Englishmen viewed as correct English were necessary conditions, they were not in themselves sufficient conditions for gentle status in Thackeray's mind.

In chapter 2 of "A Shabby Genteel Story," the narrator remarks concerning George Brandon (the earlier incarnation of *Philip*'s Dr. Firmin): "I should like to know how many such scoundrels our universities have turned out; and how much ruin has been caused by that accursed system, which is called in England 'the education of a gentleman' " (10:299). Later, in chapter 38 of *Philip*, in his depiction of the contemptible Tufton Hunt—who boozily bases his claim to be a gentleman on the grounds that he is "a university man" (16:574) who has studied Greek and Latin—Thackeray mocks the idea that education alone can make a gentleman.

In contending that Philip fails to fit Thackeray's definition of a gentleman as given in chapter 2 of *The Book of Snobs* (9:270), Baker misses the point that a crucial ingredient in this view of the gentleman according to Thackeray (as articulated both in *The Book of Snobs* and later in the lecture on George IV) is honesty—the quality which is Philip's ruling characteristic (see Baker, pp. 163–64).

64. Geoffrey Tillotson, *Thackeray the Novelist*, p. 86.

65. For complaints about the twist of the plot that brings a fortune to Philip, see Dodds, *Thackeray: A Critical Portrait*, p. 222, and Rawlins, pp. 86–87, 216–17. Despite its aura of implausibility, the climactic discovery of the will in *Philip* was apparently based on an actual occurrence with which Thackeray was familiar; see Anne Thackeray Ritchie, introd., *The Adventures of Philip*, reprinted in *The Two Thackerays*, 2:528.

66. Thackeray himself was not satisfied with the conclusion of *Philip*. He called it "rather a lame ending" (*Letters* 4:270, to Mrs. Carmichael-Smyth, 5 July 1862).

CHAPTER 9

1. Edmund Burke, *Conciliation with the Colonies,* ed. Archibald Freeman and Arthur W. Leonard ([Boston]: Houghton Mifflin, 1943), p. 118. (This speech by Burke is sometimes known as *Speech on Conciliation with America.*)

2. *Letters* 1:182, to Mrs. Carmichael-Smyth, 14–16 January 1832.

3. *Letters* 3:354, to Percival Leigh, 8 March 1854.

4. William Bradford Reed, *Haud Immemor,* quoted in *Letters* 4:137 n. 21.

5. See the "Notes" on *Denis Duval* by Frederick Greenwood (originally published in the *Cornhill Magazine* for June 1864), in *Works* 17:340.

6. Geoffrey Tillotson, *Thackeray the Novelist,* p. 62.

7. M. H. Abrams, *Natural Supernaturalism: Tradition and Revolution in Romantic Literature* (New York: Norton, 1971), pp. 356–57.

8. Bayard Taylor, "William Makepeace Thackeray," *Atlantic Monthly* 13 (1864): 373.

9. *Proceedings of the General Anti-Slavery Convention, Called by the Committee of the British and Foreign Anti-Slavery Society, and Held in London from Tuesday, June 13th, to Tuesday, June 20th, 1843* (London: John Snow, [1843]).

10. Ray, *Uses of Adversity,* p. 202.

11. Ibid., p. 275.

12. Davis, *Slavery and Human Progress,* p. 226. See also [Thomas Carlyle], "Occasional Discourse on the Negro Question," pp. 670–79, as well as Lorimer, *Colour, Class and the Victorians,* p. 123, and Davis, *Slavery and Human Progress,* pp. 219–26.

13. See Lorimer, p. 120, and C. Duncan Rice, "Literary Sources and the Revolution in British Attitudes to Slavery," in *Anti-Slavery, Religion, and Reform,* ed. Bolt and Drescher, p. 331. Dickens's *Bleak House* appeared in 1852–53.

14. Davis, *Slavery and Human Progress,* p. 277, and Lorimer, pp. 47–50, 68.

15. Ray, *Age of Wisdom,* p. 364.

16. On the idea that the topic of slavery had two sides, see the *Times* for 13 December 1850, p. 4, cols. 3–4 (quoted in ch. 4, n. 13 herein). On the feeling that it was hypocritical to criticize slavery in America while ignoring social evils at home, see the editorial for 30 March 1853, p. 4, cols. 4–6, where the *Times* compared overworked seamstresses to American slaves and urged the women who signed the Stafford House Address (discussed in ch. 6 herein) to try to do something to reduce the working hours of such seamstresses to twelve hours per day. According to the *Times,* during the season when the demand for their services was greatest, the seamstresses were often forced to work nearly twenty hours per day, making clothes for women of fashion. For an example of the *Times*'s racist assumptions in 1863, see its remark in an editorial of 15 January (in the context of a negative response to Lincoln's Emancipation Proclamation, which the *Times* contended would provoke a slave

uprising): "If the blacks are to obtain the freedom he [Lincoln] promises them, it must be by their own hands. They must rise upon a more numerous, more intelligent, better armed, and braver community of whites, and exterminate them, their wives, and children, by fire and sword" (p. 8, col. 3).

A useful recent analysis of the *Times*'s comments about America from 1850 to the early years of the American Civil War is provided by Martin Crawford in *The Anglo-American Crisis of the Mid-Nineteenth Century: "The Times" and America, 1850–1862* (Athens: University of Georgia Press, 1987). In particular, see ch. 2, pp. 15–35 ("Editors and Journalists") and pp. 54–61, 63–64, 82–83, 124–26, et passim (on slavery, which the *Times* condemned but which it viewed as a complex social problem not to be solved by immediate abolition and best left to its gradual demise as part of the inevitable progress of mankind). After the outbreak of hostilities in 1861, as Crawford observes, the *Times*—like many people in Great Britain at this point—combined repudiation of slavery with sympathy for the Confederacy (p. 126).

Selected Bibliography

The following works have been especially useful in contributing to my thinking about Thackeray and slavery. For reasons of economy, all other works employed in this study—including reviews, newspapers, and letters by or to persons other than Thackeray—are cited only in the notes.

Abrams, M. H. *Natural Supernaturalism: Tradition and Revolution in Romantic Literature.* New York: Norton, 1971.

Adams, Ephraim Douglass. *Great Britain and the American Civil War.* 2 vols. 1925. Reprint (2 vols. in 1). New York: Russell & Russell, [1958?].

Adams, Henry. *The Education of Henry Adams.* Introd. D. W. Brogan. Boston: Houghton Mifflin, 1961.

Adrian, Arthur A. "Dickens on American Slavery: A Carlylean Slant." *PMLA* 67 (1952): 315–29.

Allen, William, and T. R. H. Thomson. *A Narrative of the Expedition Sent by Her Majesty's Government to the River Niger, in 1841.* London: Richard Bentley, 1848.

Alter, Robert. *Rogue's Progress: Studies in the Picaresque Novel.* Cambridge: Harvard University Press, 1964.

Altick, Richard D. *The Shows of London.* Cambridge: Belknap-Harvard University Press, 1978.

Anstey, Roger. "The Pattern of British Abolitionism in the Eighteenth and Nineteenth Centuries." In *Anti-Slavery, Religion, and Reform: Essays in Memory of Roger Anstey,* ed. Christine Bolt and Seymour Drescher. Folkestone, Eng.: Dawson; Hamden, CT: Archon, 1980.

Arendt, Hannah. *The Origins of Totalitarianism.* 2d ed. Cleveland: World, 1958.

Baker, Joseph E. "Thackeray's Recantation." *PMLA* 77 (1962): 586–94. Reprinted as *"The Adventures of Philip." Thackeray: A Collection of Critical Essays,* ed. Alexander Welsh. Englewood Cliffs, NJ: Prentice-Hall, 1968.

Besant, Walter. *The Queen's Reign.* London: Werner, 1897.

Bledsoe, Robert. *"Pendennis* and the Power of Sentimentality: A Study of Motherly Love." *PMLA* 91 (1976): 871–83.

Bolt, Christine. *Victorian Attitudes to Race.* London: Routledge & Kegan Paul, 1971.

Boswell, James. *Boswell's Life of Johnson, together with Boswell's Journal of a Tour to the Hebrides and Johnson's Diary of a Journal into North Wales.* Ed. George Birkbeck Hill. Rev. and enlarged by L. F. Powell. 6 vols. Oxford: Clarendon, 1934–64.

Brantlinger, Patrick. *Rule of Darkness: British Literature and Imperialism, 1830–1914.* Ithaca: Cornell University Press, 1988.

Bryant, Hallman B. "The African Genesis of Tennyson's 'Timbuctoo.' " *Tennyson Research Bulletin* 3, no. 5 (1981): 196–202.

Burton, Anthony. *Josiah Wedgwood: A Biography.* New York: Stein and Day, 1976.

Carey, John. *Thackeray: Prodigal Genius.* London: Faber & Faber, 1977.

[Carlyle, Thomas.] "Occasional Discourse on the Negro Question." *Fraser's Magazine* 40 (1849): 670–79.

Chew, Samuel C., and Richard D. Altick. *A Literary History of England.* Ed. Albert C. Baugh. 2d ed. New York: Appleton-Century-Crofts, 1967.

Colby, Robert A. *Fiction with a Purpose: Major and Minor Nineteenth-Century Novels.* Bloomington: Indiana University Press, 1967.

———. "William Makepeace Thackeray." In *Victorian Fiction: A Second Guide to Research,* ed. George H. Ford. New York: Modern Language Association, 1978.

———. *Thackeray's Canvass of Humanity: An Author and His Public.* Columbus: Ohio State University Press, 1979.

"Concerning Free British Negros" [*sic*]. *Fraser's Magazine* 47 (1853): 114–26.

Cowherd, Raymond G. *The Politics of English Dissent: The Religious Aspects of Liberal and Humanitarian Reform Movements from 1815 to 1848.* New York: New York University Press, 1956.

Crawford, Martin. *The Anglo-American Crisis of the Mid-Nineteenth Century: "The Times" and America, 1850–1862.* Athens: University of Georgia Press, 1987.

Crowe, Eyre. *With Thackeray in America.* New York: Charles Scribner's Sons, 1893.

Davies, Phillips George. "The Miscegenation Theme in the Works of Thackeray." *MLN* 76 (1961): 326–31.

Davis, David Brion. *The Problem of Slavery in Western Culture.* Ithaca: Cornell University Press, 1966.

———. *The Problem of Slavery in the Age of Revolution 1770–1823.* Ithaca: Cornell University Press, 1975.

———. *Slavery and Human Progress.* New York: Oxford University Press, 1984.

Day, Aidan. "The Spirit of Fable: Arthur Hallam and Romantic Values in Tennyson's 'Timbuctoo.' " *Tennyson Research Bulletin* 4, no. 2 (1983): 59–71.

DiBattista, Maria. "The Triumph of Clytemnestra: The Charades in *Vanity Fair.*" *PMLA* 95 (1980): 827–37.

Dodds, John W. *Thackeray: A Critical Portrait.* New York: Oxford University Press, 1941.

Douglass, Frederick. *My Bondage and My Freedom.* 1855. Reprint. New York: Arno, 1968.

Drescher, Seymour. "Public Opinion and the Destruction of British Colonial Slavery." In *Slavery and British Society, 1776–1846,* ed. James Walvin. Baton Rouge: Louisiana State University Press, 1982.

Edwards, Paul, and James Walvin. *Black Personalities in the Era of the Slave Trade.* Baton Rouge: Louisiana State University Press, 1983.

Emerson, Ralph Waldo. *Journals of Ralph Waldo Emerson.* Ed. Edward Waldo Emerson and Waldo Emerson Forbes. 10 vols. Boston: Houghton Mifflin, 1904–14.

An Epitome of Anti-Slavery Information: Or a Condensed View of Slavery and the Slave-Trade. London: T. Ward, 1842.

Ferris, Ina. "Narrative Strategy in Thackeray's *The Adventures of Philip.*" *English Studies in Canada* 5 (1979): 448–56.

—————. *William Makepeace Thackeray.* Boston: Twayne, 1983.

Flexner, James Thomas. *George Washington: Anguish and Farewell (1793–1799).* Boston: Little, Brown, [1972].

Fogel, Robert William, and Stanley L. Engerman. *Time on the Cross: The Economics of American Negro Slavery.* Boston: Little, Brown, 1974.

Foot, Jesse. *The Lives of Andrew Robinson Bowes, Esq., and the Countess of Strathmore, Written from Thirty-Three Years Professional Attendance, from Letters, and Other Well Authenticated Documents.* London: Becket and Porter; and Sherwood, Neely, and Jones, [1810?].

Ford, George H. "The Governor Eyre Case in England." *University of Toronto Quarterly* 17 (1948): 219–33.

Foucault, Michel. *Discipline and Punish: The Birth of the Prison.* Trans. Alan Sheridan. New York: Vintage-Random House, 1979. Originally published as *Surveiller et Punir; Naissance de la prison* (Paris: Editions Gallimard, 1975).

Genovese, Eugene D. *Roll, Jordan, Roll: The World the Slaves Made.* 1974. Reprint. New York: Vintage-Random, 1976.

Gilman, Sander L. *Sexuality: An Illustrated History, Representing the Sexual in Medicine and Culture from the Middle Ages to the Age of AIDS.* New York: Wiley, 1989.

Gneiting, Teona Tone. "The Pencil's Role in *Vanity Fair.*" *Huntington Library Quarterly* 39 (1976): 171–202.

Green, William A. *British Slave Emancipation: The Sugar Colonies and the Great Experiment 1830–1865.* Oxford: Clarendon, 1976.

Greig, J. Y. T. *Thackeray: A Reconsideration.* 1950. Reprint. [Hamden, CT]: Archon, 1967.

Grier, R. M. *John Allen.* London: Rivingtons, 1889.

Gulliver, Harold Strong. *Thackeray's Literary Apprenticeship.* Valdosta, Georgia: Southern Stationery and Printing Company, 1934.

Hallam, Arthur Henry. *The Poems of Arthur Henry Hallam together with His Essay on the Lyrical Poems of Alfred Tennyson.* Ed. Richard Le Gallienne. 1893. Reprint. New York: AMS Press, 1973.

Harden, Edgar F. "The Fields of Mars in *Vanity Fair.*" *Tennessee Studies in Literature* 10 (1965), 123–32.

—————. *The Emergence of Thackeray's Serial Fiction.* Athens: University of Georgia Press, 1979.

—————. *Thackeray's "English Humourists" and "Four Georges."* Newark: University of Delaware Press, 1985.

—————, ed. *Annotations for the Selected Works of William Makepeace Thackeray: The Complete Novels, the Major Non-Fictional Prose, and Selected Shorter Pieces.* 2 vols. New York: Garland, 1990.

Hardy, Barbara. *The Exposure of Luxury: Radical Themes in Thackeray.* [Pittsburgh]: University of Pittsburgh Press, 1972.

Harvey, J. R. *Victorian Novelists and Their Illustrators.* London: Sidgwick & Jackson, 1970.

Hawari, Rida. "Thackeray's Oriental Reading." *Revue de Littérature Comparée* 48 (1974): 114–27.

Hodder, Edwin. *The Life and Work of the Seventh Earl of Shaftesbury.* London: Cassell & Company, 1886.

Houghton, Walter E. *The Victorian Frame of Mind, 1830–1870.* New Haven: Yale University Press, 1957.

Howitt, Mary. *Mary Howitt: An Autobiography.* Ed. Margaret Howitt. London: William Isbister, 1889.

Jacobs, Harriet [Linda Brent, pseud.]. *Incidents in the Life of a Slave Girl.* Boston, 1861. Reprinted in *The Classic Slave Narratives,* ed. Henry Louis Gates, Jr. New York: NAL Penguin, 1987.

James, Henry. Preface to *The Tragic Muse.* In *The Art of the Novel: Critical Prefaces by Henry James.* Introd. Richard P. Blackmur. New York: Charles Scribner's Sons, 1934.

Johnson, Edgar. *Charles Dickens: His Tragedy and Triumph.* 2 vols. New York: Simon and Schuster, 1952.

Johnson, Louise H. "The Source of the Chapter on Slavery in Dickens's *American Notes.*" *American Literature* 14 (1943): 427–30.

Kabbani, Rana. *Europe's Myths of Orient.* Bloomington: Indiana University Press, 1986.

Klingberg, Frank J. *The Anti-Slavery Movement in England: A Study in English Humanitarianism.* 1926. Reprint. Hamden, CT: Archon, 1968.

Knoepflmacher, U. C. *Laughter and Despair: Readings in Ten Novels of the Victorian Era.* Berkeley and Los Angeles: University of California Press, 1971.

Knutsford, [Margaret Jean Trevelyan Holland], Viscountess. *Life and Letters of Zachary Macaulay.* London: Edward Arnold, 1900. Ann Arbor, MI: Published on demand by University Microfilms, 1973.

Lester, John A., Jr. "Thackeray's Narrative Technique." *PMLA* (1954). Reprinted in *Victorian Literature: Selected Essays,* ed. Robert O. Preyer. 1966. Reprint. New York: Harper & Row, 1967.

Levine, George. *The Realistic Imagination: English Fiction from Frankenstein to Lady Chatterley.* Chicago: University of Chicago Press, 1981.

Loofbourow, John. *Thackeray and the Form of Fiction.* Princeton: Princeton University Press, 1964.

Lorimer, Douglas A. *Colour, Class and the Victorians: English Attitudes to the Negro in the Mid-Nineteenth Century.* [Leicester, Eng.]: Leicester University Press, 1978.

Lougy, Robert E. "Vision and Satire: The Warped Looking Glass in *Vanity Fair.*" *PMLA* 90 (1975): 256–69.

Lund, Michael. *Reading Thackeray.* Detroit: Wayne State University Press, 1988.

McMaster, Juliet. *Thackeray: The Major Novels.* 1971. Reprint. Toronto: University of Toronto Press, 1976.

————. "Thackeray's Things: Time's Local Habitation." In *The Victorian Experience: The Novelists,* ed. Richard A. Levine. [Athens]: Ohio University Press, 1976.

————. "Funeral Baked Meats: Thackeray's Last Novel." *Studies in the Novel* 13 (1981): 133–55.

McMaster, R. D. *Thackeray's Cultural Frame of Reference: Allusion in "The Newcomes."* Montreal & Kingston: McGill-Queen's University Press, 1991.

Manning, Sylvia. "Incest and the Structure of *Henry Esmond.*" *Nineteenth-Century Fiction* 34 (September 1979): 194–213.

Marcus, Steven. *The Other Victorians: A Study of Sexuality and Pornography in Mid-Nineteenth-Century England.* 1966. Reprint, with new introd. by author. New York: Meridian-NAL, 1974.

Masson, David. From *British Novelists and Their Styles.* Cambridge, Eng., 1859. Reprinted as "Dickens and Thackeray." *The Dickens Critics,* ed. George H. Ford and Lauriat Lane, Jr. Ithaca: Cornell University Press, 1961.

Mathieson, William Law. *British Slavery and Its Abolition, 1823–1838.* 1926. Reprint. New York: Octagon, 1967.

———. *Great Britain and the Slave Trade, 1839–1865.* 1929. Reprint. New York: Octagon, 1967.

———. *British Slave Emancipation, 1838–1849.* 1932. Reprint. New York: Octagon, 1967.

Mauskopf, Charles. "Thackeray's Concept of the Novel: A Study of Conflict." *Philological Quarterly* 50 (1971): 239–52.

Melville, Lewis [Lewis S. Benjamin]. *William Makepeace Thackeray: A Biography Including Hitherto Uncollected Letters & Speeches & a Bibliography of 1300 Items.* London: John Lane, Bodley Head, 1910.

———. *Some Aspects of Thackeray.* London: Stephen Swift & Co. [1911].

Meteyard, Eliza. *The Life of Josiah Wedgwood.* London: Hurst and Blackett, 1866.

[Mill, John Stuart.] "The Negro Question." *Fraser's Magazine* 41 (1850): 25–31.

Miller, J. Hillis. *The Form of Victorian Fiction: Thackeray, Dickens, Trollope, George Eliot, Meredith, and Hardy.* Notre Dame, IN: University of Notre Dame Press, 1968.

———. *Fiction and Repetition: Seven English Novels.* Cambridge: Harvard University Press, 1982.

Miller, Joseph C. "Imbangala Lineage Slavery." In *Slavery in Africa: Historical and Anthropological Perspectives,* ed. Suzanne Miers and Igor Kopytoff. Madison: University of Wisconsin Press, 1977.

Minutes of the Proceedings of the General Anti-Slavery Convention, Called by the Committee of the British and Foreign Anti-Slavery Society, Held in London on the 12th of June, 1840, and Continued by Adjournments to the 23rd of the Same Month. London: Johnston & Barrett, 1840.

[Mitchell, John.] "Tableaux of the Most Eminent Soldiers of the Eighteenth Century: Frederick II." *Fraser's Magazine* 23 (1841): 559–74.

Nightingale, Florence. *Cassandra.* Old Westbury, NY: Feminist Press, 1979.

Norton, Caroline. [*English Laws for Women in the Nineteenth Century,* 1854]. *Caroline Norton's Defense: English Laws for Women in the Nineteenth Century.* Introd. Joan Huddleston. Chicago: Academy Chicago, 1982.

Oddie, William. "Dickens and the Indian Mutiny." *Dickensian* 68 (1972): 3–15.

Olmsted, John Charles. *Thackeray and His Twentieth-Century Critics: An Annotated Bibliograpy 1900–1975.* New York: Garland, 1977.

Paris, Bernard J. *A Psychological Approach to Fiction: Studies in Thackeray, Stendhal, George Eliot, Dostoevsky, and Conrad.* Bloomington: Indiana University Press, 1974.

Patterson, Orlando. *Slavery and Social Death: A Comparative Study.* Cambridge: Harvard University Press, 1982.

Peters, Catherine. *Thackeray's Universe: Shifting Worlds of Imagination and Reality.* New York: Oxford University Press, 1987.

Pickwoad, Nicholas. "Commentary on Illustrations." In *Vanity Fair,* ed. Peter L. Shillingsburg. New York: Garland, 1991.

Proceedings of the General Anti-Slavery Convention, Called by the Committee of the

British and Foreign Anti-Slavery Society, and Held in London from Tuesday, June 13th, to Tuesday, June 20th, 1843. London: John Snow, [1843].

Rawlins, Jack P. *Thackeray's Novels: A Fiction that Is True.* Berkeley and Los Angeles: University of California Press, 1974.

Ray, Gordon N. *The Buried Life: A Study of the Relation between Thackeray's Fiction and His Personal History.* Cambridge: Harvard University Press, 1952.

―――. *Thackeray: The Uses of Adversity 1811–1846.* New York: McGraw-Hill, 1955.

―――. *Thackeray: The Age of Wisdom 1847–1863.* New York: McGraw-Hill, 1958.

Reed, William Bradford. From *Haud Immemor.* Philadelphia, 1864. Reprinted as "His Simple Naturalness." *Thackeray: Interviews and Recollections,* ed. Philip Collins. 2 vols. New York: St. Martin's, 1983.

Rice, C. Duncan. "Literary Sources and the Revolution in British Attitudes to Slavery." In *Anti-Slavery, Religion, and Reform: Essays in Memory of Roger Anstey,* ed. Christine Bolt and Seymour Drescher. Folkestone, Eng.: Dawson; Hamden, CT: Archon, 1980.

―――. *The Scots Abolitionists 1833–1861.* Baton Rouge: Louisiana State University Press, 1981.

Ritchie, Anne Thackeray. *The Two Thackerays: Anne Thackeray Ritchie's Centenary Biographical Introductions to the Works of William Makepeace Thackeray.* Critical introd. Carol Hanbery MacKay; bibliographical introd. Peter L. Shillingsburg and Julia Maxey. 2 vols. New York: AMS Press, 1988.

Roberts, Helene E. " 'The Sentiment of Reality': Thackeray's Art Criticism." *Studies in the Novel* 13 (1981): 21–39.

Said, Edward W. *Orientalism.* 1978. Reprint. New York: Vintage-Random, 1979.

Saintsbury, George. *East India Slavery.* 1829. Reprint. Shannon, Ireland: Irish University Press, 1972.

Sanders, Andrew. *The Victorian Historical Novel 1840–1880.* New York: St. Martin's, 1979.

Sorensen, Gerald C. "Beginning and Ending: *The Virginians* as a Sequel." *Studies in the Novel* 13 (1981): 109–21.

Steig, Michael. *Dickens and Phiz.* Bloomington: Indiana University Press, 1978.

Stevens, Joan. "Thakeray's 'Vanity Fair.' " *Review of English Literature* 6 (1965): 19–38.

―――. "Thackeray's Pictorial Capitals." *Costerus,* n.s. 2 (1974; special Thackeray volume, ed. Peter L. Shillingsburg): 113–40.

Stevenson, Lionel. *The Showman of Vanity Fair.* New York: Charles Scribner's Sons, 1947.

―――. "William Makepeace Thackeray." In *Victorian Fiction: A Guide to Research,* ed. Lionel Stevenson. 1964. Reprint. New York: Modern Language Association, 1980.

―――. "The Relativity of Truth in Victorian Fiction." In *Victorian Essays: A Symposium,* ed. Warren D. Anderson and Thomas D. Clareson. [Kent, OH]: Kent State University Press, 1967.

―――. "Thackeray's Dramatic Monologues." In *From Smollett to James: Studies in the Novel and Other Essays Presented to Edgar Johnson,* ed. Samuel I. Mintz, Alice Chandler, and Christopher Mulvey. Charlottesville: University Press of Virginia, 1981.

Stonehouse, J. H., ed. *Catalogue of the Library of Charles Dickens from Gadshill, Cat-*

alogue of His Pictures and Objects of Art, Catalogue of the Library of W. M. Thackeray, and Relics from His Library. London: Piccadilly Fountain Press, 1935.

Stowe, Harriet Beecher. *Uncle Tom's Cabin; or Life among the Lowly*. Ed. Ann Douglas. Harmondsworth, Eng.: Penguin, 1981.

Sudrann, Jean. " 'The Philosopher's Property': Thackeray and the Use of Time." *Victorian Studies* 10 (1967): 359–88.

Sutherland, John. "Thackeray as Victorian Racialist." *Essays in Criticism* 20 (1970): 441–45.

————. *Thackeray at Work*. London: Athlone Press, 1974.

Sypher, Wylie. *Guinea's Captive Kings: British Anti-Slavery Literature of the XVIIIth Century*. 1942. Reprint. New York: Octagon, 1969.

Talon, Henri-A. "Time and Memory in Thackeray's *Henry Esmond*." *Review of English Studies*, n.s. 13 (1962): 147–56.

Taylor, Bayard. "William Makepeace Thackeray." *Atlantic Monthly* 13 (1864): 371–79.

Temperly, Howard. *British Antislavery, 1833–1870*. Columbia: University of South Carolina Press, 1972.

Thackeray, William Makepiece. *The New Sketch Book: Being Essays Now First Collected from "The Foreign Quarterly Review."* Ed. Robert S. Garnett. London: Alston Rivers, 1906.

————. *The Oxford Thackeray*. 17 vols. Ed. George Saintsbury. London: Oxford University Press, [1908].

————. *The Letters and Private Papers of William Makepeace Thackeray*. Ed. Gordon N. Ray. 4 vols. Cambridge: Harvard University Press, 1945–46.

————. *Contributions to the "Morning Chronicle."* Ed. Gordon N. Ray. Urbana: University of Illinois Press, 1955.

————. *Vanity Fair: A Novel Without a Hero*. Ed. Geoffrey and Kathleen Tillotson. Boston: Houghton Mifflin, 1963.

————. *The History of Henry Esmond*. Ed. John Sutherland and Michael Greenfield. Harmondsworth, Eng.: Penguin, 1970.

————. *The Luck of Barry Lyndon*. Ed. Martin J. Anisman. New York: New York University Press, 1970.

————. *The History of Pendennis*. Ed. Donald Hawes. Introd. J. I. M. Stewart. Harmondsworth, Eng.: Penguin, 1972.

————. *The Book of Snobs*. Ed. John Sutherland. New York: St. Martin's, 1978.

————. *The History of Henry Esmond*. Ed. Edgar F. Harden. New York: Garland, 1989.

————. *Vanity Fair: A Novel without a Hero*. Ed. Peter L. Shillingsburg. New York: Garland, 1989.

————. *The History of Pendennis*. Ed. Peter L. Shillingsburg. New York: Garland, 1991.

Thomas, Deborah A. *Dickens and the Short Story*. Philadelphia: University of Pennsylvania Press, 1982.

————. "Bondage and Freedom in Thackeray's *Pendennis*." *Studies in the Novel*, 17 (1985): 138–57.

Tilford, John E., Jr. "The Love Theme of *Henry Esmond*." *PMLA* 67 (1952): 684–701. Reprinted in *Thackeray: A Collection of Critical Essays*, ed. Alexander Welsh. Englewood Cliffs, NJ: Prentice-Hall, 1968.

Tillotson, Geoffrey. *Thackeray the Novelist.* Cambridge: Cambridge University Press, 1954.

———, and Donald Hawes, eds. *Thackeray: The Critical Heritage.* London: Routledge & Kegan Paul; New York: Barnes & Noble, 1968.

Tillotson, Kathleen, *Novels of the Eighteen-Forties.* Oxford: Clarendon, 1954.

Todorov, Tzvetan. " 'Race,' Writing, and Culture." Trans. Loulou Mack. In *"Race," Writing, and Difference,* ed. Henry Louis Gates, Jr. Chicago: University of Chicago Press, 1986.

Trollope, Anthony. *Thackeray.* 1887. Reprint. New York: AMS Press, 1968.

Turley, David M. " 'Free Air' and Fugitive Slaves: British Abolitionists versus Government over American Fugitives, 1834–61." In *Anti-Slavery, Religion, and Reform: Essays in Memory of Roger Anstey,* ed. Christine Bolt and Seymour Drescher. Folkestone, Eng.: Dawson; Hamden, CT: Archon, 1980.

Walvin, James. *The Black Presence: A Documentary History of the Negro in England, 1555–1860.* New York: Schocken, 1972.

———. "The Rise of British Popular Sentiment for Abolition, 1787–1832." In *Anti-Slavery, Religion, and Reform: Essays in Memory of Roger Anstey,* ed. Christine Bolt and Seymour Drescher. Folkestone, Eng.: Dawson; Hamden, CT: Archon, 1980.

———. Introd. *Slavery and British Society, 1776–1846,* ed. James Walvin. Baton Rouge: Louisiana State University Press, 1982.

———. "The Propaganda of Anti-Slavery." In *Slavery and British Society, 1776–1846,* ed. James Walvin. Baton Rouge: Louisiana State University Press, 1982.

———. *England, Slaves and Freedom, 1776–1838.* Jackson: University Press of Mississippi, 1986.

Ward, Samuel Ringgold. *Autobiography of a Fugitive Negro.* 1855. Reprint. New York: Arno, 1968.

Welsh, Alexander. *The City of Dickens.* Oxford: Clarendon, 1971.

Wheatley, James H. *Patterns in Thackeray's Fiction.* Cambridge, MA: M.I.T. Press, 1969.

Whitridge, Arnold. "Dickens and Thackeray in America." *The New York Historical Society Quarterly* 62 (1978): 219–37.

Wilson, James Grant. *Thackeray in the United States 1852–3, 1855–6.* 2 vols. 1904. Reprint (2 vols in 1). New York: Dodd, Mead, 1909.

Workman, Gillian. "Thomas Carlyle and the Governor Eyre Controversy: An Account with Some New Material." *Victorian Studies* 18 (1974): 77–102.

Wright, Gordon. *Between the Guillotine and Liberty: Two Centuries of the Crime Problem in France.* New York: Oxford University Press, 1983.

Yellin, Jean Fagan. *Women & Sisters: The Antislavery Feminists in American Culture.* New Haven: Yale University Press, 1989.

Young, G. M. *Victorian Essays.* London: Oxford University Press, 1962.

Index

Abrams, M. H., 190
Adams, Henry, 160–61, 164
Adrian, Arthur A., 222 n.4
"Ali Baba and the Forty Thieves,"
23, 51–52
Allen, Bird, 28–29, 204 n. 24
Allen, Rev. John, 28
American Notes (Dickens), 141, 222
n.4
"Am I Not a Man and a Brother?"
(antislavery slogan), 76–78, 89,
117, 167–68
Andersen, Hans Christian, 177
Anisman, Martin J., 203 n.1
Anne, Queen, 96, 110
Anstey, Roger, 13
apprenticeship in British West
Indies, 5–6, 9, 85, 194, 200 n.19.
See also Slave emancipation, in
British West Indies
Arabian Nights' Entertainments, 23,
51–52, 43–44, 51, 130, 210 n.32
Arendt, Hannah, 12, 167
Arnold, Matthew, xv, 190, 226 n.43

Baker, Joseph E., 158–59, 165,
168–69, 178
Bananier, Le (Soulié), 29–31
Barchester Towers (Trollope), 181
Baxter, Mrs. George, 122
Baxter, Sally (later Mrs. Frank
Hampton), 124, 128–29, 136,
160–61, 164
Becher, Anne, 10
Besant, Walter, 56
Biard, Auguste-François, 24–27, 31,
33, 194
Bible, 15, 93, 105–6, 115, 157, 175,
215 n.16, 215 n.17

Bleak House (Dickens), 22, 29, 49, 78,
127, 194–95
Blechynden, Mrs. Sarah, 11, 202 n.40
Bledsoe, Robert, 92–94
Bowes, Andrew Robinson Stoney,
38–39, 206 n.41
Brantlinger, Patrick, 12, 203 n.9
British and Foreign Anti-Slavery
Society, 72
Brontë, Charlotte, 190
Brookfield, Jane, 97
Brookfield, Rev. William, 97
Brown, John, 118
Browne, Hablot Knight, 77
Browning, Robert, 2, 227 n.44
Bryant, Hallman B., 18
Buller, Arthur, 6
Buller, Charles, 6–7
Bulwer-Lytton, Sir Edward, 128,
171, 227 n.47
Bunyan, John, 84
Burke, Edmond, 188
Butler, Mrs., 11–12
Buxton, Thomas Fowell, 13, 25, 28,
38
Byron, George Gordon, Lord, 42

Caillié, René, 18
Cambridge University, 18
Carey, John, 52, 222 n.16
Carlyle, Thomas, 2, 85, 165, 190,
194, n.14, 222 n.4
Carmichael-Smyth, Anne Becher
Thackeray (mother), 1, 11, 13–15,
116, 122, 188, 190, 201 n.33, 202
n.40, 208 n.13
Carmichael-Smyth, Henry
(stepfather), 8–9, 208 n.13

Carmichael-Smyth, Sir James (brother of Henry), 9
Cassandra (Nightingale), 156
Cervantes, Miguel de, 192
Chaucer, Geoffrey, 98
Civil War (American), xvii, 159–63, 231 n.16
Clarkson, Thomas, 30
Colby, Robert A., 94, 134, 174
Collins, Philip, 224 n.18
Conrad, Joseph, 112
Constitutional, 9
Cornhill Magazine, 158, 161–62, 182, 188–89
Cowper, William, 14
Crawford, Martin, 231 n.16
Crowe, Eyre, 121–23, 138–39, 221 n.62
Cruikshank, George, 12

Darwin, Charles, 225–26 n.29
Davies, Phillips George, 11
Davis, David Brion, 3, 13, 72, 106, 118, 160, 166, 194, 201 n.32, 208 n.15
Delane, John Thaddeus, 2
DiBattista, Maria, 57–58, 61–62, 67, 210 n.23
Dickens, Charles, 29, 118, 126, 141–42, 165, 190, 194, 201 n.33; *American Notes,* 141, 222 n.4; *Bleak House,* 22, 29, 49, 78, 127, 194–95; "George Silverman's Explanation," 216 n.25; *Great Expectations,* 71, 227 n.47; *Hard Times,* 88; *Martin Chuzzlewit,* 141; *Oliver Twist,* 226 n.38; *Our Mutual Friend,* 226 n.38; *Pickwick Papers,* 77–78
Dodds, John W., xvi, 2
Douglas, Ann, 121
Douglass, Frederick, 165–66
"Dover Beach" (Arnold), 226 n.43
Doyle, Richard, 131–32
Drescher, Seymour, 200 n.19
Dunmore, Lord, 146, 148

East India Company, 9
Edinburgh Review, 24, 160
Education of Henry Adams, The, 161

Eliot, George, 72, 211 n.44
Emancipation Proclamation (Lincoln), 159, 230–31 n.16
Empedocles on Etna (Arnold), xv
Engerman, Stanley L., 218 n.22
evangelicalism, 13–15, 190
Examiner, 29, 121
Eyre, Governor, 213 n.14

Ferris, Ina, 112, 156, 176–77, 181, 227 n.46, 228–29 n.60
Fielding, Henry, 171, 192
FitzGerald, Edward, 6, 29, 42, 202 n.40
Fogel, Robert William, 218 n.22
Fonblanque, Albany, 121, 141
Foot, Jesse, 39, 206 n.41
Foreign Quarterly Review, 29
Forster, John, 214 n.1
Foucault, Michel, xvi, 34, 198 n.3
Fraser's Magazine, 20, 24, 27, 32, 85, 158
Frederick II (king of Prussia), 17, 32–33

Genovese, Eugene D., 118–119, 218 n.19, 221 n.60
Gentleman's Magazine, 189
George IV, 182
"George Silverman's Explanation" (Dickens), 216 n.25
Gladstone, William Ewart, 2
Gneiting, Teona Tone, 211 n.40
Goldsmith, Oliver, 192
Great Expectations (Dickens), 71, 227 n.47
Greig, J. Y. T., 15

Hallam, Arthur Henry, 19–20
Hampton, Frank, 160
Hannay, James, 211 n.35
Harden, Edgar F., 52, 214 n.7, 229 n.62
Hard Times (Dickens), 88
Hardy, Barbara, 75, 96, 181–82, 212 n.10, 227 n.48
Hogarth, William, 129
Holland, Sir Henry, 161
Hood, Thomas, 192

Horace, 86–87
Hottentot Venus, 57, 209–10 n.22
Howitt, Mary, 126
Hume, James, 8
Hunt, James, 165

Irving, Washington, 141–42

Johnson, Samuel, 111
Jones, John Paul, 189
Jonson, Ben, 177

Kabbani, Rana, 207 n.8
Keats, John, 2, 123, 199 n.4
Kinglake, A. W., 43
Kipling, Rudyard, 165
Knoepflmacher, U. C., 69
Knox, Robert, 165

Lawrence, D. H., 32
Leigh, Percival, 188
Lever, Charles, 123
Levine, George, 213 n.18
Lewes, George Henry, 2, 16
Lewis, John Frederick, 46–49
Lincoln, Abraham, 159–61, 164,
   230–31 n.16
"Locksley Hall" (Tennyson), 221
   n.61
Longman, Thomas, 24
Loofbourow, John, 101, 108
Lord Jim (Conrad), 112
Lorimer, Douglas A., 159–60,
   165–68, 182, 225 n.24, 225–26 n.29
"Lotus-Eaters, The" (Tennyson), 47
Low, Andrew, 160
Lund, Michael, 216–17 n.1

Macaulay, Thomas Babington, 2, 28
Macaulay, Zachary, 28, 38
McMaster, Juliet, 37, 93, 112, 147,
   172–73
McMaster, R. D., 217 n.4, 221 n.61
Marcus, Steven, 207 n.8
Marriage à la mode (Hogarth), 129
Martin Chuzzlewit (Dickens), 141
Masson, David, 179, 228 n.58
Mathews, Mrs. Charles, 57
Mathieson, William Law, 5–6, 28

Mauskopf, Charles, 123, 142
Melbourne, William Lamb, Lord,
   133–34
Middlemarch (Eliot), 72, 211 n.44
Mill, John Stuart, 60, 85, 190, 213
   n.14
Miller, J. Hillis, 112, 216 n.23
Milnes, Richard Monckton, Lord
   Houghton, 2
Mitchel, John, 163
Molière, 171
Montagu, Mary Wortley, Lady, 42
Morning Chronicle, 2, 24, 31
Morning Herald, 167–68, 226 n.39

Napoleon Bonaparte, 10
National Standard, 8
Newton, John, 14
Niger Expedition, 28–29
Nightingale, Florence, 156
Nineteen Eighty-Four (Orwell), 3, 119
Norton, Caroline, 133–34
Norton, George, 133–34
Not So Bad as We Seem; or, Many Sides
   to a Character (Bulwer-Lytton),
   171, 227 n.47

"Ode: Intimations of Immortality
   from Recollections of Early
   Childhood" (Wordsworth), 86
Oliver Twist (Dickens), 226 n.38
Orwell, George, 3, 119
Othello (Shakespeare), 112–13,
   185–86
Our Mutual Friend (Dickens), 226 n.38

Palmerston, Henry John Temple, 3rd
   Viscount, 2, 126
Paris, Bernard, J., 68, 71
Parker, Theodore, 116
Patterson, Orlando, 100–102, 105,
   214–15 n.9
Peters, Catherine, 167, 201 n.33
Phillips, Samuel, 214 n.1
Pilgrim's Progress, The (Bunyan), 84
Plain Dealer, The (Wycherley), 177
Punch, 46, 55–56, 58–59, 78
Punch's Pocket Book (1847), 45

racism, 12–13, 15, 116, 152, 157, 165–68, 195, 223 n.2
Rawlins, Jack P., 56, 156, 169, 178
Ray, Gordon N., 8, 10–11, 18–19, 24, 121, 128, 168, 193, 196, 204–5 n.25, 219 n.33; on *Henry Esmond,* 96, 97, 214 n.1; on *The Newcomes,* 114; on *Pendennis,* 212 n.2; on *Philip,* 158–59; on *The Virginians,* 221 n.1
Reception, The (Lewis), 46, 48
Reed, William Bradford, 123, 188, 222 n.2, 224 n.18
Rice, C. Duncan, 17, 25, 30
Ridley, James, 108
Ritchie, Lady. *See* Thackeray, Anne
Roberts, Helene E., 25, 27, 204 n.17
Robinson Crusoe (Defoe), 58, 69
"Rocking-Horse Winner, The" (Lawrence), 32
Rubáiyát of Omar Khayyám, The, 42
Russell, John, Lord, 126

Said, Edward W., 3, 41, 52, 199 n.10
Saintsbury, George, 76, 114, 177, 198, 204–5 n.25, 223 n.1
Sanders, Andrew, 98
Scott, Thomas, 14
Seward, William H., 161
Shaftesbury, Anthony Ashley Cooper, 7th Earl of, 126, 128
Shakespeare, William, 84, 112, 171, 185
Sharp, Granville, 13, 204 n.15
Sheridan, Richard Brinsley, 133
Shillingsburg, Peter L., 206 n.2, 212 n.1
slave emancipation: in British West Indies, 5–6, 8, 49, 118, 159, 165, 194, 200 n.19, 219 n.35; by Lincoln's proclamation, 159, 230–31 n.16
Slavers Throwing Overboard the Dead and Dying (Turner), 24–25
slavery: defined, 3, 72, 193; in British India, 9, 201 n.32; in British West Indies, 3, 5–7, 8, 17, 27, 28, 30–31, 38, 54–55, 85, 118, 159; major forms for Thackeray,

xvi, 3–4; in Near East, xv, 3–4, 38, 41–42, 44–46, 116; in Southern United States, xv–xvii, 3, 116–21, 141, 159, 221 n.60
slave trade, 5, 14, 24–27, 28, 49, 85, 149–50
Slave Trade (Scene on the Coast of Africa), The (Biard), 24–28, 194
Smith, George, 161
Smith, Goldwin, 221 n.1
Smollett, Tobias, 192
Snob, The, 18
Somerset, James, 152
Sorensen, Gerald C., 145
Soulié, Frédèric, 29–31
Spartacus, 189
Stafford House Address, 125–28, 130, 136–38, 217 n.4, 220 n.45, 230 n.16
Stanley, Lady, 127
Steele, Richard, 97
Steig, Michael, 77–78
Stevenson, Lionel, 44, 112, 169, 226–27 n.44
Stowe, Harriet Beecher, 121–27, 134, 142, 217 n.4
Strathmore, Countess of, 38
Sturge, Joseph, 13
Sutherland, Duchess of, 126–27
Sutherland, John, 78, 92, 112, 116, 158, 167, 212 n.9, 214 nn.1–2, 221 n.1, 226 nn.38–39
Swift, Jonathan, 107, 109, 189
Sypher, Wylie, 3, 41

Tales of the Genii, The (Ridley), 108
Taylor, Bayard, 164, 191
Temple, Sir William, 107, 109, 189
Tennyson, Alfred, Lord, 2, 18–20, 47, 126, 190, 221 n.61
Thackeray, Anne ("Anny," later Lady Ritchie) (daughter), 6–7, 14, 38, 120, 200 n.20, 213 n.17, 219 n.33
Thackeray, Harriet Marian ("Minny") (daughter), 7, 117, 120, 213 n.17, 218 n.23
Thackeray, Isabella Shawe (wife), 7, 193, 200–201 n.22

Thackeray, Richmond (father), 9–11

Thackeray, William Makepeace: conviction that slavery was wrong, xvi, 15, 27–32, 117, 120–21, 141, 161–62, 164, 190; early childhood in India, 9–10, 15, 115, 118, 124, 190; early professional struggles, 7; finances, 7, 219; journey to Near East, xv, 38, 43–49, 116, 194; racism, 11–13, 15, 116–17, 141; religion, 13–15; treatment of servants, 117, 193; visits to United States, xv, 1, 15–16, 115–21, 123, 140, 160, 194–96, 219 n.33

Works of: *Adventures of Philip, The,* xv, xvii, 11–12, 157–60, 164–87, 191–92, 195, 226 n.43, 227 nn.46–47, 228 n.52, 228–29 n.60, 229 nn.63, 65–66; *Book of Snobs, The,* 59, 78, 169, 229 n.63; *Catherine,* xvi, 4, 198 n.3; "Charity and Humour," 1, 169; "Cox's Diary," 12; "De Finibus" (*Roundabout Papers*), 187; *Denis Duval,* 169, 189–90; "Dennis Haggarty's Wife" (*Men's Wives*), 22; "Eastern Adventure of the Fat Contributor, An," 45–46; *English Humourists, The,* 107–8, 189; *Four Georges, The,* 10; "French Romancers on England," 29–32; *Great Hoggarty Diamond, The,* 73; *History of Henry Esmond, The,* 96–114, 130, 140, 143–44, 150, 156, 194–96, 215 n.17; *History of Pendennis, The,* 1, 39, 58, 76–97, 105, 114, 117, 158, 167, 191, 194, 196, 215 n.16; *Irish Sketch Book, The,* 196, 208–9 n.16; *Lovel the Widower,* 188–89; *Luck of Barry Lyndon, The,* xv–xvii, 17–18, 23–24, 32–40, 43–44, 113, 157, 169, 188–89, 194–96, 205 n.30, 205–6 n.34, 208 n.14; *Men's Wives,* 18, 20–23; "Mississippi Bubble, A" (*Roundabout Papers*), 162–63, 187; "Mr. and Mrs. Frank Berry" (*Men's Wives*), 20–21; *Mr. Brown's*

Letters to His Nephew, 58–60, 62, 98; "Mr. Thackeray in the United States," 219 n.35; *Newcomes, The,* 12, 35, 96, 114–16, 121–25, 127–140, 158, 188–89, 195–96, 205–6 n.34, 215 n.16; *Notes of a Journey from Cornhill to Grand Cairo,* 1, 15, 38, 43–49, 51, 208 n.11; "On a Joke I Once Heard from the Late Thomas Hood" (*Roundabout Papers*), xv, 192–93; "On Half a Loaf" (*Roundabout Papers*), 164; "On Love, Marriage, Men, and Women" (*Mr. Brown's Letters to His Nephew*), 58–60, 62, 98; "On Two Roundabout Papers which I Intended to Write" (*Roundabout Papers*), 224–25 n.20; *Our Street,* 42–43, 49, 52; "Pictorial Rhapsody, A," 24, 29–30; "Pictorial Rhapsody, A: Concluded," 27; *Punch's Prize Novelists (Novels by Eminent Hands),* 31; "Ravenswing, The" (*Men's Wives*), 21–23, 52; *Roundabout Papers,* xv, 162–64, 187, 192–93, 195, 224–25 n.20; "Shabby Genteel Story, A," 158, 172, 229 n.63; "_____'s Wife, The" (*Men's Wives*), 21; "Timbuctoo," 18–20, 23, 190, 203–4 n.9; *Tremendous Adventures of Major Gahagan, The,* 11; *Vanity Fair,* 5, 7, 40–42, 49–76, 96, 98, 109, 114, 130–31, 136, 173, 182, 193–96, 208–9 n.16; *Virginians, The,* xvi, 122–23, 140–58, 167–68, 182, 195, 221 n.1, 222 n.2; "Waiting at the Station" (*Sketches and Travels in London*), 55; *Wolves and the Lamb, The,* 188–89; *Yellowplush,* 169

Tilford, John E., Jr., 105

Tillotson, Geoffrey, 118, 180, 183, 190, 199 n.7, 208–9 n.16, 220 n.42, 228 n.56

Tillotson, Kathleen, 208–9 n.16

Times (London), 85, 124, 126–27, 136, 160, 196, 213 n.13, 217 n.8, 220 n.47, 230–31 n.16

Todorov, Tzvetan, 223 n.2
Trent affair, 164
Trollope, Anthony, 14, 38, 96, 181, 190
Turner, J. M. W., 24–25
Tyler, John, 127
Tyler, Mrs. John, 127, 136

Uncle Tom's Cabin (Stowe), 119, 121–23, 126, 142, 219 n.35

Valentine and Orson, 69, 211 n.38

Walvin, James, 5–6

Warburton, Eliot, 43
Ward, Rev. Samuel Ringgold, 225 n.25
Washington, George, 111, 124, 153
Wedgwood, Josiah, 76–77
Wilberforce, William, 13–14, 25, 28, 30, 49
Wordsworth, William, 86–87
Wycherley, William, 177

Young, G. M., 2, 196

Zong case, 25, 204 n.15

A Note about the Author

Deborah A. Thomas is Professor of English at Villanova University. She is the author of *Dickens and the Short Story* and editor of Charles Dickens, *Selected Short Fiction.*